Raymond Bryan Brown

, 973

What Kind of God?

HEINZ ZAHRNT

What Kind of God?

A Question of Faith

Augsburg Publishing House

Minneapolis, Minnesota

BT
28
. Z 2813
1972
C. 2

Originally published in 1970 as *Gott kann nicht sterben*
Copyright © 1970, R. Piper & Co. Verlag, München
Translation by R. A. Wilson
Copyright © 1971 SCM Press Ltd.
First United States Edition 1972

Library of Congress Catalog Card No. 77-176102
International Standard Book No. 0-8066-1209-6

Printed in Great Britain.

Contents

Preface

At a session of the Protestant Academy at Bad Boll recently a theology student said to me in a discussion: 'You still retain the vestiges of theism.' Previously people used to say: 'You still believe in God.' I replied that that was the reason why I still remained a theologian at all; otherwise I would long ago have become a social worker, a politician, or better still a doctor preferably a specialist in internal diseases.

This book deals with what that theology student called my 'vestiges of theism'. In plain language, it deals with God – how we can still experience and speak of God in the face of all that is said about his 'death'. Our contemporaries expect theologians to say something about this, and quite rightly so. Everything else they can find out about from somebody else, and they will find out better than from theologians. If theology at the present day is to attract any interest, it can do so only with the question of God. Apart from that it is uninteresting and dispensable.

The title of the book is also meant to point to the one unique theme of theology. It is not meant as a personal profession of faith, far less as a despairing incantation. It is simply meant to be a reminder, in the form of an objective assertion, of a simple logical fact, and at the same time to make clear the indestructible nature of the question of God. Nevertheless the book is written out of the conviction that God does not die when man ceases to ask for him, but man ceases to be man when he no longer asks the question of God.

I dedicate this book to our four sons, because although they have avoided studying theology, in spite of their father's example, they have not so far lost their faith in God.

My wife has also gone over every idea in this book, and taken down every sentence for me. I also thank Dr Maielies Jentzsch, who has taken an active part in the writing of this book. Last but not least I would like to thank Dr Michael Wegner, who in the years since he first began to read my works for the publisher has become my friend.

The Devaluation of Theological Language

It is more than the church that is at stake: it is God.

At the present day, theological language is caught up in an inflationary crisis of unparalleled severity. The church's natural currency consists as it always did of the key words, images and concepts of the bible. But in the view of most of our contemporaries, these have become paper money which is no longer backed by the experience they claim to represent. And many Christians and theologians, both ministers and academic teachers of theology, sit on a vast heap of this paper money and deny that it has declined in value at all. But there have not merely been slight variations in the rate of exchange. The standard on which the whole currency is based, God himself, has been called into question, and so the whole currency system – the whole of 'theo-logy' – is tottering. At the present day the central issue is not the question of the church, but the question of God. In so far as our contemporaries are interested in the matter at all, they are interested in this. In the language of the stock exchange we might say: Church – price falling, business slack; God: price variable, business lively. Nowadays the church is poor value, but God is still good value, and everyone knows this, from the bishop to the newest curate, from the publisher of a newspaper down to the last sub-editor.

But is the church aware of the full extent of this crisis in its theological currency? And if it is aware of it, how is it reacting to it? The following scene recently took place during the synod of one of the German provincial churches. The bishop, as he is bound, had given his report to the synod, which then went on to debate it in the usual way. But the moment the debate began to touch on theology, it suddenly started to become lively. One of the members of the synod, a pastor, explained to the synod why he believed only in Jesus, but not in God. He spoke compellingly, almost in the style of a sermon; he went beyond his time, but no one minded; many of the members of the synod, including perhaps some of those who had had a theological training, were learning for the first time what 'theology since the death of God' is all about. When this pastor had finished, an older man, a leading member of the clergy, then spoke in great agitation: 'If things like this can be said in our church and accepted as valid, then we might as well shut up shop.' After this view had been expressed, the governing body withdrew for a private discussion lasting almost an hour. The result was the usual kind of declaration that church authorities produce, probably inevitably: scrupulously fair to the individuals concerned, expressed in orthodox terms, but saying nothing. The synod did not return to the theme of 'God'. A member of the synod with a long experience of its procedure moved the closure, and the majority voted in favour. Thus the synod voted for the closure of the debate about God. On that day, it sang with good reason the hymn:

> Lord, for the honour of thy name,
> Keep us to thy teachings true,
> And in thy church the days of peace,
> Of increase, and of strength renew.

There was good reason for that synod to sing this hymn, for the 'days of increase' in the church seem in fact to belong to the past. The hope of a new beginning in the church, and indeed in Christian belief as a whole, which many cherished in 1945, has finally turned out to be false. The spontaneous, sometimes almost delirious enthusiasm manifested in the early post-war years in prison camps and amongst students, in theological colleges and church assemblies, might have given the impression that a new era was dawning for Christianity. But when we look back, we must admit that from the Christian point of view we overestimated the situation at the end of the second world war. We have since come to see that what seemed to be a new beginning was only a brief episode, an interlude. The Christian revival awaited by many has not come about.

Of course one can accuse the church of failing once again – and some people are doing all they can to make this charge heard. But this charge is so general and so justified that it is always true. The usual criticisms made of the church at the present day, therefore, remain for the most part superficial and do not touch the essence of the problem. Anyone trying to make a just assessment of the present-day situation of the church cannot simply begin with a list of its misdeeds. He must first recognize that we have never before had so active a church and so diligent a clergy as at the present day, and that there is probably no other institution which since the war has tried to review and revise its forms and practice as much as the church, or which has been so adventurous in this respect. But what has been the result? The effect seems to bear no relation to the effort that has been made. Against this background the true dilemma becomes clear. Since the war the church has made a new start in so many ways, and yet to all appearances has not made a new beginning at all.

From this point of view, the apparent new beginning which the church made after the war can be seen as a momentary pause in a decline of Christianity which has been in progress for a very long time. For a few years, and no more, the general and continuing evolution was once again interrupted. The reason for this slowing down lay in the special historical circumstances of the time. For many people, their world had collapsed around them. The social and political orders on which their lives had been based and the ideals to which they had felt committed had turned out to be false. They now longed for a new security, reliable intellectual bearings, and a new and more permanent order. At such a moment the church and the Christian faith were the only pillars which still remained erect, albeit damaged, and on which one could lean. It is this situation which led to the much abused Christian restoration of the post-war period.

But it did in fact help to bring about what people were looking for: a return to stability in every respect. But because it was only a restoration, and not a genuine renewal, the apparent new beginning after the war did not go to the heart of things, and did not last. And neither the political restoration under Adenauer nor the church restoration led by Dibelius were able to do more than hold off the intellectual, theological, ecclesiastical, social and political problems with which they were faced, and could not really get to grips with them, far less solve them.

Once this became obvious, the good will with which the church was regarded turned into mistrust and resentment, and quite often the church was blamed for its failure to do what people were unwilling to do on their own account.

Today the church's honeymoon is over, and it has to face the realities of life again. For some time the church has faced a growing animosity on a wide front, as though a long backlog of pent-up aggressions was suddenly being released. The process of disintegration, which was halted for a few years after the war, is continuing at an increased rate. Just as an hour-glass gives the impression that at the end the sand is running faster and faster through the glass, so what is still left of Christianity seems to be disappearing faster and faster at the present day. We see 'decline' everywhere. The churches are becoming empty, ordinations are fewer, the number of ordinands grows less, communities of men and women carrying out Christian service are no longer increasing, lay workers are not available and more and more people leave the church. It seems almost as if language cannot find words enough to describe this universal 'shrinkage' – at a time when the talk everywhere else is of 'growth'.

The increase in the rate at which Christianity is disintegrating is reflected in the radicalization of theological enquiry. All theological questions now lead relentlessly to the one question of God.

The decisive event which has fundamentally changed all the issues debated in theology, and which therefore determines all theological thinking at the present day, lies in the fact that not only Christian belief in God, but any concept of God at all, can never again be taken for granted without further discussion. At the present day, the starting point and constant background to everything that is said about God is provided by a concealed or explicit atheism. Many of our contemporaries already take this for granted as readily as their forefathers took for granted their belief in God. And so far as Christians are genuinely in touch with contemporary ideas, they cannot remain unaffected. Even Christians are nowadays at a loss for words when anyone asks them about their experience of God. However full their heart is, the words are no longer there.

Teilhard de Chardin caught the feeling of the present age very accurately when he said:

The fact remains that for some obscure reason something has gone wrong between Man and God *as in these days he is represented to Man*.... Hence ... the impression one gains from everything taking place around us is of an irresistible growth of atheism.[1]

Ernst Bloch once said the same thing too in these words: 'The world has no longer got its mind made up.' And the Spanish philosopher Miguel De Unamuno sees all other human questions as overshadowed by the one question, whether man is alone in the universe or not. Consequently, all theology is thrown back on the one question which is fundamental to it. Today it is God's turn.

I have in front of me a heap of books, every one a new work of theology published in recent years. Their titles are The Question of God; Who is God?; Shattered Images of God; Where is God?; Where has God Gone?; God is No More; Is God Dead? If God is Dead ...; God is not quite Dead; What Comes after the 'Death of God'?; If God is not Dead; God in the Future; To be Human – With or without God?; Atheism in Christianity; To Believe in God as an Atheist.

The common ground between all these titles is striking. They all express the same remarkable contradiction. Not only do they all mention, directly or indirectly, the name of God, but all speak in different ways – questioning, assessing, asserting – about the 'death of God'. And yet they all still mention God. This contradiction is confusing. People ask: What is going on in theology? What are these odd theologians and philosophers up to, asserting that God is dead and yet still going on talking about God? If these theologians and philosophers are right, then what is going on with God? As many of them have already replied, nothing is going on with God any more, and that is what is worrying the theologians. The great closing-down sale has begun.

Of course one can lament this situation in sermons on Repentance Day and in press statements, and one can sound the trumpet against it with every device of mass publicity, but neither lamentations nor the sounding of trumpets will help us to survive the situation. The only thing that is of any use is honest determination and more profound reflection.

Theology finds itself between an irresistible force and an immovable object. The immovable object is the situation in which it finds itself, and the irresistible force is the message it has to proclaim. What makes the present-day situation an immovable object is the fact that our present age has been formed by the experience of the absence of God. Most of our contemporaries can no longer see God at work, so that 'the word of God' no longer means anything to them. The message of theology remains an irresistible force, in that if theology is to remain Christian theology it has always to speak of *God*, and may avoid the word, but cannot keep the name silent. Ultimately both elements take the form of the question of the *content of reality* in belief in God. This has become the decisive question for all who remain loyal to the church and all who are outside it, for all who still believe in God and for all who no longer believe. The question which both ask is that of the 'reality of God'. This faces theology with a double task: it must show the present day how far God is *real*, and it must go on to speak credibly of this reality. At this point reality and credibility become identical.

Nowadays many Christians and theologians, if they are able at all to speak credibly of God, in language which represents reality, can do so only in the sphere of *society* and *politics*. They are thoroughly suspicious of all personal Christianity as a private subjective experience concerned only with the salvation of the individual, and therefore with the world to come. Consequently, they attack what they call 'religion', and press for social and political commitment on the part of the church. But since the war – much to the regret of some other Christians – the church has shown a social and political commitment, not only in Germany, but wherever it exists in the world, to a greater extent than perhaps ever before in its history. Yet this very commitment arouses the suspicions of the radical theologians and Christians, because they see in it merely an extra support given by the church to existing structures of authority. Consequently, they would like to 'change the function' of the church, for preference using it solely as an instrument of social and political action. In the face of the challenge provided by the apparent 'death of God', they identify the cause of God with

their own. They agree with the famous statement of the young
Marx in his dispute with Feuerbach:

> Thus the criticism of heaven is transformed into the criticism of the
> earth, the criticism of religion into the criticism of the law, the criticism
> of theology into the criticism of politics.[2]

Without concern for the eternal salvation of man, these
Christians and theologians apply themselves solely to his earthly
well-being. They wish to set up the righteousness of God here
on earth, as soon as possible, either non-violently or violently.
And they believe that in doing this they are following Jesus of
Nazareth. But others again deny that they are following Jesus
in this. Consequently, the present day dispute about the
existence of God also appears in the form of a disagreement
about Jesus of Nazareth.

The debates in the church and in theology about what it
means at the present day to believe in God and to follow Jesus,
and how they can credibly become a reality in what Christians
say and do, are so profound, and are conducted with such
acrimony and mutual hostility, that the Protestant church gives
the appearance of being hopelessly divided, and sometimes
almost of having split into two opposed churches.

In the weekly magazine *Die Zeit*, Rolf Zundel concluded his
account of the fourteenth German Protestant Church Assembly,
which took place in Stuttgart in July 1969, with the following
summary:

> Two groups faced one another at the Church Assembly. On one side
> there were the old-fashioned Christians who would like to keep the
> blessings of their religion safe and untarnished, but find themselves
> exposed and unprotected in the face of the demands and temptations of
> the modern world. On the other hand there are the modern Christians,
> who are trying to set up the righteousness of God upon earth, as quickly
> as possible, as perfectly as possible, and where necessary by force. The
> tendency of the former is to flee from the world into faith, while the
> latter have largely left faith behind them in order to serve the world.
> Between the two there is a large central group, which includes many
> modern theologians, which is uncertain, which has no panaceas, which
> tries to take small steps in the direction of righteousness and hopes for
> a little bit of grace – whatever that might be.[3]

These words seem not only to be a just summing up of the
Stuttgart Church Assembly, but also to be a true account of the

whole present situation in the church and in theology – even if
it is a rough-and-ready picture, somewhat over-simplified. To
this factual statement I must add here that I personally count
myself as one of the third group, the theologians who are
accused by some of being too 'modern', and by others as being
still too 'conservative'. I feel myself forced more and more into
the role of a 'mediator', and accept this role as such – with the
conscious intention of helping to overcome the false alternatives – Karl Jaspers would call them the 'raw alternatives' –
which are posed in present-day theology and society. That one
can easily find oneself between the two hostile fronts, with the
risk of drawing on oneself the anger of both sides, is a fact so
well known that once observed it is not worth complaining
about.

When we speak of 'mediation' we do not mean adopting no
point of view at all, the false mediation which blurs the situation
and blunts the truth. We hope that we are protected from such
deceitful blurring and blunting by the definite point of view
which lies behind our wish to mediate. This firm standpoint is
conviction that what matters in theology and the church at the
present day is faith in God, and that for theology and the
church the redemption of man and society can only be a
consequence of the redemption of faith. For us the alternative
lies here and it is an exclusive one: Either theology and the
church cease to speak of God and cease to exist, or else – but the
alternative is not that they should continue to speak of God,
and so continue to exist. It is this: or else they must endeavour
to speak of God in a new way; then perhaps they may also
continue to exist as well. But theology and church will never be
able to renounce the name of God.

We can do no more here than repeat what Martin Buber said
about the word 'God':

[God] ... is the most heavy-laden of all human words. None has
become so soiled, so mutilated. Just for this reason I may not abandon it.
Generations of men have laid the burden of their anxious lives upon
this word and weighed it to the ground; it lies in the dust and bears their
whole burden. The races of men with their religious factions have torn
the word to pieces; they have killed for it and died for it, and it bears
their finger-marks and their blood. Where might I find a word like it
to describe the highest? ... We must esteem those who interdict it
because they rebel against the injustice and wrong which are so readily

referred to 'God' for authorization. But we may not give it up.... We cannot cleanse the word 'God', and we cannot make it whole; but, defiled and mutilated as it is, we can raise it from the ground and set it over an hour of great care.[4]

But if we are to preserve and keep safe the word 'God', this itself makes it necessary for us to learn to speak of him in a *new way*. The whole concern of the church at the present day should be directed towards this task. To adapt Jesus's well known saying from the Sermon on the Mount, we might say: 'Seek ye first a new way of speaking of God, and a new form of the church will of itself be added unto you.'

Instead of this, we see the church at the present day pre-occupied largely not with the greater concern, for God, but with the lesser concern, for itself. Whatever one's contact with the church at the present day, one comes face to face with fear. They are all afraid: the bishops and moderators for their authority, titles and terms of office, the orthodox for the purity of their doctrine, the provincial churches – in Germany – for their boundaries, congregations for their numbers, ministers for their professional future. The classical Lutheran definition of the nature of the church is that the church is everywhere where 'the Gospel is taught in its purity and the sacraments are administered in accordance with their institution' (Augsburg Confession, article 7). At the present day one is inclined to add a third mark of the church: 'Where there is fear.'

But where there is fear, all creative imagination is cut off at the root, and there can be no free, impartial reflection upon God. And how useless such fear is in the end! Ten and twenty years ago the church was still afraid of Bonhoeffer and Bult-mann. There were great difficulties in holding Bonhoeffer memorial services, and it took a lot of effort to get a series of articles about Bultmann printed in a Protestant weekly journal. Today many church leaders would be thankful if no one had gone any further than Bonhoeffer and Bultmann.

The church is at the beginning of a *theological learning process*, in which God is both the teacher and the subject to be taught. Now there can be no learning without suffering. If the church today is to learn to speak of God in a new way, the first thing necessary is *concentration* by *reduction*, both in its inner life and in its outward aspects. It must consciously accept its status as a minority in a largely non-Christian population, and admit that it can only go on proclaiming the truth in competition with other truths. If the church can do this, it will finally bring to reality a statement by Heinrich Heine which he wrote almost a century and a half ago, and which ever since has remained an unfulfilled prophecy:

The monopoly system is as injurious to religions as to trades; they are only strong and energetic by free competition, and they will again bloom up in their primitive purity and beauty so soon as the political equality of the Lord's service, or, so to speak, so soon as the trades-freedom of the divinities, is introduced. The noblest-minded men in Europe have long since asserted that this is the only means to preserve religion from its overthrow.

But Heine continues sceptically:

But its present servants would sooner sacrifice the altar itself than the least thing that is sacrificed on it.[5]

If the church is really concerned with God, and if as a result it wishes to learn to speak of God in a new way, then it must first of all give up everything which is no longer backed by reality, which basically no longer belongs to the church, and which, if it is not now abandoned voluntarily, will rapidly be taken away from it, without the need for much force. And every theory which no longer reflects practice, all dogmas and doctrines that have become incredible, and all institutions and forms which have become empty must be confidently dismissed with the prayer: 'Lord, teach us to number our days, that we may get a heart of wisdom.' 'Honesty is the best policy' is a proverb which applies both to the church and to theology.

We are obliged to undertake this process of concentration by reduction not in self-defence, or as a tactic in apologetics, and certainly not as a reaction to a changed historical situation. The motive is the faith which will not be satisfied with anything less than God. Indeed, it is God himself who drives us to it. It is he who sends the situation. It represents more than a change in the history of human thought. It represents a new era in the history of God's dealings with man, and so, properly understood, in the history of God himself. God adapts himself to time. It is the will of God himself to participate in the changes of our age.

How else can it be that we feel our obligation to speak of God in a new way, and at the same time our inability to speak of God in a new way, as a burning fire within us?

I

The Finality of the Enlightenment –
The Starting-points of Theology

1. The Rumour that 'God is Dead'

Whatever is said about God is affected by the situation at the time. A decisive factor in the present situation is the assertion that 'God is dead'. Unquestionably, there is at the present day, even amongst theologians, an extremely ill-considered, superficial and ill-digested way of talking of the death of God, which is no more than fashionable chatter, a mere manner of speaking, without any profound reflection or personal involvement. The statement that God is dead is made in the same tone as one reads in the evening paper that the old man in the top flat has died, the one who was always so kind to the children, but didn't really quite know what was going on.

But anyone who asserts that 'God is dead' and 'religion is finished' must realize what he is saying. It is not a statement that can be made in the same way in which one can say that the buses have been taken off a particular route, or even that an era in human history has come to an end. Anyone who says that 'God is dead' is asserting that a unique, completely new, hitherto unknown and quite inconceivable event in the history of mankind has actually taken place. If you have ever gone on a Mediterranean cruise and seen the multitude of religious sites and monuments – Egyptian pyramids, ancient temples, Jewish synagogues, Christian churches, Mohammedan mosques and ancient sanctuaries, for which religion no one yet knows, as well as the brand new buildings put up to house a new religion that has just been started – only then will you realize the full implication of the statement that 'religion is finished'. When you see all this, you come to realize the force of the 'historical proof of

God' which used to be advanced, and which claimed to deduce the existence of God from the presence of religions at all periods and everywhere in the world. Or think for a moment of the unparalleled intellectual exertions and the degree of personal commitment, to the point of risking their lives, which the greatest minds of the West have applied to the idea of God: Isaiah and Job, Plato and Aristotle, Paul and Augustine, Abelard and Thomas Aquinas, Eckhart and Nicholas of Cusa, Luther and Sebastian Franck, Leibniz, Kant and Hegel, Feuerbach, Marx and Freud, Schleiermacher, Kierkegaard, Heidegger and Jaspers. This is enough to show how much is being swept away in the assertion that God is dead. If anyone can turn away unimpressed from this, the most intense current of human thought and life, if anyone can bid farewell to God without feeling pain or hatred, and from then on do nothing but operate computers and ask them about the technical or even the political and social value of the things he plans to do next, he does not deserve the heroic honours which are most improperly accorded to him at the present day. In our view he is simply an intellectual barbarian.

The great thinkers who really denied God knew what they were doing when they proclaimed that God was dead, and therefore they always despised those who clung to their coat tails and thought they could dismiss God with a pamphlet, a shrug of the shoulders or a wave of the hand. Nietzsche accused the atheism of the 'scientific and physiological gentlemen' of lacking 'passion and suffering for things'. His own denial of God was full of suffering and passion, and that was why he always had to wave God's death certificate at him. And when Heinrich Heine was struck as he wrote by the idea of the death of God, he paused and confessed in a tone of mixed reverence and mockery:

A strange dread, a mysterious reverence, does not permit us to write further today. Our breast is filled with terrible compassion; it is the ancient Jehovah himself preparing for death ... Hear ye the bell ring? Kneel down! They bring the sacrament to a dying God![1]

Sartre himself felt 'strongly opposed to a certain type of secular moralism which seeks to suppress God at the least possible expense'.[2]

But one cannot simply say that the statement which is bandied about nowadays, that God is dead, is only a 'slogan' or 'catchword', which works by its 'surprise effect' and so makes use of a 'press and TV grapevine'. This is the reply of the complacent theological assurance which is not itself wholly blameless for the start of the rumour that God is dead. The assertion that God is dead may very well have turned into a slogan or catchword, with the power of suggestion of a garish poster or a cheap intellectual cliché. Nevertheless, it accurately reflects the decisive religious experience of the present time. This consists of the fact that many people, perhaps even most people, no longer have any experience of God. Whether one says that 'God is dead', 'God is absent', 'God has failed', or 'God has gone away', or speaks of the 'darkness of God' – all these expressions refer to the same contemporary phenomenon. This is, that in our age God is no longer a phenomenon. At one time men felt they had been abandoned by God; nowadays God must feel that he has been abandoned by men.

The radical change in our present situation with regard to faith in God can clearly be seen in the distinction between the concepts of the *concealment of God* and the *absence of God*. The 'concealment' of God refers to the non-experience of the existence of God; but the 'absence' of God refers to the experience of the non-existence of God. The non-experience of the existence of God means that although God is there, he is not experienced. The experience of the non-existence of God means that God is not there, and this is what is now being experienced. The concealment of God was the experience of Abraham, Job, the Psalmists, Jesus and Luther. The fate of our present age, on the other hand, seems to be the absence of God.

Whereas the concealment of God is like a passing storm which one can hope to live through, the absence of God is like a change of climate, which no one is able permanently to escape. The image of a change of climate illustrates once again the character of the atheism which is so widespread at the present day. In most cases it is not a matter of a conscious personal decision against God, but of an unconscious acquiescence in a general contemporary attitude. A person does not give up belief in God after due consideration, he slips out of it without noticing. It simply evaporates like water from a puddle. Good Friday sermons rightly tell us that it was not the Jews alone who crucified Jesus Christ, but that we would do just the same ourselves today, so that the cross might just as well have stood on the Venusberg outside Bonn or on Hampstead Heath as on Golgotha outside Jerusalem. This is fair enough, but I sometimes wonder whether we would really crucify Jesus Christ again today, not because we believe in him, but because we are indifferent.

Atheism at the present day is adopting a point of view that takes it beyond the problem of the existence of God. Sartre's definition of atheist existentialism is typical of this:

> Existentialism is not atheism in the sense that it would exhaust itself in demonstrations of the non-existence of God. It declares, rather, that even if God existed it could make no difference from its point of view.[3]

Camus, in his story 'The Outsider', has portrayed the essence of this atheistic standpoint, beyond the problem of the existence of God, in an impressive scene. A man condemned to death, shortly before his execution, tells the prison chaplain that he does not believe in God. The priest asks him several times whether he is quite sure of this. He replies that he does not need to ask himself whether he is quite sure of it, but he finds it totally unimportant. He has only a little time left and does not want to waste it with God. All he had ever been bothered about was what existed at the moment or was coming today or tomorrow.

The statement that 'God is dead', when it is taken in *deadly* earnest, signifies more than merely the end of conceptions and representations of God which have hitherto been valid. It also means more than a private, personal matter of individual experience. Throughout history, temptations of this kind have always accompanied faith, so that there have always been situations and times in which men experienced existentially the absence of God, and as a result lost their faith for a time or for ever. But the situation with regard to God is more serious than this! The present-day assertion that 'God is dead' does not imply merely a transitory subjective experience of the absence of God on the part of individuals, but a final, public, objective event rooted in the very basis of the historical process. Even if on closer examination the assertion can be shown to be superficial and perverse, because it is self-contradictory, the theologian's first task is nevertheless to come to terms with this radical interpretation of the statement that 'God is dead'. Only then can he give honest consideration to the problem of how to speak of God in a 'contemporary' way. To elucidate rumours, you have to investigate them.

2. The Negative Consequences of the Enlightenment for Faith in God

Why has the question of God become so radical that the actual death of God is asserted? The answer can be given in a simple historical affirmation: *The final and ultimate encounter between the enlightenment and Christian faith has come about.* This statement gives the fullest reason for the event which is summed up in the idea of the 'death of God'. The enlightenment claimed many notable victims. But the greatest and most notable was God. Because he was the greatest, and the loftiest, he fell the furthest. That is why, in the course of time, the speed of his fall has grown greater. The Newtonian laws of gravity seem to hold not only in nature, but also in history.

In his famous essay 'What is the Enlightenment?', Kant described the enlightenment as 'Man's leaving behind the immaturity for which he himself was to blame'. He calls on man 'to make use of his reason without anyone else's guidance'.

'*Sapere aude!* Be brave enough to use your own reason.' This for him is the 'slogan of the enlightenment'. Kant's call to man to free himself by the use of his own reason from servitude to authorities and institutions outside himself was by no means explicitly directed against belief in God. But the gathering pace of man's enlightenment has brought with it the consequence that God is pushed further and further into the background.

In our age this movement has reached its final goal. We describe its finality by using the expression 'the second enlightenment'. One might describe this metaphorically by saying that we are no longer the son who has just arrived in the far country, we were born in the far country. Thus we must think twice about interpreting our situation by means of the theological category of 'revolt against God'. For a start, not everything that has happened in history is the fault of man – the process of inexorable fate and misfortune can also be found in the his-

tory of the intellect. Secondly, our contemporaries at least are
not to blame for the enlightenment; it is quite impossible for
them to decide for or against it. For them the enlightenment is
as complete and irreversible as the release of atomic power or
the landing on the moon.

If we consider the very complex process of intellectual history
which we call the 'enlightenment' from the point of view of
the questions we are discussing, the only prominent feature at
first sight is its destructive consequence for belief in God. The
attack of the enlightenment on faith in God has been like a
pincer movement. The left wing has attacked intentionally and
directly, formally denying the existence of God, while the attack
of the right wing has been unintentional and indirect. It has
infiltrated nature and history with the aid of human reason,
and in this way has indirectly deprived God of his footing in
the world. Here as so often in history the indirect attack from
the right has turned out to be the greater, the really fatal danger.

This breaking-down process has been due to the combined
effect of a whole series of different but related factors. We shall
now distinguish and give a brief account of them, in order to
achieve an increasingly concrete picture of the meaning of the
'death of God'.

(a) The Subjectivity of Man

The moment the discoveries of Copernicus removed the earth
from the centre of the universe, man became the universal point
of reference in the world. This 'anthropocentric revolution' of
the enlightenment is characterized by Descartes' well known
phrase *cogito ergo sum* – I think, therefore I am. If the only
support that man can find to confirm his own existence is that
in his own act of thinking he experiences himself as existing,
it necessarily follows that all truth in the world is relative to the
human subject which knows it. From this point on, then, every
truth either on earth or in heaven must be submitted to human
judgment, to see whether it is fit to be admitted into his consciousness. The process of direct commonsense experience is
replaced by that of conscious reflection, in which man adopts
an attitude, to himself and to the world, of standing back and
making a critical analysis. He carefully tests every link and
accurately draws the limits of every certainty. With a com-

bination of tolerance and scepticism he regards truth as constantly in balance. He sets more store by the question than the answer and always sees himself as in the figure of the doubter – as Bertolt Brecht describes in a poem:

Whenever we seemed to have found the answer to a question, one of us loosened the cord of the ancient rolled-up Chinese canvas on the wall, so that it fell open and you could see the man on the seat, who doubted so much. I, he said to us, I am the Doubter.

Thoughtfully and curiously we looked at the doubting blue man on the canvas, looked at each other and began again from the beginning.

Anyone who has been bitten by the bug of doubt in this way is never rid of it. He would rather doubt than return to feed on the 'milk of pious thinking'.

Even in discussing the truth of God, man's subjective consciousness is henceforth always there to pass judgment. Man may still stand face to face with God, but God no longer asks man: 'Adam, where are you?' Instead, man asks God, 'God, where are you?' One must not overlook the note of challenge in this question. The doctrine of justification seems to have been turned upside down. It is no longer man who has to justify himself before God, but God before man. In the modern age, all theology becomes a hidden theodicy.

(b) The World becomes Worldly

Before final encounter between the enlightenment and Christian faith, history was like a window through which one could look at God, and nature was like the forecourt of a temple as it were the forecourt of God, in which man would work and go about. Together nature and history formed a numinous, and therefore both glorious and terrible marginal zone of God's holiness. The acts and intervention of God penetrated the world in a thousand ways, as light penetrates a prison.

But nowadays, when an aeroplane crashes at 11.46, because at 11.45 a fault developed in its engine, or when someone is killed in a road accident because someone else did not observe the right of way, no sensible person dares any longer to state that God caused this misfortune by direct intervention, and that it was his will from eternity. And when people are hungry when the fortuitous link between two persons leads to the birth and suffer under the oppression of unjust circumstance, or

of a child, no responsible person any longer dares to assert that
the wrong or misfortune is ordained by God, to comfort those
concerned by the promise of eternal life, or to terrify them
with the threat of eternal punishment.

The reason for this 're-interpretation' of the world lies in
the process of *secularization*. There is no primary religious
cause for secularization, but it has secondary religious consequences. We disagree with the present-day tendency in theology to place more weight on the concept of secularization than
it will bear. It is important to restrict it to its proper limits,
that is, to certain partial aspects of man's picture of the world.
Secularization is neither a consequence, consciously drawn, of
Christian faith, nor an intentional revolt of man against God.
It is 'the natural consequence of the discovery and gradual
extension of the rational horizon of human understanding'.[4]
This, of course, brought with it to an increasing degree a 'loss
of function on the part of religion'.

In the past everything that took place in the world was
derived from God as the *causa prima*, the first cause, the prime
mover of everything. But this *causa prima* was encountered
within what took place in the world in the form of *causae
secundae*, that is, as it was mediated in the world through
secondary causes. But as science extended the causal nexus to
all phenomena, explained the world in a 'natural' way and
formed it according to human plans with the aid of technology,
God was forced out of the secondary causes and lost his foothold in human society and existence. Nowadays man looks for
natural causes in the weather, the outcome of battles, sickness,
the institutions of government and the changes that take place
in society, and so divests them of their divine character. Functions which hitherto have been fulfilled by God are being taken
over to an increasing extent by human society. Faced with
catastrophe, we no longer pray, but make plans, and the success
rate seems to be higher than when they prayed in the past.
Artificial manure brings visibly better results in agriculture
than sprinkling with holy water. Divine providence is replaced
by rational plans, divine help by protective measures against
disasters, the driving out of demons by psychiatry. People protect themselves against infection by immunization, from the
prospect of a failure of the harvest by importing wheat in good

time, and against inflation by the appropriate economic measures. And perhaps we may even succeed, with the aid of the new scientific study of the causes of conflict and the conditions for peace, in ridding the world of war.

Thus as a result of human scientific investigation and technological planning the *causae secundae*, the secondary causes, have become autonomous and have gained ground. There has been as it were a 'revolt of the instrumental causes'. In the midst of mere *causae secundae*, mere secondary causes, investigated, established and wherever possible produced by men, the *causa prima*, the first cause, God himself, is no longer recognizable.

In the words of Ernst Bloch: 'The address where those who have brought about and continued this process can be found has become very well known in the process.'[5] It is no longer the Father and creator above but man below! The 'divinized world' has become the 'hominized world'. The world of God has become the world of man. 'Wonderful are thy works,' sang the Psalmist. The pronoun 'thy' now refers to a different person. The *homo faber* with his technology has replaced God and his creation. And when he looks about him, he no longer sees the 'footprints of God' everywhere but only the 'footprints of man', the consequences of his own transforming action upon the world.

Max Weber called the consequences of man's increasing ability to put everything to his own use the 'disenchanting of the world'. The parallel process to this is that God is increasingly dislodged from the world. God seems no longer to 'occur' in the world. As a result of secularization religion has undergone a decrease in its functions; the 'religious sector' has grown narrower and narrower. Above all, present day man is no longer able to experience God in nature; here religious experience has as it were been deprived of the substructure that underpinned it. In the past, the earthquake at Lisbon had a shattering effect on people's minds, and led to an intensive period of religious and philosophical questioning in Western Europe. Although natural catastrophes nowadays arouse our sympathy for the victims, and although we may be willing and ready to help, such natural events scarcely ever raise any theological questions. Nor is the experience of nature any longer a source of religious feeling for us. The moon still exists for lovers and astronauts, but not for the religious.

But this loss of the function on the part of religion applies not only to nature, but to the whole universe and its history. Imagine the apostle Paul delivering his famous address upon the Areopagus (Acts 17) at the present day, in one of the capitals of the modern technological world, in New York, Moscow, London or Tokio. His hearers would not wait until he spoke of the resurrection of the dead before they protested. They would interrupt him before that, when he spoke to them of their experience of God in the cosmos and laid down the premiss that God made the world and everything in it, and that he is not far from each one of them. Secularization has made the world no longer an abode of God; it has turned it into a 'city without God', a *cité des hommes.*

(c) *From the World Beyond to this World*

The Anglican bishop John A. T. Robinson tells how during a conversation late at night with a Jewish student in Chicago, the student admitted: 'If I could really think, like our fathers, of this life as a mere few seconds preparation for eternity, it would make a lot of difference. But I can't. Can you?' Robinson goes on: 'I had to agree. I couldn't.'[6] And for our part, we must agree with the English bishop and admit that none of us can either, if we are true contemporaries.

The loss of the world to come does not affect merely Christian belief in eternal life, nor is it restricted in its effect to belief in God. It affects all metaphysical thought whatsoever in the West. Before the work of the enlightenment was concluded, all theoretical and practical knowledge of the world and ordering of life in the West was determined by a cosmic dualism which derived from the syntheses of Hellenism and Christianity and which had endured throughout the middle ages into modern times. According to this dualism, there stand opposed to each other two different worlds, thought of as each possessing substantial existence: the higher and the lower, the supernatural and the natural, the spiritual and the physical, the heavenly divine world and the earthly human world. Of these the higher, supernatural, spiritual divine world was regarded as the only real and true one. It defined the horizon of the lower, natural and physical world, and was set above all earthly and human life like the light of the sun above the earth, lighting it from above and making it what it is. But as the process of the enlightenment, that activity on the part of man which illuminated and changed the world, came to its conclusion, the ends of the world as it were grew together over our head – perhaps even, one might say, getting on top of us – and became our new heaven. This happened in the process of secularization which has just been described, by which the world became worldly. Through this process the world beyond, the supernatural divine world, which hitherto had been regarded as the only real and effective world, has become unreal and ineffective. It has lost its power and no longer gives life.

There are more and more people who no longer believe in heaven, hell and eternal life, and yet live and act responsibly here in time. The background to their attitude is a shift of consciousness from the world beyond to this world. The orientation of human life has swung through exactly 180°. New priorities have been substituted for old, and a real 'revaluation of all values' has taken place. It seems as though what the young Hegel said is now being fulfilled:

> Apart from some earlier attempts, it has been reserved in the main for our own epoch to vindicate at least in theory the human ownership of the treasures formerly squandered on heaven.

But, he continues sceptically,

> What age will have the strength to validate the right and make itself its possessor?[7]

Whether our present age will be strong enough remains to be seen. In any case, in this age man has begun to build himself a house in a world which has ceased to be divine, to make himself 'at home' on earth.

(d) The Revolution in Authority

Before the enlightenment, undisputed authority was accorded to what had either been 'handed down' horizontally from the fathers or 'laid down' vertically by God – God and the fathers normally being in agreement. But today people are no longer prepared to accept a truth as binding on them solely on the grounds of a guarantee from outside, either from above or from the past, from God or from the fathers. The enlightenment has subjected the traditional authorities to a comprehensive scrutiny, picking holes in them with its critical questions. By so doing it has as it were shot its way through the door, 'out of the immaturity for which man himself is to blame'.

This has largely been the work of historical criticism, in association with the scientific study of the world. With a sharp scalpel in its hand it has fallen upon every tradition, every dogma, legal system, social sanction, tradition, commandment and general assumption, and dissected them to see what they are worth, and whether they are still worth anything at all. Not only are historical traditions tested to see if they are genuine, to see if they can be shown to be good and reliable; their content is also examined to see if one can agree with it. The result of this has been a change in the concept of truth and authority. Truth has come to be regarded as historically conditioned and therefore as changeable. Only what is sufficiently convincing of itself to gain spontaneous acceptance can claim any authority. So all values become matters of judgment, and the result is relativization, pluralism and tolerance.

The crisis of tradition brought about by the enlightenment was bound to tell particularly upon Christian faith, for it was faith above all which based its truth on an appeal to an already existing, objective, absolute authority. This authority lay in certain particular words and acts of God in history, and especially in the coming of Jesus Christ, all these acts being handed down in the bible and the tradition of the church. The two latter were dissected by the scalpel of historical criticism and all that still remained valid was what could be shown to be historically genuine and credible and acceptable in content. Henceforth even Christian truth can no longer appeal for its basis to an objective external norm, whether this norm is 'It is written' or 'Rome has spoken' – even the party is no longer always right!

Henceforth, a saying by Lessing can be applied to the Protestant appeal to the bible:

Religion is not true because the evangelists and apostles taught it, they taught it because it is true. Written traditions must be explained on the basis of the inner truth of religion, and all written traditions are incapable of giving it truth if it possesses none.[8]

The point of this saying is that the truth of biblical statements about God is not sufficiently guaranteed by their historical origin, even if it is supposed to be divine. The only guarantee is that what they state brings an inner conviction to the hearer or reader. The effects of the revolution in authority have been the same for Catholics, with regard to the church's teaching office, as they have for the bible amongst Protestants. Catholic theologians used to hawk around the cynical dictum: 'What do I believe? Ask in Rome!' Nowadays it may well be that 'Rome has spoken', but the matter is far from being concluded. Discussion continues apace, and indeed it is only at this point that it becomes really lively.

For Catholics and Protestants at the present day there is nothing that can be said about God which still has an official backing and from which it derives its authority.

Instead, the distinction made by Karl Jaspers between philosophical and religious language is nowadays true of the statements of theology:

> No one who speaks of God does so in an official capacity, but speaks on the same level as anyone else, with no claim to authority, and counting only on the human power to convince.[9]

(e) The Ideological Criticism of Religion

The revolution in authority in the modern age has been accelerated by the ideological, social and economic criticism of religion. Just as science, by its investigation of the causal structure of nature and history, destroyed the religious idea of heaven above and turned the universe from a monarchy into a republic, so Marxist ideological criticism dealt it a new blow, doing the same thing with the aid of its penetrating examination of economic and social structures. The destruction of the urge to speculate about things on high, or, as Ernst Bloch jibed, 'to fish in muddy water' was implicit in the uncovering of the economic and sociological roots of this urge. Religion came under suspicion of being an ideological superstructure, a reflection of the existing economic situation, the 'halo round a fallen world'; in short, it was considered to be the 'opium of the people'. All heavenly theocracy was rejected, while at the same time all earthly hierarchies were deprived of any metaphysical, heteronomous character they possessed. And by a reverse process, once the partriarchal ordering of society was replaced by a democratic structure, man could no longer look past and above earthly authorities and rest his gaze upon heaven: 'Where there is no earthly throne, there is no social basis for a heavenly throne.'[10] And thus man began to get up from his knees and stand erect – both before God and before the king, before the heavenly Father and before his earthly fathers.

Modern social science has been able to show, with the aid of theologians themselves, how the image people hold of God is repeatedly formed and overlaid by the concerns of those who believe in it. Because agricultural societies have an interest in good weather, God becomes for them a 'weather God'; because soldiers desire victory, they call upon God as the 'Lord of Hosts'; because rulers try to establish their power more firmly they appeal to God as the 'guardian of the social order'; because property owners wish to retain their property, they call God 'the giver of all good gifts'. Everyone had his own fish to fry, and unconsciously tried to fry them on the fire of the altar of God. But the demonstration by sociological and theological criticism of this link between belief in God and the ideologies of human interest gave rise to a vacuum. Once God is no longer the guarantor of people's main concerns in their lives, or even if he has only ceased to be the guarantor of their party and group concerns, many people no longer know what there is to talk to God about, nor why they should still worship him.

(f) *Facing the Future*

The disintegration of the world beyond this world and the revolution in authority has led to a decisive change in man's orientation. Not only does he no longer look up to heaven, he also no longer looks back into the past. He now looks forward, in the direction of the future. Since the enlightenment the movement that has mattered for man is 'progress'. The dollar notes of the 'New World' still bear the word *Novus ordo seclorum*. These words express the attitude to life which is characteristic of the modern age. Modern man does not dream of the past, but looks forward actively and creatively to the future. The 'golden age' is not behind us, but in front of us: 'The new age goes where we go'.

What interests our contemporaries at the present day is not

so much *quod factum est* – what has happened – but *quod faciendum est* – what has to happen. The dispute about man's physical origin has long been over, and he has very little time to concern himself with his intellectual ancestry. What pre-occupies him is the question of his future. He tries to plan the future, as though he wanted to write the history of the future, as once people wrote the history of the past. As a result of this, there has been a shift in the centre of gravity in the world of academic study. The greatest weight is no longer placed upon the alpha faculties, as the humanities are called in America, and this means that theology, firmly linked as it is to a revelation which took place in the past, no longer occupies the place of honour. Instead, the greatest weight is placed upon the beta and gamma faculties, natural science, technology and be-havioural studies. But as a whole these are mainly orientated towards the future. And thus the dominant position, both intel-lectually and in practice, is held by the future, not by the past. The guiding principle is not 'memory' but 'hope'. Man seeks not only to know and explain the world, he also wishes to plan and alter it. He is simultaneously both producer and product.

(g) The New Humanism

Because they are orientated towards the future, science and technology have taken on a political and social aim. This aim consists of the Utopian vision of a 'better', 'more human' world. Secularization can be described as the hominization of the world, but is not yet the humanization of it; although through this process the world has become the world of man, it has not yet become a human world. People have recognized this and wish to change it. Some unrealistic Utopians would like to do so, if possible, in opposition to science and technology, while the more realistic make their attempt with the aid of science and technology. But they would like to relate them more closely to the good of society, and place them more fully at the service of society. And therefore scientific investigation and technical planning are nowadays combined in a political and social commitment.

If a survey was conducted today, particularly amongst young people, to find out what they regarded as the highest value, which they would regard as most worth fighting for, they would probably reply not as in the nineteenth century, freedom, but peace and justice, or freedom only in the sense of the liberation of man to be more human by the establishment of peace and justice in a more perfect society. If one were to go on to ask what it is that causes so much unrest amongst men throughout the world at the present day, and what makes students grow rebellious in places as far apart as Berlin, Frankfurt, Tübingen, Tokio, Paris, Prague, Rome, Madrid, Berkeley and Mexico City, we would receive the same answer. As the enlightenment has continued, whole classes and races have discovered that their sufferings have not been ordained for them by a higher divine authority, but result from human intentions and failures, so that they are not inevitable. It is this which has led to world-wide unrest. The world is filled today with a longing for justice, peace, freedom and humanity. Men have been seized by a new humanism, not an academic humanism, but a scientific human-ism, and above all a social humanism. This is true regardless of the race or nation to which they belong, or of the philosophy or religion which they profess. For many people today, if the question of God ever occurs to them at all, it takes the form of the search for justice in the world. And because they do not regard justice in the world as guaranteed by God, they no longer believe in him. This is a 'troubled atheism', as Karl Rahner once called it.[11] It is nourished by grief at the injustice and suffering of the innocent in the world. The things that once happened in Auschwitz, Dresden, Stalingrad and the Warsaw Ghetto, and which are now happening in Vietnam, South America, Greece, China and in slums throughout the world, seem to be an accusa-tion against Almighty God and to call for his deposition.

Because modern atheism is basically a new humanism, it possesses a powerful political component. If God is the Almighty who can be taxed with all the wrong and suffering in the world, and who justifies and backs everything that happens in the world with his authority, then belief in this God prevents men from changing existing political and social conditions – and this is why he must be abandoned. This can only happen if men are freed from the false awareness they have of their posi-tion in the world, and brought to a proper understanding, so that they can once again claim as their own original and legitimate property the values and goods which they have for so long lavished upon God.

This is the situation with which Christian faith finds itself faced at the present day, and with which theology too is faced – not only Protestant theology, but Catholic theology, and not only in Germany, but wherever Christianity exists.

3. The End of Theism?

When we draw together in this way the various factors which characterize the process of the enlightenment from the theological point of view, we can see how the rumour that 'God is dead' could get about. And it is clear why only this extreme expression seems adequate to many of our contemporaries to describe the total effect of the enlightenment on Christian belief in God. One thing is certain. As the premiss in a collective world view, as an assumption which everyone in the Western world understands and takes for granted, as the moral prop of society and politics and the working hypothesis of natural science and the humanities, God has ceased to exist. There is no longer agreement that 'there is a God'.

And we must state once again that the so-called 'death of God' is not merely a private, subjective individual experience, a kind of pietistic negative experience. It is not as though people were formally converted to God through certain experiences they are now converted away from God by opposite experiences. The expression 'God is dead' refers to a process which goes far beyond the experiences of the individual.

What is this process, and how are we to interpret it?

In German theology at least it is usually called 'the end of theism', and similarly refers to itself as 'a-theist'. The concept of 'theism' has been developed against the background of dualistic Western metaphysics, and against this background can be seen to include two separate conceptions. The first is belief in a supernatural world beyond the present world, and the second is the concept of God as a personal being. When these two conceptions are combined, the 'theism' that results is belief in a God, thought of as a personal being, who creates nature and directs history by intervening from beyond, from outside or from above in the course of the world, and similarly

in the fate of individuals, in acts of wrath or mercy. A believer
has a direct personal relationship with him and experiences
him as a person whom he confronts, as the 'You' with whom
he can speak, who speaks to him and whom he answers.

A-theists claim that this concept of God has vanished once
and for all, taking with it every direct religious experience on
the part of man. In her book *Stellvertretung* (English title:
Christ the Representative) which she explicitly sub-titles: 'An
Essay in Theology after the "Death of God"', Dorothee Sölle
writes:

> What happened to Moses at the burning bush belongs to an irrevocable
> past. What St Francis felt and experienced is no longer open to us to
> experience as something immediate. Luther's anxieties can be explained
> by the psychoanalysts and stripped of their unconditionality. The
> progressive awakening of the consciousness has excluded these possi-
> bilities of attaining certainty about God.[12]

But if theism comes to be regarded as out of date, more is
lost than merely a certain conception of God; all biblical faith
in God vanishes with it. For an essential element of belief in
God in the bible is that God is another person whom man encounters and to whom he speaks face to face, who stands in a
direct personal relation to man, who speaks to him through
his word and to whom he can reply in prayer. Thus this
'a-theism', in the sense of the mere end of theism, has a powerful
tendency, whether voluntary or not, to become 'atheism' in
the sense of the total denial of God, or at least of biblical faith
in God.

The justification for the end of theism and all direct religious
experience of God is found in the enlightenment. As the enlightenment has proceeded the scientific explanation and technological planning of the world by man has, step by step, made
God 'unemployed'. And so all direct access to God, every naïve
and unselfconscious relationship with him has been destroyed,
and man has been wholly forced back on what is immanent in
a closed system.

Thus the death of God seems to be the necessary result of
the process of secularization in the modern age. But the problem
is this, whether the modern process of secularization has actually
had this result. Or is the idea that 'God is dead' not a theologically exaggerated interpretation of it? One thing cannot be

denied, and that is that since the enlightenment there can no longer be a blind, naïve, unselfconscious belief in God. From now on faith and selfconsciousness are inseparable. After his encounter with the natural sciences, history, ideological criticism, sociology, psychoanalysis, etc., the theologian walks with a permanent limp. But apart from his limp, the question is whether, after this encounter, he is still a 'theologian' at all.

Everything turns here upon the careful observance of certain distinctions both in regard to belief in God and also in regard to secularization. That there is a connection between the two is indisputable. Belief in God always exists in a certain social and cultural context which gives it a particular form and appearance. Nowadays this context is different from that which existed before the enlightenment. There is no doubt that before the enlightenment belief in God was nourished from sources which have dried up as a result of the process of secularization. Science and technology have enormously enlarged the scope of human life. They have helped man to overcome his powerlessness and relieved, if not altogether removed, many of the numerous restrictions and limitations which previously surrounded him. In so far as religious experience was determined by the social and cultural situation, and was therefore conditioned by the age in which it took place, one can in fact say that God is 'dead'. But the statement that 'God is dead' is for this very reason only a partial one. Once it is understood as a statement of universal scope, it becomes false. For it then conceals the theologically exaggerated interpretation of secularization which mistakes a partial aspect for the whole. The partial aspect conceals the fact that secularization is a process in the history of civilization, which has in fact brought with it a change in religious practice. But if secularization is interpreted in a wholly atheistic sense, and if its result is proclaimed to be the 'death of God' understood in a universal sense, then one is guilty of an ideological interpretation of a phenomenon in the history of civilization. The sociological and theological spheres are being confused, a procedure which is unscientific.

Moreover, such an interpretation is made on the basis of the very 'metaphysics', the end of which is so loudly proclaimed. For the assertion that 'God is dead' is just as much a metaphysical statement, and is as little capable of verification, as such a statement as 'there is a God'. Again, the question arises whether secularization, and therefore the death of God as a partial phenomenon, do not represent a development which itself forms a consequence of Christian belief in God.

4. Atheism – Is it a Consequence of Christianity?

The basis for the secularization of the world can already be found in the two creation stories in the Old Testament. In particular, they foreshadow two characteristics of the later process of secularization. Firstly, nature is deprived of its magical power. Secondly, man takes responsibility for the creation. In both elements there is a tendency towards a 'partial atheism'.

One example of the way in which nature is no longer regarded as imbued with magic power is the fact that God creates the sun, the moon and the stars and hangs them like lamps in the heavens. This is certainly a primitive concept, but the demythologization of the world begins with this primitive concept. At that time, the sun, the moon and the stars were regarded as divine powers. The statement that God created them and set them in the heavens explicitly denies that they possess any divine character of their own. Moreover, they are consciously referred to by the prosaic and disrespectful term 'lamps', and their functional purpose is described in a very rational and formal way. The result of all this is that they cease to be divine beings who receive personal worship, and become non-divine, natural things, available for man to study. The creation story in Genesis has therefore with some justification been described as a piece of 'atheist propaganda'.

Nature is divested of its magical power; and at the same time, man is made lord over nature. God's command to the first human pair is: 'Be fruitful and multiply, and fill the earth and subdue it' (Gen. 1.28). The secularizing and atheist tendency present in this command is clear when it is seen against its background in comparative religion. In the world of the ancient Near East, the earth was worshipped as the 'mother', and yet men are now to rule over the earth. Devout heathens must have regarded this as virtually the rape of their mother.

The entrusting of lordship over nature to man in the first creation story was taken further by an important feature in the second story. There we read: 'So out of the ground the Lord God formed every beast of the field and every bird of the air, and brought them to the man to see what he would call them; and whatever the man called every living creature, that was its name.' (Gen. 2.19). The meaning of this naming is that it is man who, by an act of appropriation, gives meaning to the creation round about him. Thus the names, relationships and coherent structures of the world are not simply present from the start, so that man has only to discover them. It is he himself who calls them into being and forms them. One cannot but contrast Plato's doctrine of ideas with this 'nominalism'. In Plato, the ideas are timelessly present, they are as it were stored up in heaven, waiting to be sent for, and man apprehends them by memory and intuition. But in the bible God allows man to co-operate with him as his partner in ordering the world; together God and man plan the signs and give the meanings which turn chaos into order. But in this way the world ceases itself to be divine.

With respect to the question of how far secularization and atheism are a consequence of Christianity itself, the Old Testament creation narrative seems almost to be a prophecy of the revelation in Christ. Here man is finally adopted as the 'son' of God, and receives as his inheritance the world, over which he has to rule in mature responsibility (Gal. 4.1ff).

It seems almost as though in its gradual development, Christianity has undermined itself in two ways. First of all, from his stance in God, man can look at the world from outside, fearlessly investigate it and put it to use, and so create for himself an independence and freedom which seems to make him less and less in need of God. Secondly, the diffuse and naïve piety present everywhere in the world is concentrated and focused by Christian faith on the revelation in Christ, so that the world is as it were drained of its natural religious tendency.

It is certainly an exaggeration to say that atheism is a consequence of Christianity, and that, consequently, Christianity is only a transitional phase between polytheism and atheism. But it is true to say that only where God is proclaimed and believed in so radically as in Christianity, can he be so radically denied and rejected. There is no comparable phenomenon in non-christian religions. To this extent one can say that modern atheism is a post-christian phenomenon.

In the assertion that 'God is dead' Christian faith sees itself reflected in a negative image. If this fact is taken seriously, the conflict between Christianity and atheism is one between two hostile brothers, who, as long as they continue to dispute the inheritance, make it obvious that they are sons of the same father. And anyone who tries to be rid of God shows that he is not yet rid of him.

2

God Cannot Die

1. Theology Concentrates on the Question of God

Since the end of the second world war, the change in the nature
of theological enquiry has proceeded at an increasing pace,
and has become more and more radical.

The main preoccupation of theology and the church during
the years immediately after the war, apart from the problems of
reconstructing the church and the first attempts and temptations in the process of becoming aware of Christian social and
political responsibility, was the inherited problem of the relationship between revelation and history, Christian faith and
historical thought. The questions faced were those raised by
historical criticism: the reliability of biblical tradition, the
authority of the Old and New Testaments and the church's
creeds, the question of the historical Jesus, the virgin birth, the
divinity of Christ, the crucifixion, the resurrection, the empty
tomb, the ascension and the second coming. As early as the
end of the first world war Karl Barth had asserted of the theological arguments raised by historical criticism that 'this battle
is over'. But he was ahead of his time.

After the flood of dialectic theology had run its course, all
these unresolved problems came once again to the surface. Since
the debate initiated by Rudolf Bultmann about the 'demy-
thologizing of the New Testament', if not before, theology and
the church have again been heavily entangled in the problems
of theology and history. For almost twenty years, from the end
of the war to the middle of the 1960s, this discussion has pre-
occupied theology and the church. For a short time it even drew
the attention of the public outside the church, to an astonishing

extent. The bookshops were flooded by it; the press, the radio and the television were full of it. But public interest in the subject has long since declined, and in fact the main problems can be regarded as settled. What had to be said has been said; nothing startlingly new can be expected on the subject. On the whole, only rearguard actions are now going on, a game of ping-pong inside the church. Only the church public which provides the regular audience for this kind of discussion still follows the game, and with much diminished interest. There will always, of course, be those who never learn. They are only dangerous when their intractability is expressed in propaganda and, if they are able, in terror, be it in the church or in politics.

It is not that the problems of the bible and of christology have been 'solved' for us. This will never be so. But nowadays they occupy a different position in the context of theology. We face them in connection with the question of God. This has meant that they have lost some of their force as questions in their own right, but have at the same time become more radical through their new link with the question of God.

What is at issue at the present day is not one or other partial aspect of Christian faith, but the whole of Christian faith. The argument is about the existence of God. For if those who speak know what they are talking about, the statement that God *exists* forms the content of all Christian faith and preaching. The word 'God' sums up everything that is contained in faith. And therefore theology has for some time been undergoing an intensive process of concentration. God himself has once again become the central theme of theological study, and theology has once again become *theo*logy in the strict sense of the word. How could this be otherwise, if theology is to take its task seriously?

But this concentration on God has also meant that theology has 'returned to first principles'. One of the favourite charges made against 'modern theology' is that of 'reduction', of trimming its message. The word has become almost a term of abuse. But reduction can be understood in a positive sense, as a return to origins, to the 'kernel in the nut', to the 'germ of the wheat' (Luther). In this sense it does not mean cutting down the Christian message by deleting part of it, but concentration by compression – and at the same time by simplification. In the context

of the debate over Robinson's book *Honest to God*, a reader
wrote to the Guardian:

> The best thing about being a Christian at the moment is that orga-
> nized religion has collapsed.... Stripped of our nonsense we may almost
> be like the early Christians painting their primitive symbols on the
> walls of the catacombs – the fish, the grapes, the loaves of bread, the
> cross, the monogram of Christ – confident that in having done so they
> had described the necessities of life....[1]

2. 'God is Dead' – A Logical Contradiction

How can we speak of God today, in the face of the statement
that 'God is dead'? This is the question which has deeply pre-
occupied numerous theologians for years, especially the intellectually honest amongst them. Amongst some of them, it
is true, one can already hear the undertones of another question: Can we speak about God at all today, after the death of
God? They faithfully endeavour to do so, as before. And they
try with all seriousness to draw up the outlines of a theology in
the face of the assumption, or indeed on the very basis of the
assumption, that God is dead.

This so called 'theology after the death of God' does not
form any kind of unity, but presents an extremely obscure and
even confused picture. One of the main reasons for this is that
it uses the word 'God' and the concept of the 'death of God'
in an astonishingly careless and embarrassingly contradictory
way. A simplified and schematic distinction between the two
tendencies in this movement can be made by describing one
group as Christian atheists, and the other as Christian a-theists.

The Christian atheists ask whether it is possible to be a
Christian without believing in God. They answer this question
by the assertion that only by affirming that God is dead is it
still possible to be a believer in the conditions under which we
live in the twentieth century. They have given up any attempt
to save the concept of God by re-interpreting it. They set out
to be conscious atheists, without compromise, without any use
of the name of God, without worship and prayer. This is the
most radical challenge with which theology has ever presented
itself, an experiment which has never previously existed in this
form. Here, for the first time in the history of Christianity, the

death of God is proclaimed by theology as the programme it has set itself.

This attitude is roughly that of the radical wing of 'God is dead theology' in the USA. It was set in motion in 1961 by the theologian Gabriel Vahanian in his book *The Death of God. The Culture of our Post-Christian Era.* The title of this book gave the signal to others. Simultaneously with Vahanian's book, or shortly after, a whole series of similar essays and books appeared in America, all turning on the same theme: They were pure obituaries for God. But they varied a great deal, so that in America, too, the 'God is dead theology' became a general term covering widely different and even contradictory views.

Since then a similar theological school, stimulated by the American example, but of native origin, has come into being in Germany. It refers to itself as 'theology after the death of God'. But there is a marked difference between the German and the American form of this theology. One might express this in a rough and ready way by saying that in Germany we have a theology 'with nothing up above', while in America we have a theology 'with nothing at all'. A better way of putting this would be to say that the American school consciously intends to be a theology of the death of God, where the death of God itself is made the object of theology. The German school, on the other hand, sets out to be a theology *after* the death of God; here the death of God is regarded principally as determining the situation.

Thus most German 'God is dead' theologians can be described as Christian a-theists. If one attempts to express in carefully defined terms the rambling and imprecise way in which they speak of God and his death, one would not go far wrong in saying that for them the death of God does not signify the end of any belief in God, his total non-existence, but only the end of a particular concept of God. They do not wish to be tied down either to philosophical atheism or to religious theism. They regard both standpoints as belonging to the past, for in their view both have been shown to represent a naïve and discredited philosophical world-view. Instead, this 'theology after the death of God' asks what the word 'God' means today, how one can still experience God today, how God happens today – now that the continuing process of the enlightenment has made man wholly dependent upon what is immanent in the world. God as immanent in a closed world is the problem with which this theology is faced, and the programme according to which it works.

But it is clear that they do not stop at mere a-theism. The attack on theism is the first step along a path which leads irreversibly to total atheism. The position which the 'theology after the death of God' tries to adopt between atheism as a philosophical world-view and religious theism is not maintained, but abandoned in favour of atheism, when Dorothee Sölle calls on Christians to take the place of the 'absent God' in the world, and accordingly concludes her book *Christ the Representative* with this appeal:

> When the time was fulfilled, God had done something for us for long enough.... From now on, it is high time for us to do something for him.[2]

Here the lament for the absence of God is answered by a moral appeal to man. Certainly, of course, we can do something for God. Almost every page of the bible tells us this. But if our human acts for God consist of taking the place of the absent God in the world, then something inhuman is being asked of us. An element of breathlessness, fearfulness, frantic activity and constant over-exertion is introduced into Christianity – as though it were the business of Christians to help God, like a weak old man, to walk, or at least to get back on to his feet.

If the statement that 'God is dead' is more than a mere metaphor, and more than a mere human experience which in principle is subject to correction, and instead represents a final historical reality – in short, if God is really dead – then no human being, taking his place however perfectly, and no theologian, however contemporary, can ever bring him back to life. But then God would never have lived!

'God is dead' theologians of all schools seem to me to be like faithful soldiers who keep a guard of honour around the coffin of their dead general, and in their hearts cannot yet realize that he is actually dead. But neither piety nor tact are of any use in the face of the death of God, only logic and honesty. And anyone who thinks logically cannot avoid the honest alternative;

either God is dead, in which case he has never lived; or
else God has lived, in which case he is not dead. *For God
cannot die!* 'A god who can die deserves no tears,' says Harvey
Cox.[3] We would go on to say: because he has never existed!
The assertion that God is dead contradicts the inner logic of
the idea of God, which is binding even on non-believers when
they think of God.

The basic error of the 'God is dead' theologians lies in the
fact that they have taken an epistemological statement about
God and turned it into an ontological one. Because they no
longer experience the living and personal presence of God, they
declare that he is absent and dead. Their experience is comprehensible, but the proposition they deduce from it is not
logically conclusive. Can anyone put the sun out by closing his
eyes? Any person of understanding whose heart is in the right
place will sympathize with Dorothee Sölle when she writes:
'How, after Auschwitz, anyone can praise the God who o'er all
things so wondrously reigneth, I cannot understand' – or when
she says elsewhere: 'There is no way back to the father of his
children, who through waves and clouds and storms, gently
clears the way.'[4] Yet there is an immediate answer to this kind
of refutation of God. The two quotations above contain refer-
ences to two hymns which were written in or shortly after the
Thirty Years' War. Was the amount of suffering, senselessness
and injustice in the world at that time less than today? And
even if it was actually less in quantity – did people experience
the horrors of the Thirty Years' War with less pain than we
did those of the second world war? And yet they experienced
God and actually praised him! Even more to the point, if someone faced with the sufferings of Auschwitz should declare:
'Either there is no God, or God is a sadist', an almost verbal
parallel can be found in Martin Luther. In his work *De servo
arbitrio* Luther writes that if human reason were to consider
how God rules the world, it would be forced to the judgment
that either there is no God, or God is unjust.[5]

This historical comparison forces us to the following theological conclusion. Faith in God has always been exposed by the
world as it is to endurance tests and objections which have been
just as powerful and just as severe in all ages. Faith in God is
something which men have never been able to 'take for granted'.

They have always believed in God against the outward appearances presented by the world. Their faith has always had to say 'nevertheless' and 'in spite of all': 'Nevertheless I am continually with thee' (Ps. 73.23).

It is possible to assert that man's belief in God has at all times been a deception and an impossibility. But one cannot allow that belief in God was possible in the past and at the same time declare that it is impossible in the age in which one lives. If belief in God is an illusion today, then it was before. Sigmund Freud's assertion that in all essential respects religion is complete, and that if it was a mistake, it must remain one for ever[6], can also be put the other way around: If religion is an error today, it always was so in the past. But if this is so, then at all ages men have lived under a great illusion, and there is in truth no more urgent task now than finally to disillusion them.

A theology without God is either pure anthropology or nonsense. At least it is no longer theology, neither *theo*logy in so far as it no longer speaks of God, nor theo*logy*, in so far as it no longer proceeds by logical argument. Theology without God is a theology which has disembodied itself!

Here we have a standard by which anything that is said about the 'Death of God' can be judged. The legitimacy of language about the death of God depends upon whether it is dialectic or non-dialectic.

Basically Nietzsche spoke non-dialectically about the death of God. He coined the phrase: 'God hath died: now do *we* desire the Superman.'[7] Here there is no dialectic; one thing is being exchanged for another. Thus Nietzsche, too, is guilty of an inner logical contradiction. One cannot speak of the death of God in the way Nietzsche does. All that can ever die is a concept or an illusion which man has cherished with regard to God – and a person's faith can also die. But a God who dies or is killed by man has never lived or is not God.

Almost a hundred years before Nietzsche, Hegel subjected the atheism of the modern age to a critical examination. Hegel discusses the death of God dialectically, by relating it to the events of Good Friday, and at the same time taking the resurrection into account. When he speaks of the death of God he quotes Luther's hymn: *O grosse Not! Gott selbst ist tot (O* great sorrow! God himself is dead!) and he continues:

> The consciousness of this fact expresses the truth that the human, the finite, frailty, weakness, the negative, is itself a divine moment, is in God Himself; that otherness or Other-Being, the finite, the negative, is not outside of God, and that in its character as otherness it does not hinder unity with God; otherness, the negation, is consciously known to be a moment of the Divine nature. The highest knowledge of the nature of the Idea of Spirit is contained in this thought.
>
> This outward negative changes round in this way into the inner negative. Regarded in one aspect the meaning, the signification attached to death is that in it the human element has been stripped off, and the divine glory comes again into view. But death is itself at the same time also the negative, the furthest point of that experience to which man as a natural being and consequently God Himself are exposed.[8]

Hegel understands the death of God as something that happens within God himself. It is not, therefore, something man does to God, but a movement on God's own part. 'The feeling that God himself is dead' may only be taken 'simply as an element and no more than an element in the supreme Idea'.[9] And so for Hegel the death of God signifies only a transitory process within God. Thus one cannot do what is sometimes done nowadays by the 'theology after the death of God', and call upon Hegel as principal witness in favour of a Christian atheism. The reverse is true: he is talking about 'Christianity taking atheism into itself'.[10]

And therefore one can only speak properly of the death of God when one also takes into account the resurrection. But when the death of God is spoken of without regard for the resurrection, it is not God who is being spoken of. This brings us to the paradox that the assertion that 'God is dead' is at bottom an expression of faith, and that only where there is belief in the living God can one legitimately speak of his death. Walter Hartmann has expressed this paradox most strikingly:

> The death of God can be proclaimed only in the name of the living God ... Only in the light of the resurrection is it possible to give a sufficiently profound consideration to his death ... Anyone who has nothing to say about the new life of God in the history of the present day is likewise incapable of talking about his death in the past.[11]

That the resurrection has been taken into consideration in relation to the idea of the death of God, does not mean that our worries are over. Things are not yet back in order again. We must not be deceived into leaving everything as it was – everything here meaning God. Nothing is in order, and nothing can be left as it was. Christians share in the blame for the statement that is made today, that God is dead, because their faith in God and their language about him has been too narrow and tied far too long to the world view, the political institutions, and the whole social and cultural reference system of a bygone age. And they have not succeeded in making the break between their faith and this system in time for others to be set free by it.

In Bertolt Brecht's stories of Herr Keuner we read the following:

> A worker who had to give evidence before a court was asked whether he wished to take the oath or make the affirmation. He replied 'I am unemployed'. 'This was not simply confusion,' said Keuner. 'By this answer he made it known that he was in a situation where such questions, and perhaps indeed the whole process of the trial as such, no longer made any sense.'

The same has happened to theology and the church with respect to what it says about God. In its interpretation of texts it has overlooked the context, the connection with the life of men, and because men have become unable to recognize this connection, the whole procedure no longer seems to make any sense to them.

Understood in this way, the statement that 'God is dead' is a judgment on theology and the church, and therefore a call to repentance. The form this repentance must take is for theology to begin the process of coming to terms with the 'transformation' of God in history and of believing in him in a new way, and so of speaking about him more credibly.

The new way of speaking about God which is required of theology and the church at the present day is of course more than merely a problem of language, in the sense of a better mutual agreement about the language to be used. The question of how we are to speak about God in a new way in the context of the 'death of God' cannot be solved by a mere manipulation of vocabulary, either by dropping or replacing the word 'God'. We will certainly not be able to use the name of God as much as before, but we cannot simply give it up. We have no right either to talk God to death or to bury him in silence!

A renewal of the church will not happen by the clergy taking their robes off and preaching in ordinary dress; nor can theology be renewed simply by a change of clothes, that is simply by changing the words and concepts in which its statements are dressed up. 'Make-up alone does not make a country girl into a woman of the world.'[12] It must be a *human* language, not jargon, just as Jesus was a human being and not an ignorant clod.

Unless theology and the church 'make a move' they will never learn to speak about God in a new way. Not until they are once again 'on the spot', doing there what men need, will they once again have the chance of finding a new language in which to speak about God. Perhaps it is now necessary for the temple of theology and the church to be broken down, as Jesus said the temple of the Jews had to be broken down. But the least that is required of them is an exodus, like the exodus of Israel from Egypt or the passage of the Apostle Paul from the Jewish to the Hellenistic world. This will not be an 'exodus from God', as Bloch prophesies, but it will be an exodus from the old sanctuaries where the fathers found and worshipped God to a new historical dwelling place. It will be an exodus to the place where human, social and political life is at its most intense, with the aim of encountering and serving God there. In the words of Rosenstock-Huessy: 'God is the one who says, "From now on you must look for me somewhere else." '[13]

3. In Praise of the Enlightenment. Its Positive Consequences for Belief in God

To look for God again somewhere else – that is what the enlightenment adds up to. But there is by no means only a negative side to the enlightenment; there is a positive side as well. It is a challenge. And therefore we must scrutinize the process of the enlightenment once again and try to find out how far it represents a 'transition' on the part of God. That is, can we see in the enlightenment only the 'death' of God, or is his 'resurrection' there as well?

In our first scrutiny we showed how, as the enlightenment of man increased its scope, it had the effect of restricting God to an increasingly limited sphere. In recent years this process has frequently been described. The emphasis has been limited mainly to its negative aspects, those which are destructive of belief in God. But in fact the enlightenment has an ambivalent character with regard to God, a negative and a positive side. The negative side lies in the fact of the constant limitation of the sphere in which belief in God is operative. But the result of the positive aspect which accompanies it is that thought and language about God has been purified and made more profound, undergoing a continual process of cleansing. It is as though Kant's famous statement from his *Critique of Pure Reason* has been fulfilled in the history of the modern age: 'I have therefore found it necessary to deny *knowledge*, in order to make room for *faith*.'

Properly understood, even the modern atheism which originates in the enlightenment has had a purifying and refining effect on theology. Think of the things we took for God! Think of the things we claimed to be the work of God! Think of the things we have said and done in the name of God! How often have we made God in our own image! From now on, this kind of idolatry is impossible. The positive achievement of modern atheism is the vigorous purification which Christianity, together with its theology, has undergone, bringing the rejection of every kind of idolatry. The French Christian Jean Lacroix once expressed this in the words: 'I am grateful to my atheist friends, for they have taught me not to cheat.'[14] Thus the presentation of the negative aspect of the enlightenment must now be followed by the *praise of the enlightenment*. We shall do this by working through the seven factors we have already identified, but this time pointing to the positive ways in which they have purified belief in God and made it more profound.

a. The first negative factor we identified was that as a consequence of the 'anthropocentric turning point' of the enlightenment all truth is related to the human subject which knows it, and the critical, judging, and doubting ego of man claims a right to share in all judgment upon the truth, even when it is a matter of the truth of God. We must now add as a positive factor that as a result of this very subjectivity the 'involvement' of man is ensured. This is what Hegel, in his *Encyclopaedia*, demands for the experience and acceptance of any truth:

The principle of experience comprises the infinitely important condition that man himself must be involved in the acceptance and belief in a matter, or, more accurately, that he finds such a matter incorporated in his self-awareness.[15]

Jesus of Nazareth said the same thing eighteen hundred years before Hegel, but in a simpler, more telling and more practical form. According to an apocryphal tradition, he said to a man working on the land on the sabbath, 'If you know what you are doing, you are blessed. If you do not know what you are doing you are cursed.' Man must know what he is doing when he believes! This awareness is a requirement which is common both to belief in God and to the enlightenment.

In this way 'second generation Christianity', based largely on birth and upbringing, becomes a 'Christianity of choice', based upon a conscious personal decision. But this discovery itself is not as modern as it looks. The Church Father Tertullian said: *Fiunt, non nascuntur christiani* – one cannot be born a Christian, one has to become one. In short, one does not become a Christian by birth, but by choice. Thus the days of the early church are returning today, at the end of the enlightenment.

But choice always implies a selection as well, in a dual sense. First of all, a selection has to be made between the systems of values, ideologies and religions which face contemporary man every day in an age of philosophical pluralism. But a choice must also be made with regard to the whole mass of Christian faith itself. No one can believe everything that Christianity offers him. Neither pope, professor, bishop nor prelate can manage that! And that is why a selection is necessary. Everyone must and may select only what 'suits' him. There is no faith without understanding and no understanding without decision. The age in which one could say 'Yes and Amen' to everything are past. Nowadays one must also be able to say 'No and Amen'. Sometimes it is no longer sufficient to use the favourite method of quoting conflicting authorities as a means of looking objectively at church tradition. At certain points, a conscious break must be made with this tradition.

b. We identified as a negative factor the way in which, as a result of the extension to all phenomena of the causal nexus and the rational ordering of the world, God was increasingly forced out of the world by scientific investigation and technological planning, losing his foothold in human society and existence. We must now affirm as a positive aspect that science can also function as a kind of 'negative theology', by showing everything that God is *not*. It unmasks the false and facile identification of the events of nature and history with God, and helps us to think more clearly about God. The exclusion of God from the secondary causes of the process of nature and history results in God's being led into direct and unmediated contact with man. If man encounters him at all, it is in a more personal and intimate way. The decline of magic brings an increase in the transcendence of God and the personal commitment of man. At the same time, the purging of all elements of any philosophical world-view from belief in God results in greater intellectual honesty. Anyone in the field of science who nowadays takes refuge in God is being unscientific. Anyone in the field of political economy who tells man in his misery to seek comfort in God is merely prolonging an existence which is beneath human dignity. Anyone in the field of psychology who tries to bring man peace through God is misusing God by making him the instrument of human wish fulfilment.

Of course one must not overlook the fact that as the concept of God is made more spiritual, and is more intimately and profoundly apprehended, it can also become rarefied to vanishing point. The other side of the rediscovery of the 'deity of God' is that it becomes increasingly difficult to experience and conceive of him. Pure intellect without flesh is always a bloodless, feeble and therefore suspicious, almost embarrassing matter – like so-called 'platonic love'. Intellectualization often occurs as a sign of fatigue at the end of an era of civilization.

c. The shift of consciousness from the world beyond to this world has brought about a decisive change in man's feeling for life, and means that from henceforth man exists only in a *single* reality, with his feet firmly on the ground in this world. We saw this as a negative element, but it is complemented by the positive factor. It has meant that the significance and intensity of earthly life has increased, in so far as man's encounter with God, if it takes place at all, takes place here, in the midst of human life and in the reality of the world. There is no more 'pie in the sky'. Faith in God must be vindicated here and now on earth – it is no longer any use to point to eternity. The same lesson was taught in the parable of the rich man and Lazarus:

'Neither will they be convinced if someone should rise from the dead' (Luke 16.31).

d. A fourth negative element was the fact that the critical interrogation of all traditional authorities by the enlightenment has also cast doubt on traditional belief in God, so that it is no longer undisputed and taken for granted as it was before. On the positive side, if God is no longer an automatic and authoritative premiss, both the dignity of man and the honour of God are increased. From now on religious faith is associated with critical awareness, and this link is good for religious faith, at the very least. Man is no longer prepared to give unconditional recognition in advance to any 'divine' authority and to sign a blank cheque. He reads the small print before he signs. And he can afford to! Because the progress of secularization has enormously extended his freedom of action, he no longer needs God as a mere 'source of sustenance'. Thus when man seeks God at the present day, it is really God whom he is seeking. His motive is not a concern for his well-being, nor even for his well-being in the world to come, but solely the search for truth. And when he accepts the truth of God he does not do so because he is ordered to by someone else, but spontaneously, of his own accord.

But this 'personalization' of authority also means that the honour of God is greater. For the honour of God lies in the fact that he does not want slaves who are forced to serve, but witnesses who testify of their own free will, 'friends of God', who have let themselves be won over, who have not been over-powered by some external force, but who are convinced from within, who do not merely assent, but believe 'from the heart'. Paul speaks of the 'slaves of Christ', but John speaks of his 'friends'. In his gospel, Christ says: 'You are my friends.... No longer do I call you servants, for the servant does not know what his master is doing; but I have called you friends, for all that I have heard from my Father I have made known to you' (John 15.14 f.). Schleiermacher seems to prefer John to Paul when in his *Discourses on Religion* he said: 'It is no slavery and no captivity. You must belong to yourselves. Indeed this is an indispensable condition of having any part in religion.'[16]

The kind of Christianity which has resulted from the transformation of authority by the enlightenment is often called 'undogmatic Christianity'. We accept this, and believe that it represents the rediscovery of something basic in Christianity.

e. We saw that the ideological criticism of religion, which has investigated its economic and sociological roots, has revealed the hidden link between belief in God and the ideologies in which human interests are expressed. The discovery of this link created a vacuum for belief in God. But the positive side of this is that the 'twilight of the gods' initiated by this ideological criticism of religion has at the same time had a wholesome and purifying effect. In the words of an ancient rabbinic saying, the second best thing after believing in Yahweh is not to believe in God – meaning the rejection of idolatry. The ideological criticism of religion brings with it this resistance to the setting up of false idols. And therefore, voluntarily or involuntarily, it shares the concern that God should not become a human artefact, but should remain the 'Wholly Other'. It is as though at the present day God was ridding himself increasingly of every confusion of his person with human interest, and every attempt to camouflage and deform his image with human ideologies.

f. Man lives nowadays with his face turned towards the future, and because in part he has abandoned his memories of the past, he no longer looks back to historical revelations. Against this negative assertion we must set the positive factor that this new orientation towards the future has restored an attitude to time which is an original element in Christian faith. The enlightenment has played its part in helping theology to re-discover primitive Christian eschatology. In the first place, it has enabled theologians, with the aid of historical criticism, to read with new eyes the texts that bear witness to the Christian revelation. Secondly, the idea of progress which characterizes the enlightenment, but which preserves Christian eschatology in secularized form, has enabled theologians in their turn to look towards the future, and to consider the future of the world and of man from the point of view of the future of God.

g. Modern 'humanists' are resolved to come to grips on their own with the suffering and injustices in the world, either without the help of God or even in conscious hostility to him. They are taking the future of human society into their own hands. But there is a positive aspect of this. This commitment on the part of humanists has, as it were, challenged Christians to compete with them in the field of social policy. They can no

longer afford to blame the providence of God for all the evil and
unrighteousness in the world, but are obliged to recognize that
in part at least it is due to their own failure, and to concern
themselves in the future not only with the renewal of human
hearts, but also with the renewal of human society.

When we see the beautifully written manuscripts of ancient
monastic libraries, we praise and marvel at the patience of the
monks, who worked for years to complete them. And we regret
that such patience is no longer to be found in our own age. But
this is false. For one thing, a scientist who carries out a repeated
series of experiments over many years is no less patient than a
mediaeval monk who spent year after year writing out a manu-
script. Secondly, a 'consecrated life' at the present day requires,
besides prayer, not the calligraphy of the past, although it is
still widely practised in the church, but the practice of righteousness in whatever way is needed. And this too requires patience.

4. Is God Concealed or Absent?

Having once again scrutinized the process of the enlightenment, to discover its positive aspects, we must turn again to the
question whether, in order to give the right theological interpretation to our present situation, we have to speak of the 'concealment' or of the 'absence' of God. In the past scarcely any
distinction was made between these two concepts. The background to both was the presence of God, even when it seemed to
be obscured. Not until, in the present age, God seemed to have
withdrawn into an increasing darkness, was a distinction made
between the two concepts. At present the preference is for the
concept of the absence of God. In distinction to that of his concealment as a transitory event, it implies that the situation is
final, that God has not temporarily withdrawn, but has gone
away for good.

But we have seen from our second scrutiny of the process of
the enlightenment that it shows evidence not only of the 'death'
of God, but also of his 'resurrection'. This means that we have
to revise the distinction between the 'absence' and the 'concealment' of God. If there is an inner logical contradiction in speaking of the death of God, and if the enlightenment does not
merely destroy belief in God, but at the same time purifies it

and makes it more profound, then the distinction vanishes. It can now be characterized as follows – and indeed there is no other way: 'The fool says in his heart, "There is no God"' (Ps. 14.1); but Jesus cries out on the cross 'My God, my God, why hast thou forsaken me?'

The world has become worldly, heaven has closed over our heads, and it hangs low and inpenetrable over us. Yet is there anything which really gives us the right to claim so vehemently for our own age that it is exceptional? Does our relationship to God really depend so much upon the change in our picture of the world? Is our trust in God seriously lessened by the fact that our houses have lightning conductors on them? From the very earliest times, has not the greatest threat to belief in God been not so much the way man's picture of the world has changed, as the fact that the reality of the world has remained the same? People often go on nowadays as if the world had previously been full of the revelation of God, but is now completely empty of it. But has not the revelation of God always brought with it his concealment?

Why, then, did Job suffer so much? Because God was so far from him or because he was too near to him? Surely because he was so near him, and for that reason he suffered from his remoteness. If Job had not believed in God, he would not have been any better off, and would still have been sitting on his dunghill. But the source of his bitterest suffering would no longer have been there. It is the very nearness of God which makes Job's suffering so painful. Without belief in God his life would still have been meaningless, but it is belief in God which gave the meaninglessness of his life its real cruelty, to the point where it was intolerable.

Even if God reveals himself in the world, his concealment does not stop. In his revelation he is to be found in things that are indistinguishable from other things in the world: the Bible is a book, Jesus of Nazareth a rabbi, the church an institution and the Christian an ordinary man.

Whether he is present or absent, God always exists, as long as man takes any account of the fact that he exists. Only when we have this general background clearly in our minds can we sketch upon it the distinctive features of our own present age. And then we can even speak of the absence of God, not to express the assertion that his concealment in our own age is a final one, but to show how profound it is. But we are now looking at something deeper than mere historical change. Only at this point can anything that is said about the concealment or absence of God be a serious theological statement. We now have to take into account the possibility that God himself has withdrawn into a more profound concealment, and that this is why at the present day we live remote from God. In fact God does not always show himself in the same way. He is not always equally present, far less is he always available to us. Although we have his promises, we have no guarantees. That is why there are different periods in the history of God's dealings with men: periods where the cry is 'Look, now!', and periods when the cry is 'Look, not now!'

But we must take care not to console ourselves by treating this idea as though it were a philosophical category for interpreting history. Even when interpretations of history proclaim the decline of the West or even the death of God, they can have a marvellously consoling effect. They bring the age under our control and God within our grasp. When the bible talks about times when God is absent, it does so with fear, terror, the confession of man's own guilt and a new, more urgent expectation of God.

Thus we cannot speak of the absence of God in a world which has become worldly with the complacent approval, displayed by some theologians, of modern atheism or of our own interpretation of the history of thought. We can speak of it only with terror, and in the hope that God will come back to us. Perhaps such terror and hope is the most intense witness Christians can give their contemporaries of the presence of God today. It could be, however, that in this terror and hope God is actually making himself known again, so that what we regard as the death of God is in reality only the preparation for a new transformation.

3

Transformations of God

1. Is the Image of God Opposed to God?

'Transformations of God' is an expression of which Ernst Barlach has made use, and which Ernst Troeltsch was already using before him. Significantly, it was an artist and a philosopher of history who first spoke of transformations of God. For both deal with the variety of forms and phenomena presented by life, with the changing expression of the infinite in constantly renewed and visible finite forms. The artist expresses this process in his pictures, while the philosopher of history reflects upon it through the written word. For both it is a short step to speak of 'transformations' even in respect of God.

As a matter of experience, the concept 'transformations of God' provokes two opposite reactions. Some reject it as too dangerous, while others accept it too hastily and uncritically. In both cases we suspect that they do not really appreciate what the expression 'transformations of God' really signifies. We shall therefore explain it by arguing against these two opposite reactions.

We begin with those who are scandalized by the expression 'transformations of God', and who feel afraid and reject it on grounds of orthodoxy, the illegitimate daughter of fear. Is God not the 'Eternal'?, they object. But how can the Eternal be 'transformed'? Does not Psalm 90 say of him: 'Before the mountains were brought forth, or ever thou hadst formed the earth and the world, from everlasting to everlasting thou art God'? And did not God say of himself at his encounter with Moses at the burning bush: 'I will be what I will be' (Ex. 3.14;

RSV margin)? These 'defenders of the faith' can call upon Karl Barth as their principal witness among theologians, with his blunt assertion that 'God is God', and the advice he accordingly gives with regard to all church practice, that the church can only fulfil its 'true task ... by proclaiming something that is above all human possession'.[1]

To begin with, we shall make two brief points in reply to this appeal to the unchangeable eternity of God and the rejection of any statement about the possibility of 'transformations of God'.

In the first place, the very God who is said to have existed from eternity and to remain the same for eternity is also called in the bible the 'God of Abraham, Isaac and Jacob'. Whatever detailed exposition may be given of this title of God, it introduces an element of movement, and perhaps even of change, in God by the very fact of the way in which he himself has chosen to be related to man and his history. Here we have the first stage of a dialectic which we must take into account when speaking of God. It could be that the basis of this dialectic is in God himself, and in his wish to enter into a dialogue with men.

Secondly, the expression 'transformations of God' once again explicitly excludes any statement about the 'death of God'. For a transformation never implies an end and a death, but on the contrary assumes something permanent. Something can only change which within and in spite of every change continues to exist through the change.

But these two points might easily lead to a premature and false reassurance. And here we turn to the second group, to those who accept the concept of 'transformations of God' too hastily and uncritically. They betray no suspicions of this expression. On the contrary, they are reassured and almost encouraged by it. When they hear tell of 'transformations of God' they think only of the transformation of the concepts, images and concept of God which men make for themselves, not of a transformation of God himself. And they are reassured and comforted by this. For as historical experience shows, men's concepts and images of God have often changed in the course of time. Thus, they conclude, things may not be too bad for God at the present day!

But this reassurance is dangerous, its comfort it offers is too facile. Underlying it is a suspicious attempt to avoid the pressing problem by playing the image of God off against God himself. But anyone who argues like this oversimplifies the question of God. He takes the sting out of the expression 'transformations of God' in a way which is not permissible. For the expression does not simply refer to changes that are always possible in the conceptions, images and concepts of God which man makes for himself, but also refers to changes in God himself. This interpretation is unavoidable if we take seriously the debate about the relationship between subject and object which has gone on for many decades, and do not simply cast away what it has established.

The decisive outcome of this debate lies in the *overcoming of the subject-object pattern* in thought. A subject which knows does not stand apart from the object which is known as a neutral observer. Subject and object have a living relationship with each other. They are joined together in the act of knowledge.

This is perfectly evident in all the 'hermeneutic sciences', that is, in all branches of study which are concerned with understanding and values, and above all in the sphere of history. The object which a historian is studying is not there in front of him like a body on an anatomist's or pathologist's dissection table. Rather, he is face to face and in constant dialogue with it, and the more he is subjectively involved in it, the more he will know about it objectively. This is the reason why every generation has to re-write history: not only because new sources have been discovered and the material has increased, but above all because there has been a change in the point of view from which we begin and as our own subjectivity has changed. But for a long time the overcoming of the subject-object pattern has applied not only to the so-called 'hermeneutic sciences', but more and more to the natural sciences as well – those to which the adjective 'exact' has been applied, to emphasize their objective character. Even in the so-called 'exact sciences' there is no pure objectivity, 'without regard to' the subject which knows. Here, too, the final result is always influenced by the particular viewpoint of the observer. The investigating scientist does not remain an outside spectator, but joins in. He is as it were drawn into the experiment. The answer he receives from nature is partly dependent on the way he formulates his question. One can say that what one shouts into nature is echoed back. The method applied does not leave its object unchanged, so that different aspects of nature result from different points of view and methods. The best known example of this is that of light, which behaves as a wave or as a corpuscle, depending upon the way in which it is observed. Thus even the exact natural sciences no longer present us with a picture of nature in isolation from the observer, but, in the words of Werner Heisenberg, only 'a picture of our relations to nature'.

This overcoming of the subject-object pattern can also be encountered in psycho-analysis. Freud's requirement that a psychoanalyst should be analysed himself as a necessary condition for undertaking the analysis of anyone else, and the conjunction of transference and contra-transference in the healing process of psychoanalysis, assume that subject and object are not separated and opposed to each other, but are independent of each other and must co-operate if anything is to result.

If we apply the outcome of the subject-object debate to theology, and therefore to the *relationship between man and God*, it appears that here too the knowledge of the object is never independent of the subject which knows it. A part is always played in the knowledge of God by the kind of relationship in which man stands to God on any given occasion. Apart from this relationship of man to God there is no knowledge of God at all.

No one has expressed this truth in such radical terms as Martin Luther. He has used expressions which are so bold as to recall Feuerbach, and which Barth has accordingly suspected of being anthropological, and has therefore severely criticized. Thus for example in a lecture on the Epistle to the Romans given in 1515/16, Luther says *Deus est mutabilis quam maxime ... Qualis est enim unusquisque in seipso, talis est ei Deus in objecto.*[2] Freely translated this means: 'God is changeable to the utmost degree ... As anyone is in himself as subject, so God is to him (as negative to positive image) as object.' Luther expresses the same thing even more drastically in a sermon on the 18th of June 1534 on Matthew 8.13: 'As Adam believes, so is his God; as he paints him in his heart, so he finds him ... Therefore God says: If you portray me right, you have me right, if you portray me badly, you have me badly ... As you believe, so you have! If you want to have me as the devil, you will have me as the devil, but it will not be my fault.'[3] This is why Luther was able to set up the famous rule for man's knowledge of God which he constantly repeats in different forms: 'If they believe, they possess.' 'If you believe, you possess; if you do not believe, you do not possess.'[4] Everyone always has as much of God as he believes. This rule of Luther's is backed by the saying which Jesus so frequently uses in the New Testament: 'According to your faith be it done to you.'

This does not mean that for Luther God is merely a projection of man and has no reality outside faith. In the passage quoted from the Epistle to the Romans Luther explicitly adds: *Verum haec mutatio extrinseca est* – but this change takes place only outside him. And in the sermon we have quoted he adds, 'But it is not my fault'. But it means that for Luther God is only real and effective through the function of faith; outside the function of faith, in Luther's view, man can have no relationship at all to God, and God does not even exist for him:

Faith is the creator of deity, not in person, but in us. Outside faith God loses his righteousness, glory, majesty and so forth, and nothing of majesty or deity exists where there is no faith.[5]

Thus for Luther God and man are 'combined in a field of force in which a change at one point brings about a change in the other.'[6] Or to use another image, just as in the natural sciences the investigator is drawn into the experiment, so man is always involved in the experiment with God.

Thus the expression 'transformations of God' is revealed to us in all its profundity. We can now say, of course, that God himself does not change, 'only' man's experiences of God and the images in which he expresses these experiences actually change. But we are no longer able to play the images of God against God himself. For what is the force of the word 'only' here? It is in his experience of God that man 'has' God, and in no other way, and therefore the expression 'transformations of God' refers in the end to God himself. Where man's experience of God changes, God himself changes for him; and where a person no longer has any experience of God, their God has ceased to exist for him. There is a Jewish saying: 'If you do not bear witness to

me, I am not.' We repeat, 'as anyone is in himself as subject, so
God is to him (as negative to positive image) as object'. The
expression 'transformations of God' must be taken as seriously
as this.

But we must not make these ideas carry more weight than
they can bear. The rediscovery of primitive Christian eschatology has led to an emphasis at the present day on the coming
of God, understood in historical terms – by contrast to the
static idea of the existence of God. This is certainly right and
proper. But the fact that God is coming must not lead to the
conclusion that he is only 'on his way' and is therefore 'not yet
ready' in himself. The 'coming' of God is due to the fact that it
is his own will to make himself known. Because it is his will to
enter into relationship to man and the world, God adapts himself to every age, and therefore submits to a historical process.
But we can neither say in the words of the young Rilke that
men work on God like builders on a cathedral, nor may we
assert that God 'develops'. The image of building makes God a
work of man, while the idea of development brings with it the
concept of a beginning and an origin. The idea of an 'origin' of
God is as logically absurd as that of his 'death'. But the concept
of 'transformations of God' expresses the paradox of the
presence of God in history through forms which are constantly
renewed.

2. Transformations of God in the Bible

The idea that God changes is not so frighteningly new as it
seems at the present day to many timorous orthodox Christians.
In fact it is wholly in agreement with the biblical evidence. We
can see in the bible how, under the pressure of actual experiences, and in the fluctuation between tradition and situation, there took place a continuous process of theological innova-
tion and progression, in the course of which the changes were
far from affecting merely outward forms, but also altered the
content of faith in God. It is not difficult to demonstrate the
existence of such 'transformations of God' in the bible. We shall
give three examples.

1. Our present Old Testament begins with the creation narrative, and also contains other lengthy statements about God the

creator. But all these texts are relatively recent in date. In the early days of Israel's religion faith was in Yahweh not as God the creator, but as the God of history. This began with the exodus from Egypt. 'I am the Lord your God, who brought you out of the land of Egypt, out of the house of bondage' (Ex. 20.2). This was the historical saving act of God which was the foundation of the 'covenant', Israel's first creed. A belief in God as creator was not developed until after the Israelites had entered Canaan. There, in their new environment, the tribes came into contact with the cultic worship of creator gods, together with the related creation myths. They were faced with the question whether the power of these foreign creator gods could possibly be of wider extent than that of their own God of history, Yahweh. Israel's reply to this challenge was to take the idea of creation into its covenant faith. But this did not happen simply by placing the two ideas side by side, but by a process of integration and adaptation. The non-Israelite creation myths were critically interpreted. Many mythical elements, especially the deification of sexuality and fertility, were excluded, and instead belief in God as creator was related to faith in him as the God of history. The history which God ruled was 'backdated' to the creation, but this divine history was made to begin with the creation. In the view of the Old Testament scholar Gerhard von Rad, 'theologically, this was a great achievement'. We do not hesitate to speak here of a 'transformation of God', and Gerhard von Rad agrees with this when he writes: 'It goes without saying that the expansion of the old Credo by means of such a preface tremendously broadened the theological basis of the whole thing.'[7] As a result of this, faith in Yahweh was both extended to a wider area of experience and became more profound.

2. How anyone can propose to adhere strictly to the bible without the idea of a transformation of God seems incomprehensible in the face of a contradiction such as the following. Throughout Trito-Isaiah – and not in some single fugitive passage – Yahweh speaks in words such as these:

> I have trodden the wine press alone,
> and from the peoples no one was with me;
> I trod them in my anger
> and trampled them in my wrath;

> their lifeblood is sprinkled upon my garments,
> and I have stained all my raiment.
> For the day of vengeance was in my heart,
> and my year of redemption has come ...
> I trod down the peoples in my anger,
> I made them drunk in my wrath,
> and I poured out their lifeblood on the earth. (Isa. 63.3 ff.)

But on the cross Jesus said: 'Father, forgive them; for they know not what they do' (Luke 23.34). When these two passages are taken together, one begins to see why Karl Holl has spoken of a *'new* concept of God' on the part of Jesus. Anyone who tries to reconcile these two passages must be a theological conjuror. True enough, a lot of theologians have as big a belly as the church is said to have; they can digest as many huge intellectual inconsistencies as the church can digest all kinds of worldly goods. But anyone who tries to get round the two passages that have been quoted without thinking historically, that is, without making use of the idea of a transformation of God, is not merely a theological conjuror, he is a confidence trickster. There is a straightforward alternative here; either we accept that 'transformations of God' are possible, or we do away with the whole bible as a testimony to God.

3. In late Judaism the law of God, the torah, was as important as a way of salvation as the gospel is in the Christian church. But the commandment to keep the sabbath was the backbone of the law. Rabbinic tradition declares that in the heavens God himself, with all the angels, keeps it with scrupulous exactness, and that if the whole people of Israel could only once keep the sabbath according to the law, the Messiah would come and the kingdom of God would begin. But Jesus says: 'The sabbath was made for man, not man for the sabbath' (Mark 2.27). This signifies that the ritual commandment to keep the sabbath has been replaced by the commandment of love.

In addition the Jewish law contained numerous provisions about food and ritual purity. The underlying principle of these was the distinction which is characteristic of all cultic religions between clean and unclean, sacred and profane. But Jesus says, 'Not what goes into the mouth defiles the man, but what comes out of the mouth, this defiles a man ... to eat with unwashed hands does not defile a man' (Matt. 15.11 ff.). From the point of view of the history of religion this represents a revolution; from the point of view of the history of man it is a liberation. The distinction underlying all cultic religion between clean and unclean, between sacred and profane, is abolished, and man is set free from a constant fear of transgression and guilt. In future, the service of God has not to take the form of cultic worship at a specified place and a particular time, but of a test undergone in the midst of the world and at every moment, in which one will not even know that one has encountered God, and will ask with astonishment: 'Lord, when did we see thee hungry and feed thee, or thirsty and give thee drink?' (Matt. 25.31 ff.). A religion of endeavour is turned into a religion of love and grace. If this does not represent a transformation of God, then I do not know what a transformation is.

These examples demonstrate only 'transformations of God' which can be found in the bible, each of which came about under the pressure of changed situations and the experiences and dilemmas they brought. The objection may be made that this only applies to the Old Testament and late Judaism, before all previous revelations of God were fulfilled in Jesus Christ. Now, it might be agreed, this no longer holds good. This objection is false. Even in 'Christian times' God has not ceased to change himself for men's sake. This is one of the subjects of this book.

3. *The Suspicion of Projection*

All we have said about the 'transformations of God' is threatened from the start by an objection which we must now examine critically. This is the charge of *projection*, that is, the suspicion that all human belief in God is nothing more than the projection of man's own desires into heaven, an ideological super-structure built upon his social relationships, the transference of his own imperfections upon another figure who is thought of as perfect. There is no greater threat to belief in God at the present day than the suspicion that it is merely a projection in this sense.

It is by no means a new idea. In antiquity it occurs as early as Xenophanes, who observed that the gods of the Ethiopians had flat noses and black hair, while those of the Thracians had blue eyes and red hair. He suspected that if oxen, horses or lions were able to paint or carve, they would certainly represent their gods as oxen, horses or lions. Today the charge of projection is a combined one made by philosophy, sociology and psychology, by Feuerbach, Marx and Freud and their followers. But whether it is Feuerbach who asserts that man portrays himself in his gods 'not as he is, but as what he wishes to be', Marx who sees in religion the 'halo round a fallen world', or Freud for whom a personal God is 'psychologically nothing more than an exalted father', the basic charge is the same. However different the arguments may be in each case, the same pattern of thought is always implied, the conversion of divine revelation 'from above to below' into a human fiction 'from below to above'. Man's belief in God is seen here not as relating to a reality, but as based upon an illusion; it is not God who has made man in his image, but men who have made God in their image. Religion and theology are nothing more than a 'fantastic projection of light in the sky'.

As long as man was in his childhood, he could be allowed to indulge in such illusions and fantasies. But now that he has left his childhood behind and has grown up, he must be brought back to reality; his illusions must be destroyed and he must be confronted with reality as it is, and not as he has imagined it. 'Men cannot remain children for ever.' 'Experience teaches us that the world is no nursery.'[8]

Because the images in which belief in God is expressed make many of our contemporaries feel in fact that they are back in the nursery, they not only reject the images of God, together with other conceptions from their childhood days, they also suspect that belief in God as a whole is an illusion of man, a hangover from the stage of his development before his puberty.

Thus suspicion of projection forces theology at the present day to reconsider the question of the content of *reality* in belief in God. What is the reality to which faith corresponds, and does it correspond to any reality at all? We shall discuss the problem of belief in God as projection in five stages.

a. There is no possibility of a belief in God which is completely free of the suspicion of projection.

This is true not only of belief in God, but of all belief, all love, all hope, and every personal experience without exception.

However vigorously I protest that I believe in God, that I love my country, that I am attached to a person, and whatever I do to demonstrate this faith or this love, someone else can always make the objection that all this is clearly imagination or illusion on my part – that in reality I am only projecting myself into my counterpart. All we have left in the end is the appeal to our own experience and the certainty based upon it. And no one is sure of himself.

b. The problem of projection faces us with a dilemma which we cannot resolve logically, but can only endure existentially.

Another example from personal relations will make the nature of this dilemma clear. If I have a friend, should I have an image of him in my mind or not? Both alternatives seem equally inhuman. If I have no image of him, our friendship remains something purely abstract, without memory or recollection and without any living participation of one in another. Basically, each is leaving the other to himself. But if I create an image of my friend in my mind, I run the risk of fixing and indeed of manipulating him, because I will try to make him fit my conceptions and wishes, and so deprive him of his own proper nature. The consequence will be that our friendship will ossify or even die, because the image that I have set up of my friend interferes with his own free development, and it deprives me of the chance of a new, open-ended encounter with him.

The same thing happens between us and God. On the one hand the stern commandment: 'You shall not make for yourselves any image or likeness of God' still holds force. There is accordingly, throughout the bible, a rejection of any attempt to tie God down to any name or conception (e.g. Gen. 32.30; Ex. 3.14; Judg. 13.18), until finally, in Judaism, the name of God was no longer even uttered. A similar phenomenon in the history of Christian theology is the tradition of *theologia negativa*, which only dares to say of God what he is *not*. *Nescio, nescio* – I do not know, I do not know, was the answer of Bernard of Clairvaux to every question about God, and Master Eckhart distinguishes between 'God' and 'deity'. By 'God' he means the imperfect conception in the form of images which man makes of God, while by 'deity' he means the unnameable, indescribable divine ground of being itself. The consequence is that *theologia negativa* is something totally abstract. A personal encounter with a concrete counterpart is lacking. It is no accident that in the history of religion there is frequently a close link between mysticism and atheism.

But where there is a personal encounter with a concrete counterpart people make images. Thus the same bible which contains the strict prohibition of images, and repeatedly rejects the naming of the name of God, is at the same time full of crude and detailed anthropomorphic images and conceptions of God. What we say about God can never be free of this dialectic. It is simply impossible for man to experience and understand anything without verbalizing or 'wording' it. Just as everything that King Midas touched turned to gold, so everything that man knows and experiences turns to words. But words immediately bring images on to the scene. There is no language without images, for otherwise, in our attempts to express the truth, we would be restricted to mathematical formulae.

Thus it seems that we can only speak of God in words – and therefore only in terms of images. The second commandment does not forbid this when it says that we must make no image or likeness of God. But it does forbid us to equate the words and images in which we speak of God with the reality of God. They can only be transitory 'outlines' which are the product of our experience of the reality of God. But they are never sufficient to encompass that reality, and as soon as they are formed, they always become obsolete and have to be corrected as a result of new experiences. Yet what are outlines if they are not 'projections'?

c. Because the revelation of God is directed towards men, it is quite impossible for human knowledge about God to get away without projections.

The biblical revelation itself does not exclude partial human projections, and in fact it makes them necessary. It always has an objective and a subjective side. The objective element in it is God's action, while its subjective side is its reception by man. One does not exist without the other – otherwise there would be no revelation of God at all! But where something divine is revealed, it enters 'into the flesh', that is, into human conceptions, images and concepts. The reception of divine revelation always takes place *secundum hominem recipientem* – in accordance with the man who receives it.

Thus in the first instance at least we can speak of the encounter with God only through analogy with our human relationships. Thus, for example, if we are trying to make clear what is meant by the 'love of God', we must in the first place use as a model the encounter between two human beings – that is, if we are to be comprehensible at all. Thus anthropomorphic language about God is not merely justified, but quite simply indispensable – unless we propose to give up any attempt to speak about God.

Thus the statement that human language about God consists of projection is not automatically an atheist attack. From the psychological point of view the structure and content of belief in God is always that of a projection. Every image of God reflects a variety of human features. The shadow of man always falls across the portrait which he sketches of God. Just as every reality which we perceive is coloured by our senses, so is the reality of God. If belief in God is really the belief of a living person of flesh and blood, it is always to some extent coloured by this fact. It is difficult to exclude this extraneous colouring except at the expense of a personal and living belief. Thus the 'non-theological factors' in belief in God should not be too much despised. By contrast to chemical experiments, a slight 'contamination effect' does no harm in theology. On the contrary, an exaggerated concern for the purity of our concept of God is inappropriate. If orthodoxy is too perfect it easily becomes sterile.

But one cannot give a seal of approval to the process of projection without at the same time being aware of the danger which it conceals. All our human conceptions of God constantly threaten to replace God and so to direct our gaze away from him. Thus for those who believe, the objection that their faith is a projection is always a timely one.

d. The charge of projection requires and makes possible the purification of human conceptions of God.

Basically, Feuerbach, Marx and Freud have done theology a service with their criticism of religion. They have forced it to observe the first and second commandments – to have no other gods besides God, and to make no images and likenesses of God himself – more strictly than before. It has led to a process of 'refuse disposal', in the course of which numerous worn out and indeed false human manifestations of God have been swept away, and belief purified with increasing vigour from alien elements. For example, when sociology reveals that the religion of a group is the reflection of its social circumstances, or when psychoanalysis makes it clear that a person's belief consists of projections of his infantile father or mother images, a Christian who is intellectually honest can only be grateful for this. A faith which is as vulnerable as this to sociological or psychological analysis is shown by that very fact to be false.

And whenever God has become too familiar to us, in fact almost 'a good acquaintance', it is appropriate to emphasize once again the other theme which runs throughout the bible: the fact that God remains unknown and unnamed, however much he is known and named. He cannot be thought of in human conceptions, and he cannot be comprehended in human terms. He is concealed in every revelation, he is the abyss in every firm foundation, he is the deity in God. The warning against projections reminds us that all our human images, ideas and conceptions of God are only symbols and ciphers, and are therefore always inadequate and ephemeral. Using them is like jumping from one ice-floe to the other. To stay too long means death – not the death of God, but at least of our conception of God.

e. To argue that projections are possible is not to assume that contact has been lost with reality; it assumes that it is present. Let us suppose that a child has projected all kinds of qualities, desires and experiences on to his father – does this mean that his father does not exist? It would be unjustifiable to make this assumption in advance. But it is an assumption implied in all theories of projection once they cease to be partial and become universal. The reply that, in the case of belief in God, the father is only a 'figment of belief' is not conclusive. It immediately provokes the argument that unbelief might also be the result of particular psychological constraints. May not the rejection of religion be no more than a reaction to errors in upbringing and education committed by parents and teachers? Might not atheism itself be only a projection, that is, the reflection of the desire to be rid of one's own father? Here objection, reply and counter-objection show that the truth of belief in God cannot be decided by psychological means. The argument is always a circular one.

Psychology, sociology and philosophy may well explain and criticize certain features of belief in God as partial projections, but they cannot obliterate the experience of God as a whole. They must first of all recognize that, like every other human experience, it is a directly experienced phenomenon. And even if they go on to declare the divine partner in this experience to be a projection and the whole experience itself an illusion, because there can be no real relationship to an illusory partner, the experience itself still exists as a phenomenon, even if it has been reduced to the level of an illusion; and it still needs to be interpreted. But the question then arises whether theories of projection, regardless of their origin and the methods they use, are themselves able to do justice to the phenomenon of religious perception.

Paul Tillich reminds us that projection always is projection *on to* something, a screen or a wall, which receives it. Tillich's purpose here is not to use the physical image of projection for the apologetic purpose of salvaging the existence of a supernatural world beyond this world. But he wishes to suggest that there is a sphere of the unconditional, the search for ultimate, absolute being beyond which no question can be asked, the direct experience of an 'ultimacy' of all life and being, which can no longer be explained as a projection, but is rather the assumption on which all projections are based.[9] Tillich's fundamental attack on the projection theory is supported by observations from human history. In particular, this historical argument has been applied by Wolfhart Pannenberg in his disagreement with Feuerbach's hypothesis of projection. According to him the history of man has taken precisely the opposite course to that asserted by Feuerbach. Man has not broken off a piece of his secular experience of himself and of the world and set it up as an alien, divine being; rather, the men of all ancient civilizations first understood themselves and the world in the light of the divine reality which they perceived. Pannenberg sums up this observation in the words: 'The history of man's understanding of himself is a function of the history of man's religion.' Religious experience must therefore be accorded 'historical priority' to every conception man has of himself: 'Religion is not a secondary addition to man's humanity. Rather, religion seems from the very first to have been as characteristic of man as the use of fire and tools and the power of speech. Thus it possesses the same fundamental status, as one of the foundations of man's distinctive position amongst the higher animals, as do the other characteristics of human behaviour.'[10] But we must reapply Pannenberg's historical argument on a more fundamental level.

What actually compels man to project part of himself upon a higher being? This obvious question is ultimately never answered by any of the advocates of the theory of projection. Feuerbach says of man, 'What he is not himself, but wishes to be, he imagines in his gods.'[11] But how does man ever come to have such wishes and conceptions? How does his imperfection come to be a source of suffering to him, so that he longs for perfection? And how does he come to suffer from the knowledge that he is mortal, and desire immortality? He could not do this, if he did not have some sense of perfection and immortality. Thus the charge of projection itself contains the germ of its refutation, in the undeniable fact that man reaches out towards an 'ultimacy' of being, to which he tries to attain by transcending his present state.

For Christian faith this readiness on the part of man to reach out towards the transcendent is based on the fact that God has created man according to his image (Gen. 1.27). It is this alone which enables man to set up images of God with any prospect of their providing an acceptable analogy. Whether these images are 'true', both in regard to the reality of God and also to the reality of the world, must be 'shown'. That is, they have to be verified.

In conclusion, then, we return to our first point, that our conceptions of God can never be cleared with complete certainty from the suspicion of projection. For verification never means logical proof. It does not replace faith, but gives power to faith, while at the same time it demands of faith that it should show itself to be true. But verification of this kind cannot be obtained within the closed circle of psychological argument, but only in the whole expanse of our experience of the reality of life and of the world. It must begin by paying attention to the questions which modern man is asking, and in particular to the questions he is asking about God.

4

What Kind of Questions are Men Asking about God?

1. Questions on Content and Meaning (The Scope of Questions)

The question: What kind of questions are men asking about God? straight away provokes the more radical question: Do men today ask questions about God at all? Indeed, we should perhaps first ask another question, more radical still: Do men still ask questions at all?

There is an image which involuntarily comes to mind. Anyone who has walked through a suburb on Sunday morning and has seen people washing their cars, working in the garden, reading their papers and playing with their children, gets the impression that this is such a closed, self-sufficient world that nobody in it is asking any questions, far less asking questions which look beyond it. Oscillating between factory and suburb, clamped in place between production and consumption, and driven by purely material forces, present-day man seems no longer to have any questions to ask.

Of course present-day man still asks questions. He has to know about a whole multitude of things, many more than his forefathers, in order to keep alive. In order to keep his life under control he needs information in increasing quantities, and information is obtained by asking questions. This covers such questions as which is the best bus to school in the morning, how to operate a machine or how to organize a business. Questions of this kind may even be about the future ordering of society. But all these are questions which ask about men's immediate needs and purposes. They are questions of practical knowledge, technical functioning and rational organization. In short, they are

questions about what is under human control. Naturally, man
asks such questions at the present day with great frequency
and so he will continue to do, as long as he lives. But when many
critical observers nowadays doubt whether present-day man
asks questions at all, they are not referring to this kind of question. When they claim that present-day man no longer asks
questions, they are saying that he does not ask questions which
go beyond his immediate needs and purposes, beyond practical
knowledge, technical functioning and rational organization, beyond everything, in short, that is simply under his own control.
He no longer asks, they claim, about the nature of things, about
his responsibility for society, about the meaning of his existence
and the destiny of his life. In short, he no longer asks questions
which go beyond all detailed, material, specialist, and technological matters and are concerned with the human person and
with totality; he no longer asks questions which contain something unconditional and absolute, and at first glance seem almost
useless and pointless.

This complaint, which becomes almost an accusation, conceals a distinction between two classes of questions which correspond to Heidegger's well-known distinction between calculating
and meditative thought. Calculating thought is concerned with
what can be controlled and computed, and is satisfied with what
is correct. Meditative thought asks about the meaning of things
and is concerned with the truth, even if it is of no apparent
value. The only question is whether this distinction between
two kinds of thought, and so between two kinds of question, can
be so strictly maintained for very long.

In the first place, it cannot be denied that there is a connection
between our smoothly functioning technological civilization and
our assertion that present-day man does not ask questions. The
greater the triumphs achieved by calculating thought, the
greater the extent to which it parts company from meditative
thought and sets out along the path of thoughtlessness. The
apparent ease with which everything can be controlled and
planned tempts one to take everything for granted, whether it is
a car or a bunch of roses. But where it seems possible to take
everything for granted, there is nothing left to ask. Man's total
control of the world threatens to destroy him as a being who
asks questions. Someone who no longer comes into conflict with

reality no longer asks about it. He leaves unopened the letters that life writes to him every day. Instead of accepting an absolute claim and indulging in a great longing, or even a dream, he remains satisfied with the appeasement of his immediate needs and comes to terms with the world as it is, at most agreeing a few rules for living with his fellow men.

Of course the much abused affluent society should not be made a whipping boy for all the wickedness in the world. Nevertheless, it shares the blame for the way our present age asks so few questions. An interest in consumer goods creates an atmosphere in which there is a growing lack of interest in the question of truth, while in its turn a growing lack of interest in the question of truth increases the interest in consumer goods. Prayer is not learnt from poverty, but he who has does not ask.

Against this background the old parable of the rich farmer – in spite of its country village atmosphere – is surprisingly applicable to our modern industrial society. The farmer said, 'I will do this: I will pull down my barns, and build larger ones; and there I will store all my grain and my goods. And I will say to my soul, Soul, you have ample goods laid up for many years; take your ease, eat, drink, and be merry' (Luke 12.18).

In the same way, many people at the present day seem to be in a permanent coma, and to wake up only now and then to be fed. It seems difficult, almost impossible, to approach people like this with the question of God. In this totally unquestioning atmosphere, consider the effect of a biblical saying such as this: 'Do not fear those who kill the body but cannot kill the soul; rather fear him who can destroy both soul and body in hell' (Matt. 10.28). You feel at once that there is not the slightest basis for any understanding of such a saying, even if it is not taken of God, but of some other unconditional claim. Because many of our contemporaries have no really demanding questions of their own to ask, they do not even know how to begin to ask about God. But they are unaware of this, and boldly assert that there is no question to ask.

There can be no questioning without a certain intellectual wakefulness. Consequently, before any questions about God can be asked, they must be preceded by an act of general intellectual awakening. Man must be woken up out of his acquiescent attitude to reality, out of the sleep in which he never questions his existence. This is true not only of questions about God. All questions about truth begin with a kind of 'awakening' of man. This is as true in philosophy as in religion and theology; Jesus, Buddha and the gnostics knew this as well as Plato, Marx or Heidegger. For man to wake up and ask questions is equivalent to his waking up to be human. It is not a matter of gaining a new human faculty, but of releasing a faculty which is potentially present. When man is woken up to ask questions, a learning process begins which on the one hand assumes that certain educational requirements have been fulfilled, but on the other hand requires of the individual a personal commitment even to the point of suffering, and which lasts all his life. What is known as 'the final conclusion of wisdom' does not exist.

The learning process begins with one's nearest neighbour. The most radical question about the 'ultimate meaning of the universe' always starts with the individual and the concrete, with a particular matter and a real object. No one has ever yet sat down, his chin on his hand, looked round and asked: What is the meaning of life and of the world? The question of the meaning of life is asked at the conveyor belt or at a funeral, in the middle of work, when one loses a job or is involved with another person. Mostly, in fact, it is not consciously posed, but 'comes up', like a ship on the horizon.

This is why it is questionable whether one can really make so strict a distinction between calculating and meditative thought, and therefore between questions of content, functional questions, and questions of meaning or essential questions. Such a distinction can easily betray the out-of-date attitude of an intellectual *élite* which looks haughtily down upon everyday affairs and the practical questions of the 'apparatus of existence', the 'framework' or 'tools', as though these things could be understood and dealt with without any trouble. The usual consequence is a disregard for real life, an idealistic spiritualization, a thoroughgoing remoteness from facts, and the 'jargon of essentiality'. Calculating and meditative thought, and questions of content and meaning, or functional and essential questions, are related at every point, so that it is never possible to say with certainty where one finishes and the other begins. The result is that all individual questions, however everyday, material, technical, practical and even pragmatic they may be, have their place within an all-embracing horizon and are related to the meaning of the totality of the world.

The way which questions of content and meaning are related at every point can be clearly shown from two examples.

First example: Before us lies a tool, say a hammer. What is a hammer for? To knock in nails. When I knock in nails with a hammer, I am joining boards or beams. But the joining of boards and beams may be, for example, part of building a house. And what is the house being built for? So that a family can live in a house. And so the questions lead on to the final question: Why does man live on earth at all? What is the meaning of his existence?

Second example: A workman stands in front of a machine. He asks how this machine functions and how he is to operate it. He is taught to operate the machine properly; the machine functions and produces. Let us suppose that it produces textiles. Question: What are textiles for? Answer: To clothe people. New question: Why do people wear clothes? A whole series of answers are possible: First, to cover their nakedness; secondly, as a protection against the weather; and finally, to adorn themselves and to show themselves off. Each of these answers leads to further questions: covering one's nakedness to the question of human shame, protection against the weather to questions of practicability and demand, adornment and display to questions of fashion, of ways of life and prestige. These in their turn lead to new questions. The question of shame leads on to the question of custom and morality, the question of practicability and demand to questions of economy and society, the questions of fashion, way of life and prestige to questions of the nature of man, his relationship to others, including the other sex, and of the purpose and the final aim which a person sees associated with his life.

What these two examples have shown is true of every tool, every machine, every activity, every product and every event. One question always leads to another, and every question widens the horizon. Through questions existence is clarified, in the true sense of the word. One question leads on to another, until we come to the question of the meaning of the universe; the horizon is pushed back, the space in which we can see becomes wider, and at the same time existence is clarified and illuminated.

Thus all human questioning contains an impulse which leads to something absolute and unconditional. Man cannot be content to ask only about the purposes and consequences of his actions, he is always concerned with their meaning as well. His first question always contains the seeds of the ultimate question, and its horizon is always that of the universe. Although science can affirm the existence of this demand of man for a final and absolute meaning, it cannot satisfy it. No less a person than the philosopher and social scientist Max Horkheimer, whom it is impossible to suspect of any tendency to abstract metaphysics, has affirmed this: 'When men act thoughtfully, they ask about the purpose of the consequences of their action. But in such questions which can be answered by understanding, knowledge and science, there is always another factor at work. This is, that actions also have a significance which is not merely relative, a significance which we cannot penetrate at once with the resources of our own understanding, but which we have no right simply to reject.... Not only professional life, but especially science, is becoming increasingly specialized, and this makes it necessary constantly to remember that what matters in the end is not merely skill but truth. The important question is the one Kant asked: What is truth? What ought to happen? What ought we to do?'[1] Characteristically, Horkheimer made this affirmation in a discussion of the function of theology in society!

2. *The Social Link (The Context of Questions)*

Many Protestant theologians at the present day have a profound mistrust of all 'ultimate questions', amongst which they include not only the question of the meaning of the world, but also questions about guilt, suffering, and death. Their mistrust derives from the widespread hostility in present-day Protestant theology to all 'metaphysics' and 'religion' which sometimes virtually becomes an anti-metaphysical or anti-religious complex. Thus these questions fall under suspicion of being 'metaphysical' or 'religious' questions. Hans-Dieter Bastian in his book *Theologie der Frage* (Theology of Questioning) makes a dig at them every time he looks at them.[2]

There are two principal reasons why theology is ill at ease with what are supposed to be metaphysical or religious questions. There is the fear of an inadmissible attempt to create a point of contact for statements about God, either by building up a gradual and predetermined pathway to God by moving from one question to another, or else by ambushing man at the frontiers of his life with so-called 'ultimate questions', so that when he seems to have no way out he can be presented with God. These so-called 'ultimate questions' are regarded as a typical expression of the individualistic and inward-looking religious feeling of the bourgeois age which is coming to an end, if it is not already gone.

This brings us to the second reason why theology is ill at ease with 'ultimate questions'. It consists of a protest against the way Christian belief is 'isolated from the world' in existentialist theology. This theology tried to express belief in the Christian revelation with the aid of Heidegger's categories of thought, with the result that it restricted it to the private existential life of the individual, and so forgot that man is also an 'ensemble of situations' (Marx). As a result of this process of abstraction, faith lost touch with the world. Theology became purely interpretative, a 'philology of belief', and thus turned into a theory without any practice. But nowadays we do not want just to understand the world in love, we would also like to alter it out of love! Thus there is a suspicion of any kind of 'metaphysics of questioning' which would attempt to bring about a gradual ascent of man to God, understanding the world in the process, but leaving it behind unchanged.

On the whole, we sympathize with the objections underlying both themes, but we believe that the consequences that have been drawn from them are too one-sided and therefore ultimately false.

We certainly do not think that to proceed from individual practical questions to final, absolute questions of meaning represents a gradual 'ascent' of man to God. The question of meaning cannot of course be allowed to turn without further ado into the question of God. We must of course consider whether and to what extent the question of God is actually implicit in the question of the meaning of the universe which man asks.

But we would point out at once, that it is high time that the discussions of the 'point of contact' of divine revelation, which for some time have been neglected, should be taken up again. Moreover, if there is no point of contact, then everything that man says about God is either left hanging helplessly in the air or contains a magical element. In the latter case, we would run the risk not of speaking of God, but of conjuring him up.

We also frankly admit that there is a danger in asking 'ultimate questions' – about the meaning of life, about suffering in the world, about the guilt and the death of men. It is all too easy to overlook the social circumstances which actually exist. People discuss the problem of suffering in the world and feel that this excuses them from reducing the suffering that is going on in the world at the moment by changing social circumstances. There is no doubt that Western philosophy and theology have long succumbed to this danger – this is why Karl Marx came on the scene.

But does this mean that one should no longer speak of the 'boundaries' of human life and go on to talk at these boundaries about God? Does this mean that the 'religious questions' which so many theologians nowadays despise were merely questions which belonged to the bourgeois age, and should therefore no longer be raised in the future? It must be pointed out that the bourgeois age has not lasted two and a half centuries, but more than two and a half millennia, since the beginning of Karl Jaspers' famous 'axial period'. For since that time people have asked questions about who man is and about the totality of the world. And we must also point out that guilt, sin, suffering and death in the world have not ceased; it is simply that a few theologians have ceased to think and speak about them, or at least have ceased to think and speak about them in relation to God.

Of course the questions which are concerned with human existence and 'totality' – questions of guilt, suffering, love, righteousness, the meaning of life and death – do not exist in suspended animation as 'ultimate questions', as 'questions in themselves'. Nor is every one of them relevant in the same way in every age. These questions are always linked to the historically changing intellectual standpoint of the person who poses them, and occur in a particular system of social and cultural coordinates; they always have their concrete social 'situation in life'.

The way in which all religious questions and answers are rooted in the social environment of their time is very clear in Luther's Shorter Catechism: 'House, garden, fields, cattle, money, goods, a devout wife, devout children, devout labourers, devout and honest masters, good government, good weather, peace, health, propriety, honour, good friends, loyal neighbours and so forth' – all this reflects the world of the small farmer, obedient to those set in authority over him, in the sixteenth century.

We have only recently become aware that behind all questions about God, and therefore behind every ecclesiastical or theological system of answers, lies a particular social and cultural pattern with which they are co-ordinated. The much despised *Kulturprotestantismus*, the Protestant theology of the early part of the century which was concerned with the connection between theology and the problems and issues of contemporary civilization, is once again fashionable. But dialectic theology and existentialist theology have long ignored it.

Existentialism works with an 'abstract ego' (Gollwitzer). As the discoveries of the new sciences of human relationships – sociology, political science, psychology and so forth – have come to be accepted, this ego has once again been given a concrete 'social content'. We have recognized that, even as an individual, man does not exist in an abstract private realm, but always in a social context, determined by his environment. Thus we are never dealing only with an individual; the life of the individual is always woven into a whole network of political and social structures. Here are two examples of this 'social content' with which the former 'abstract ego' has been filled.

First example: Existentialism set the irreplaceability of the individual on a lofty philosophical pedestal, to the point of extolling his loneliness. Nowadays we see the other side of this, the way in which the individualization of man is largely also a product of social conditions, just as the growth of his isolation keeps pace with that of the anonymous world of the great cities. Existentialism could almost go as far as to welcome the death of man, as the moment when no one else any longer takes his place, and his uniqueness is indisputably manifested. But we today can scarcely bring ourselves to utter such a statement, in view of the fact that the dying today can be sedated under morphine and left to themselves in the bathrooms or other siderooms in our hospitals.

Second example: What existentialism has to say about the 'essentiality' or 'inessentiality' of man is largely restricted to abstractions and to the private sphere, and is so reduced to the 'jargon' mocked by Adorno. But when they are transposed into a social context, these abstract qualities of an individual's existential life are filled with concrete content. The inessentiality of man becomes his 'self-alienation', which is caused amongst other things by certain economic and social circumstances, such as the way in which he is enmeshed in a consuming and producing society; and the essentiality of man becomes his 'liberation', due in large part to the alteration and overcoming of these circumstances.

Thus all man's religious questions are always rooted in a particular social context. And at this point we find ourselves back with our first question, whether and in what way man still asks questions about God at the present day. For today it is this social context which claims his most intense interest – it is this which concerns him absolutely.

If we try to give a statistical answer to the question whether and in what way men still ask questions about God at the present day, we have to admit that men very rarely ask such questions, or that very few ask them. But if we ask about the content of such questions, the answer is that man does not ask questions about God at the present day, but about *man*, and if he still is asking about God, he is doing so as a consequence of his questions about man.

It is far from true that the completion of the process of the enlightenment in our own time has imbued men with a spirit of unqualified optimism about the future. Man knows perfectly well what he has done. He no longer recognizes the hand of providence; he has to look to his affairs himself. His fate is in his own hands. He has to plan and create his own future as never before.

But once again, as a result, he is faced with the inevitable question of the meaning of his life. It originates and is located for the most part at the present day within the triangle formed by the three great forces of the present day: science, technology and society. The kind of question we ask is what the consequences will be for human society of the increasingly close link between science and technology, and how a meaningful life can be possible at all in a society formed in this way. The result of this is that questions about man himself are asked with a new intensity. Man is well aware of the threat to his humanity posed by the scientific and technical world which he has created, and by the society which owes its structures to this world of science and technology. He is aware of the risk of being drawn into the wheels of his own machinery and of becoming a product like everything else. This is why, when present-day man asks about what concerns him absolutely, he asks about man.

Instead of being horrified at the irreligious nature of this question, we should be sensitive to the urgency with which it is posed, and realize that it implies a demand for a meaningful human life. We may go as far as to affirm that at the present day even those who are 'outside the church' are looking for meaning and truth in the world with a total commitment and a passion which has long gone unrecognized. At the present day, particularly amongst those who are aware of larger issues, a search for meaning seems to be under way which once again, in reaction against the general relativization of standards and values, is looking for answers of absolute significance. And this in fact one can call the religious need 'of our time', even if the name of 'God' is never mentioned, or even if there is actually an experience of his 'absence', which itself gives rise to a new search for absolute meaning.

At this point our discussion of the question of whether and in what way man at the present day is asking questions about God has turned full circle. We said that at the present day man hardly ever asks any questions about God; his questions are almost without exception only about man. But his new and passionate enquiry about meaning and truth in the world, about the absolute and unconditional – an enquiry provoked by the universal experience of a relativization of standards and values – is in fact concentrated on this very question of man. We must now go on to ask whether man's new and passionate study of mankind may perhaps conceal an unexpressed search for God.

And this brings us back to the familiar problem of the 'point of contact'.

3. *The Problem of the Point of Contact*

The problem of the point of contact is concerned with the question whether human existence is in any way inherently orientated towards God, in such a way that man's questions are indirectly asked about God, even if he does not explicitly state this, or is actually ignorant of it.

We come from a theological tradition which for the sake of the greatness and purity of the revelation of God has not only forbidden all statements about a point of contact on man's side but has bitterly attacked them. But the very assertion of a revelation by God assumes the existence on the human side of a point of contact for this revelation. For if man were not already concerned with the question of God, when God revealed himself to man he would be quite unable to recognize God as God in such a revelation. How could man understand anything if he did not already possess some general idea, some 'prior understanding'? How could he perceive an answer as such, if it was not an answer to a question which, consciously or unconsciously, he was already asking? Augustine has given classical expression to the problem of the point of contact in his famous statement: *Tu nos fecisti ad te, et cor nostrum inquietum est, donec requiescat in te* – You created us for yourself, and our hearts are restless until they rest in you.

We have said that at the present day man is particularly concerned with a passionate enquiry about man himself. This means that man is not only asking questions, he is the question himself. But this brings us to the ultimate fact of human existence, beyond which our questions cannot go. The only thing about us which is beyond question is that we ourselves are questionable. Thus we can no longer affirm the certainty of our own being as Descartes did: *Cogito ergo sum* – I think, therefore I am. We must now begin with a more radical statement: *Interrogo ergo sum* – I ask, therefore I am.

Thus we shall deal with the problem of the point of contact by dissecting the act of human questioning itself, to find out what it contains. We find three elements in it.

Firstly, when I ask a question, I do so in order to receive an answer, and if this answer leads to a new question, I also ask this question in expectation of an answer. As long as a person asks, he expects an answer. Thus questions always assume a conscious or unconscious *trust*. One expression of this is the fact that in asking my questions I use speech. I do so, trusting that it will express my question and convey it to my interlocutor. The most blatant example of such a trust in language is the last message of a suicide. At the moment of the utmost mistrust, the suicide still trusts language to express his mistrust and to convey it to those he leaves behind.

Secondly, when I am asking a question, I am looking to the *future*. 'The temporal environment of questions is the future.'[2] This is so even when I am asking about the past. When a doctor goes over the case history of a patient and asks about the illnesses from which he or his forebears have previously suffered, he does so because he is concerned with the cure that lies in the future. One element in questions is always that one is planning the future of one's life. Besides the trust that one will receive an answer, there is also the hope of a change.

Thirdly, when I ask a question, I always assume both *need* and *possession*. I assume a need, in so far as I can only ask for something which I lack. I only ask a question when I am at a loss. But it implies possession, in so far as I can only ask for something which I already possess in part – otherwise it would never occur to me to ask for it. Thus a question already betrays a certain degree of prior knowledge. For example, I ask the name of the capital of a country because I do not know it; but I can only ask its name, because I know that this country exists and also that there is such an institution in the world as capital cities.

But both my lack and my possession point to a *totality*, and assume the possibility of a totality. When I observe that I lack the courage for something, and ask for courage, I am assuming that such full courage exists. Or if I ask about a single organ of the human body, such as the heart, this single organ is related as a part to the totality of the human organism.

Trust; openness to the future; relationship to a totality through lack and possession: these three elements, which form the structure of the human act of questioning, imply something of great importance about man himself. They lead us to an answer to our question of the point of contact.

Man is the questioning animal, the being who cannot stop posing new questions which take him further on, so that he constantly transcends himself. At first, gliding along on the surface of reality, he asks what he should eat, drink, wear, learn, do in his work or make, how he can refresh and enjoy himself and what he has to pay for all this or gets paid for it. All these are good and honest questions, and no one should despise them. But they cannot give permanent satisfaction. And therefore man penetrates the surface of reality and goes on to ask where he comes from and where he is going, what he is and what he ought to be, what good and evil are and what endures. Finally, he breaks through every layer of reality in turn and asks about the ultimate reality: what is the ground and meaning of all being? What is the ground and meaning of my being? Why do I exist? Why does anything exist at all?

Man, then, is radically questionable, and this means that everything, not least his own existence, is a proper subject for his questions. But the same fact makes him capable of asking questions, and its basis lies in his 'openness to the world', to which modern anthropology bears witness. It compels him constantly to press his questions and to go beyond what is known and at hand, into the unknown and the open-ended. That modern neo-Marxists, regardless of their particular tendency, are neither willing nor able to give a concrete picture of the future for which they hope and struggle, is an indirect proof of this openness on the part of man; in this field there is no 'final solution'. To this extent man's questions betray the fact that his existence is orientated towards a *totality*, which he can only approach, but can never finally reach. But since when man asks questions he is always asking at the same time about himself, about his destined purpose, this orientation towards a totality is manifested as his own *inherent concern with what transcends him*.

But man could not ask about the totality of the world, or about the reality of the world at all, nor about the destined purpose of his existence, if something of all this were not already present in his existential life. He would not 'try' all this if he had not already 'tried it'. He can only ever ask about a reality which he has already known through experience. His questions can only reach out beyond himself to the foundation and meaning which sustains all reality, because he already knows that he is sustained by it. Thus in his very questions, man shows that he is 'dependent'.[3] Just as there is no answer without a question, so there is no question without an answer. Man could not ask questions in confident expectation of an answer if he had not already had answers. He could not aim at the future if the future was not already drawing him on; he could not reach out for totality, if the totality was not already driving him forward. The parable of the Prodigal Son provides an illustration of this: even in the foreign country he lived on his father's inheritance, and the idea of returning could never have occurred to him if he had not remembered his father's house, even in the foreign country.

Here we have made a final and ultimate statement about the possible point of contact for what God says to man, and therefore for what man can say about God. If we replace the 'totality' towards which man is orientated, and for which he is reaching out in his questions, by the name 'God', we can say that the question of God is concealed in man's existential life, but not the answer. And the answer cannot be deduced from the question. A continuous and progressive process of questioning will not lead us to the answer. Camus rightly speaks of 'that hopeless encounter between human questioning and the silence of the universe'.[4]

Not that the world faces us with total silence. Just as the earth sometimes bursts open and brings forth what is within it, so the ground of being opens up in many ways and displays something of its secret to us. It reveals itself in numerous different ways, and speaks constantly to us through reality. It speaks to us in signs; it writes the truth in cipher. These ciphers must be interpreted by prophets, wise men, scholars, philosophers, artists and poets, and sometimes they succeed. We are not without all knowledge, but our knowledge is fragmentary. All we ever have in our hand is parts, and we can never succeed in putting the parts together in a meaningful whole. We can never get to the meaning of the whole by adding the parts together. Thus at the end the questions remain: What is the ultimate ground and meaning of being? Above all, what is it like? Is it good or evil? Or is it without all attributes, indifferent, like a monster constantly giving birth to new life from itself, in order to swallow it up again? The reality of being is multiple in its significance, and therefore the significance of its ground and meaning remains ultimately unknown. The Preacher admits with resignation: 'Man cannot find out what God has done from the beginning to the end' (Eccles. 3.11).

Thus we can only call man's questioning a 'point of contact' if we already know about revelation. We have already pointed out that anyone who speaks of a revelation of God assumes that there is a point of contact for it in man. We must now assert the reverse: Anyone who speaks of a point of contact in man assumes a knowledge of revelation. Man's questioning can only be seen as a possible point of contact in the light of God's answer. But in its turn, the revelation of God can be understood as an answer only when it is seen to be the answer to a question which man is already asking, consciously or unconsciously.

4. *The Question Takes Precedence over the Answer*

The church today is largely an 'answering church'. As before, men expect it to give answers, but they no longer expect its answers to mean anything to them. The reason why our contemporaries regard what the church has to say as so irrelevant is not so much that the church's answers have been handed down from the past. This is also true in part of the 'hermeneutic sciences'. The reason is rather that the church is answering questions which are no longer asked by our own time. The usual punctuation mark in the church's statements is the exclamation mark, not the question mark. Its statements usually take the form of an appeal, not an argument. And the principal virtue it preaches is obedience, not thinking for oneself. The church hurls its answers at men's heads like meteorites from a distant star.

This is what seems to have been in the mind of an English reader of John Robinson's book *Honest to God*, when she wrote:

Ever since I can remember I have had doubts – I have never been able to go to a church service without having a wild desire in the middle of the sermon and sometimes the lessons to stand up and start asking questions ... There seemed to be so many things which I was expected to believe and accept unquestioningly if I was to be a true member of the church.[5]

There must be a connection between questions and the answers they receive, and this should lead theologians to call an immediate halt to certain discussions which are at the moment in progress within the church and even at church conferences, because the questions and answers underlying them no longer relate to real life. They only distract attention unnecessarily from the questions which preoccupy our contemporaries. The necessity for this is even greater, we believe, because at the present day the church no longer exists as a 'Sunday duty', but only as a possible spare-time activity. But there are numerous other claims on our spare time. Many other activities have something to offer, and what they offer is by no means always valueless. If the church is to survive this competition for people's free time, it must offer something which they can see is genuinely important in their lives; and the offer must be made in an attractive way. But this means that the church must ask 'convincing questions', in which present-day man can recognize himself. For him the timely questions are the practical questions, and if he does not consider something of practical importance, he has no time for it.

Bertolt Brecht's stories of Herr Keuner include the following tale, which he characteristically entitles 'Convincing Questions': ' "I have noticed", said Herr K., "that we frighten many people away from our teaching by having an answer to everything. Could we not, in the interests of propaganda, draw up a list of questions which seem to us to be completely unsolved?" ' In its own way, theology should take up Keuner's suggestion of asking 'convincing questions'. For it is the world which gives theology its agenda, and not the other way round! And the principle that we lay down for what theology has to say about God at the present day is that *the question takes precedence over the answer*. Look at the questions that are asked in the bible! The prophets and psalmists assail God with questions, not merely the conventional questions of theology, but also with very unconventional, undevout and almost blasphemous questions! God is asked: Why do you not hear? Why do you sleep? What good will my life be to me? Why did you bring me forth from the womb? Why did I not die at birth? Why do you not look away from me and let me have a moment's peace? (Hab. 1.13; Ps. 44.24; Gen. 27.46; Job 10.18; 3.11; 7.19). And Jesus himself asks 'My God, my God, why hast thou forsaken me?' (Matt. 27.46). But the questions in the bible are by no means always so emotional and dramatic; sometimes they are very quiet and rational. Jesus's questions appeal to man's understanding: 'Is it lawful on the Sabbath to do good or to do harm, to save life or to kill?' (Mark 3.4), and many parables are introduced by questions, in order to shake the hearer out of his accepted pattern of teaching and to provoke him to think for himself.

But where are questions really asked in the church at the present day? Does not the church share in the *malaise* of our age, which we described above, and which lies in the fact that it does not ask questions? Are the words of Hans-Dieter Bastian not true?

Those Protestants in Germany who pay their church tax are simply being drawn into the social automatism of established churches, which carries them on a conveyor belt from baptism through various ceremonies and a few annual church festivals to the grave, without ever motivating them to ask questions.[6]

To bring to an end the situation in which no questions are asked in the church, it is not enough to make a good resolution to make more room for questions in the church. If questioning is ever going to be anything more than personal initiative, an example of exceptional daring, and is to become a normal process which is taken for granted, then it must be institutionalized in the church. This must apply to sermon preparation groups, discussions in or after services, and 'critical synods', and must lead on to the transformation of the pastoral ministry and of theological training. Franz Rosenzweig's statement in the early 1920s to the *Jüdisches Lehrhaus* (Jewish Academy) in Frankfurt seems to me to point the way for the Christian church: 'Learning must no longer follow the path from the torah [the bible] into life, but the other way around, from life ... back into the torah [bible]. This is the key signature for the present day.' And Rosenzweig goes on to describe one who teaches theology as the 'conductor of the choir of questioners'.[7] The most important office of a theologian at the present day is not to be a 'prayer leader' but a 'question leader'.

Where theology exercises this office of 'question leader' it accepts a share in the responsibility for the intellectual steward-ship of the age. We live in an age of expansion in every direc-tion; our energies are constantly stretched to their limit, and our questions hardly ever go further than immediate political needs or social purposes. This gives a powerful forward urge to our lives, but also threatens to deprive them of any foundation. It is not only that we no longer have any ultimate aims and guid-ing images – and indeed our age is not likely to produce them; but we virtually ask no more questions either. We hardly ever ask questions about our intellectual bearings, that is, questions which go beyond our immediate needs and purposes and ask about the total meaning of things: where we come from and where we are going; why we are doing what we are doing; why the world is as it is; and whether death does not make every-thing meaningless in the end. But these questions remain questions which man has to ask, even in the most perfect order-ing of society, unless man was to stop being the *animal quaerens cur*, the creature that asks why. But that would mean that he had ceased to be man.

If theology and the church do not keep these questions alive and ask them, who else is to do it at the present day? From this point of view, even the official ceremonies, the baptisms, wed-dings and funerals, which so many ministers moan about today, can be seen in a new light and take on a different quality. They are always concerned with the crucial moments of human existence, and therefore with its basic questions, with birth, puberty, marriage, death, etc. and are an attempt to give an answer which does not merely satisfy man's intellectual need, but also his justifiable demand for ceremony and even solemn-ity. Ministers should not regard themselves as reduced by this to masters of ceremonies, but as being called to be the advocates of man's humanity. I might almost say that the church would have to be invented for this reason, if it did not already exist.

The demand that the question should take precedence over the answer should not be dismissed as the 'adaptation of the word of God to the service of man' (Karl Barth) or written off as a 'theology of human deficiencies', in which God is demoted to the position of one who answers human questions and makes good human deficiencies; man dictates and God obeys. This would be a theology without love, taking no real account of what man requires. The church cannot simply talk of making good deficiencies like a psychologist or a politician. But it is a disastrous theology which is not interested in human need, in what is needful for man! Of course in this respect there is a true and a false theology. A false and vulgar 'theology of need', scarcely worthy of the name, is expressed in the saying of the singer Frank Sinatra: 'I am for everything that helps anyone through the night, whether it is a prayer, a sleeping pill or a bottle of whisky.' What is shocking in this statement is not the random way in which prayer, sleeping pills and whisky are lumped together – why should they not be lumped together in a Christian's life? But the reason why they are lumped together in a random way is that here human need is made the sole criterion, and no longer subjected to the judgment of truth.

A true theology of need begins with man's questions and needs, and demands that they should be answered and satisfied. But it subjects man's questions and needs to the influence of the answer and satisfaction offered by the Christian gospel, in order to purify them, correct them, and make them more profound. But if this is to happen, I must first have heard the gospel; and yet if I am to hear the gospel as an answer, I must first have asked my questions. Thus man's questions come first, although only as a matter of method, not as a matter of fact. For the fact is that God has already begun long ago. But this must be verified!

5

The Reality of God in the Reality of the World

The Method of Verification

1. The Invisibility of God

On October 18th 1931, Dietrich Bonhoeffer, who was then twenty-five years old, expressed the following ideas to a friend in a letter, after a long stay in America: 'There is one great country I should still like to see, where perhaps the great solution might come from – India. Otherwise it all seems to be over, the great death of Christianity seems to be here. I wonder if our age is past and the gospel has been given to another race, perhaps to be preached in different words and actions? ... I am now student chaplain at the Technical University, and how can you preach this sort of thing to these people? Who still believes it? The invisibility does for us. If we cannot see in our personal lives that Christ is present, then we would like to see it in India at least, but this madness of being constantly thrown back on to the invisible God himself – nobody can endure that any longer.'[1]

His work as student chaplain at the Technical University in Berlin was leading Bonhoeffer to lament the invisibility of God – and to long for India. What is the connection between the two? The same motive underlies the complaint that God is invisible and the longing for India: it is the desire for what is tangible and visible, for new evidence of the reality of God; the wish that a more credible proclamation of the Christian faith might once again show that it is real and true. And if this cannot be done here and now, at the Technical University in Berlin, perhaps it can be done one day in distant India. The complaint and longing expressed by the young Bonhoeffer in this letter later became the theme of his theological life's work.

He gave his life for it. To this day it has remained the fundamental problem faced by theologians in their work and their
experience.

Almost forty years later, on the 20th June 1967, the lecturer
and tutor Rolf Schäfer gave his inaugural lecture in the Faculty
of Protestant Theology in Tübingen on the theme 'God and
Prayer – the Common Crisis of Two Doctrines'. At the beginning of his lecture he justified his choice of theme by pointing to
the present dilemma of theology: 'This lecture has grown out
of the consideration of how to deal with the principal difficulty
of theological study: the fact that the verification which is
sought so intensively cannot be found ... Christian faith seems
to be an uncommonly relevant and attractive hypothesis, but
it remains a hypothesis, which refuses to be turned into an
apodeictic certainty, even in part. The reason why talented
students so often abandon theology is that they become convinced of another apodeictic certainty: that Christianity is an
ideology which is thrust upon man without regard to his consciousness of truth. A wholesome and honest feeling for truth
resists this....'[2]

These words express the same insoluble problem as Dietrich
Bonhoeffer's letter. The problem is how faith in God can be
uttered and accepted in such a way that it does not seem to be
a hypothesis, a law imposed from outside, or an ideological
superstructure, but a certainty which can be experienced in the
reality of one's own life, and therefore a truth which is worthy
of belief. Since Bonhoeffer's time this difficulty has grown
greater rather than less. Modern man is quite obsessed with
the experience of reality. He can only regard as credible what
is real and accessible to experience: 'The proof of the pudding
is in the eating.' And therefore our contemporaries seek the experience of God, if they seek it at all, in the reality of their life
and their world.

The problem of the laity in the church, so much discussed
at the present day, must also be seen against this intellectual
background and at this profound theological level. But it too
casts a revealing light on the problem of the direct experience
of God. The laity, or at least the best and most able amongst
them, are claiming equal rights in the church not merely in the
administrative sense, but above all in the theological field. They

would like to be independent in their belief, and to experience God in the world themselves. Consequently they are ill at ease with theological abstractions and niceties which they feel bring them into a state of dependence upon theologians. The theologian's only duty, they consider, is to show them what concrete form faith in God should take in the world.

The following conversation is characteristic of this. A doctor was discussing with a minister the task of the layman in the church. They were talking about the possible forms of Christian activity open to a theologian at the present day. The minister spoke with great assurance; he tried to explain to the doctor how an important change had taken place, and how the first steps had been taken towards a new recognition of the task of the laity. But the doctor interrupted: 'Basically, we laymen only matter to you ministers after knocking-off time, when we come to your bible groups and talks, sit on the church council or come to your men's evenings.' And then he added, more quietly, 'But I would like to have a clear conscience in the mornings when I am operating.'

This conversation reflects the basic dilemma of theology, and not only of modern theology. That doctor wanted to be a Christian, he wanted to act and live in a Christian way, but he wanted to do so not solely 'after knocking-off time', not only in the ecclesiastical sphere, but in the daytime, in his work, in the operating theatre – in short, in the *world*.

But how can this be: God in the world, or more precisely, the invisible God in the visible world? This brings us back to Bonhoeffer's complaint about the 'invisibility of God' and to the 'basic difficulty' of young theologians at the present day. In fact the invisibility of God is everyone's basic difficulty. But this is an age in which almost without exception truth is accorded only to what can be seen, measured, tested or weighed. In such an age, the invisibility of God is clearly the most pressing professional problem of those 'whose business is God', regardless of whether they earn their living by this calling or not.

How can I believe in anything which I cannot see? This is always the first and most telling objection which is made to belief in God. But things are not as simple as that. In the first place, we rely in our life on other experiences which we cannot test by direct 'inspection'. Secondly, someone who believes in

God can point to experiences which come from his belief. Thus the problem of the 'invisibility of God' comes down to the question of the kind of experience involved in belief in God, the relationship of this experience to our other experiences of reality, and the degree to which the experience of belief can be elucidated and verified. Our present-day concern is with the verification of belief in God. Of course this demand is not as new as is sometimes claimed at the present day. Faith has always had to give an account of itself to the world. In the New Testament itself Christians are exhorted: 'Always be prepared to make a defence to anyone who calls you to account for the hope that is in you' (I Peter 3.15). But since the full effects of the enlightenment on Christian faith have been felt in our own time, and faith as a result has lost its sole rights, the task of verification has been given new urgency.

2. *The Method of Verification*

If all the different factors which constitute the process in the history of human thought known as the enlightenment are considered from the single point of view of the question of God, two main themes emerge. The first is the revolution in authority and the autonomy of man which results from it. The second is the breakdown of all conceptions of a divine and supernatural world, leading to the secularization of the world.

These facts have two important consequences for traditional belief in God:

Firstly, God is no longer an authoritative premiss. As the assumption behind the world view and institutions of Western society, understood by everyone and largely taken for granted, God has ceased to exist.

Secondly, the God who strikes down like lightning into the world from above or outside, as a supernatural being, not of this world, and who is transcendent and personal in this sense, is dead. He was too much above this world, and therefore too unworldly, to live.

Drawing together these two consequences of the enlightenment, we find that they lead to a further twofold requirement for responsible and credible statements about God.

Firstly, theology at the present day has a duty to *verify* all its statements about God.

Secondly, this verification must take place within the *sphere of experience of contemporary secular existence.*

To sum up, we can only give a good account of our belief in God, if we take account of the world.

Once the full effect of the enlightenment on Christian faith had been felt, the period of quoting and handing down tradition, of repeating and affirming the statements of the past, was over. Faith can no longer survive by making the same assertions as before, only louder. Loudness is no guarantee of truth. The age of the polemic credal style which characterized the church struggle of the 1930s is also past, particularly as this style, in Western Germany at least, no longer carries the conviction which comes from the fact that the speaker is risking his life. It is no longer possible to do as a bishop recently did in his report to his synod, and thunder forth the statement: 'The louder the death of God is proclaimed, the more he is manifested as the living God!' At the present day such a statement does not even have the quality of a testimony of faith; it sounds to people more like the spell of a heathen medicine man than the theological statement of a Protestant bishop. One is involuntarily reminded of the 'Laconic Remarks' of Heinrich Wiesner: 'They speak in tongues, but not in the Spirit.' Even churchmen, whether bishops or professors of theology, no longer have the right simply to fire off a handful of arbitrary statements and then appeal to the Holy Spirit as though to say, 'He will see to it!' In such a case, the Holy Spirit sees to nothing. He too no longer allows official proclamations, but requires arguments that are to the point – even from bishops and even from the Pope.

Anyone who uses the word 'God' at the present day must make clear what he means – not in the sense of a philosophical and theological definition, but with the intention of showing how his ideas can be given concrete expression in the world. As our guide for what we have to say about God we can take the basic principle laid down by Lenin: 'There is no abstract truth, truth is always concrete.' When he was in exile in Denmark, Bertolt Brecht pinned this statement on the beams of his study, and we should post it up on all the pulpits, platforms and lecture rooms where anything is said about God.

The requirement that what is said about God should be capable of concrete expression immediately excludes another way of presenting the truth of God to men. We can no longer preach the revelation of God in Jesus Christ at people from outside, as if it were a self-contained drama of salvation taking place somewhere above us, and then go on to add that it is this that they have to accept. How can they accept something when they do not recognize that it is taking place in their own world and happening in their own lives? What has this business in heaven got to do with me? I live on earth, in space and time, and my life takes its own course. The arch of divine revelation stretches from eternity to eternity – isn't it far above my head? I imagine myself lying in a field on the grass and looking at the sky. All at once I hear roaring above me and notice an aeroplane. But what I really see is not the aeroplane, but only the vapour trails behind it. Involuntarily I think: who is inside it? Where is it coming from and where is it going? But I never find out. The plane flies on above me and finally disappears out of sight. For a time I can still see the vapour trails which it has left, but gradually they break up and I am left there by myself in the field, with perhaps a few white clouds left above me. Is this not the way we feel about the revelation of God, whenever it is described for us as something taking place high in heaven? Even the subsequent assurance that we are drawn into this heavenly drama of salvation, and that it affects our own existence, is no longer sufficient. We want to know how far it affects our existence, and want to be shown *what this effect looks like.*

The mere repetition of the word 'God' or the mere assurance of his revelation is no longer of any use to us today. It seems just pious talk, a pure illusion, if not nonsense, unless it is backed by the concrete experience of reality. It is for this purpose that the *method of verification* is needed, that is, the proving and testing of biblical statements about God in the sphere of experience of our present-day existence in the world.

At the present day there has to be a practical 'foundation' for what is said about God. But this foundation is not provided by pointing out that what we say is rooted in God's revelation. We have to go further than this, and show the connection between the revelation of God and the reality of the world, so that belief in God and his revelation, and the experience of the reality of the world which surrounds us, penetrate each other, and sustain and prove each other. The word 'God' can never be uttered except in the context of human life. We can perceive what God is saying in the vertical plane only within our commitment on the horizontal plane. As a result, credible and comprehensible statements about God are made at the present day only when belief in him no longer looks like an assumption made on the basis of eternal authority or an ideological superstructure, and only where, within the reality and experience of present-day secular existence, it can be shown to be 'correct in practical terms'. In this field there is no longer any theory without practice.

To make clear what is being said, let us consider an example of the very reverse of what we are calling for. The 'principles for the restructuring of secondary education' in Lower Saxony lay down that wherever possible the division of the curriculum into separate and distinct subjects should be avoided. 'Basic instruction' is allocated to sets of subjects grouped together. The only subjects which still appear in isolation on the timetable are religion and sport! The same is true of the model syllabus in both Berlin and North Rhine-Westphalia.[3] This is in blatant contradiction to what is required by the method of verification. A more total misunderstanding of the task of religious instruction and of the way it should speak of God is scarcely possible.

Characteristically, the bible contains no doctrine of God as a distinct article of dogma. It does not begin with a chapter or a book which discusses the nature of God as such, but begins with the creation narrative. This shows that the bible discusses God only in his relationship to the world and man. What we say about God must follow the same pattern. We cannot say who God is in himself, but only what God does to us. And therefore we cannot describe God as he exists in himself, but only as he occurs in his actuality – where and how God in his acts becomes present and real to us. The starting point of the experience of God is not the authoritative assertion that God 'is' or that he 'exists', but the practical demonstration of how God 'happens' at the present day. We only become certain of the reality of God in what he does.

Consequently theology, in speaking of God, must maintain

an endeavour, which is never brought to perfection and never concluded, to manifest the reality of God in the reality of the world. The question of God only occurs to us in the problems of the world, the acts of God only in the facts of history. If we were to speak of God in any other way, we would be like archaeologists who have dug a few pieces of broken pot out of the rubbish dumps of a past civilization and displayed them to a mildly interested public. Either what we sing on Sunday in church, 'God is here', is true in the everyday life of the world, or it is not true at all.

The method of verification is the reply to Bonhoeffer's complaint about the invisibility of God. The word 'invisibility' brings involuntarily to mind the contrary word 'evidence'. Evidence means confirmation, demonstration, understanding through experience. It is this which Bonhoeffer was calling for with regard to God, not only on his own account, but in the name of all his contemporaries. And it is this which the method of verification tries to provide. It is trying to give certainty to belief in the invisible God by making visible its relevance to the reality of the world. Without such insight one cannot demand that any person should believe. 'Blind faith' is always suspicious, and has to take care that it does not lapse into superstition.

Thus when theology speaks about God it is basically 'showing' God – as in the bible an important truth is often introduced by 'Behold!' The purpose of verification is achieved when a person lifts his eyes above what is shown to him and cries out, 'I believe, Lord, help my unbelief', or, in more modern theological jargon, 'Honest to God, it's for real!'

At this point, if not earlier, the fearful cry of all orthodox believers will make itself heard. Is God not being dragged before the bar of human experience and subjected to human judgment, so that his reality is measured by human reality? This objection on the part of orthodox believers is simply the other side of that made by unbelievers: How can I believe in something which I do not see? The reply of the method of verification can be summed up in the paradoxical thesis: The experience of God is contrary to the outward appearance of the world, and therefore must be shown to be true in the experience of the world.

We shall develop this thesis in four points.

First, the method of verification does not try to derive what is said about God from the reality of the world, but to demonstrate it and make it comprehensible in that reality.

The practical starting point for its argument is not man, as would be the case if an anthropological method was being employed, but the witness which God has borne to himself in Jesus of Nazareth. Thus its method is a strictly theological one. This testimony which God has born to himself is taken up by the method of verification in such a way as to show what divine revelation signifies within the sphere of human existence. This is done by relating the revelation of God to the reality of the world, and showing its significance in the context of human life. Its methodological starting point, however, is in human existence, and in the questions which derive from it. But it only does this in order to show how the revelation of God can give an answer to these questions, so that through it man receives a new vision of himself and of the world.

Secondly, the method of verification is not trying to prove the reality of God, but to demonstrate it in the reality of the world.

Here as ever it remains true that all experience of God, in so far as it is really experience of *God*, is contrary to the outward appearance of the world. Its watchword is 'nevertheless'. The basic failing in the 'theology after the death of God' is to forget this, or to pay too little attention to it. But the mature man of the present day demands – and to this limited extent the 'theology after the death of God' is right – that even if the experience of God is against the outward appearance of the world, he should make it only within the reality of the world, and that its truth should be demonstrated to him in this way.

Thirdly, the intention of the method of verification is not to give man a manifest demonstration of belief in God in such a way as to make faith unnecessary for him. Its purpose is to give concrete expression to belief in God.

The verification of belief in God never results in unequivocal certainty. With every attempt to make the relevance of belief in God 'visible' in the reality of the world, the reply can always be made, 'I don't see.' The New Testament story of Pentecost is an example of this. While some believed on hearing Peter's sermon and recognized the working of the Holy Spirit in what was happening before their eyes, others were totally unimpressed: 'They are filled with new wine' (Acts 2.1ff.).

Fourthly, the method of verification provides only an *indirect* experience of God, but precisely because it is indirect it can be seen to be an experience of *God*.

This indirect experience is in accordance with the invisibility of God. This does not mean that God does not exist, but that he exists in the reality of the world only in an indirect way. This does not mean that I undergo all kinds of experiences in life, including amongst others the experience of God. What it means is that I experience God only in and through the experience of my life, which is why the experience of God is always indirect. For this reason, then, one can never tell with certainty of any experience that it is an experience of God. The experiences which believers and non-believers have in their lives are the same. The only difference between them is that the believer 'integrates his experience of life in a specific way'.[4] This specific integration consists of seeing his experiences in the light of faith, and so discovering that the reality of the world is the reality of God. A striking example of the indirect nature of the experience of God is provided by the New Testament story of the healing of the ten lepers. Jesus healed ten lepers, but we are told of only one of them that 'when he saw that he was healed, he turned back, praising God with a loud voice'. All ten lepers underwent the same experience, but only one of them experienced God in it. To him Jesus said, 'Your faith has made you well.' This does not mean that the other nine once again became infected with leprosy. But it means that only this one 'discovered' God in what happened to him (Luke 17.11ff.).

Thus the method of verification does not subject God to human experience, but only tries to show man how, in and through his experiences of the reality of life and of the world, he can experience the reality of God. It therefore assumes faith – not in others, but in the person who is employing the method, and shows that theology is the 'science of faith'. To practise theology is to give an account of faith. This is not done in denominational declarations of faith, as in a certain kind of pietistic religion, nor by logically convincing demonstrations, as in the field of the exact sciences. Theology works out by a process of later reflection what is implicit in the existential experience of faith. Theology is the conversion of faith into thought.

At this point we must pay our respects to the memory of the old *proofs of God's existence*. It is wicked calumny to say that they simply set out to prove the existence of God by means of human reason. They were always rational means of demonstration in the hands of believers. In them the believer affirmed, full of astonishment, albeit with apologetic zeal, that if he had been reasonable, he would have been bound to perceive the reality of God previously in the reality of the world. Admittedly, he was trying to impose upon others before they believed what had not occurred to him till after. And the result of this was that the proper nature both of reason and of faith was lost.

The germ of truth contained in the traditional proofs of the existence of God can be seen at the present day in the fact that faith has always to give an account of itself to the world. This leads to the dialogue of belief with unbelief. The theme of this dialogue is the world: which of the two perceives the reality of the world in the right way – for both, not only unbelief, but belief too, belong to this reality. And therefore theology always takes place at the meeting point of belief and unbelief, in a kind of no-man's land, which for the time being does not wholly belong to either, neither to belief nor unbelief. And theology is not trying to conquer this no-man's land for itself – how can it do so, when it believes that as a part of the reality of the world it already belongs in any case to the reality of God? But it is this which theology is trying to demonstrate – not by proving logically, but by developing the existentialist experience of faith with regard to the world in such a way as to make it appropriate to the world and meaningful in itself. Theology too can be said to propose 'hypotheses', and attempts to present any given hypothesis as a meaningful and therefore convincing solution of a problem. It does so in the hope that in the process of converting belief into thought, it will as it were infect and carry with it the thought of others, so that this too becomes the conversion of belief into thought.

In this way the no-man's land becomes a transitional zone, in which belief and unbelief are in dispute about the true understanding of the reality of the world. This dispute is the familiar opposition between faith and reason, faith and thought, faith and knowledge or even faith and science.

3. *Faith and Reason in the Dispute about Reality*

In the course of the modern period the feud between faith and reason has become more and more violent, and they have grown further and further apart. But it is questionable whether either side has properly understood the other, and whether the opposition that undoubtedly exists is really as profound and total as it seems. In recent years, both on the side of faith and the side of reason, a growing number of voices have called for a revision of the hostile attitudes which have prevailed hitherto. Summing up in a single phrase the new relationship that seems to be coming into being between faith and reason, one could describe them as distinct but co-existent. That is, although a distinction must be made as before between faith and reason, they can no longer be strictly separated from one another, but must be related to each other. In discussing the method of verification, we have shown how far this is true of faith in its attitude to reason. Now we must look at the other side of the matter, and show how this method also casts a new light on the relationship of reason to faith. We shall develop this in three steps.

1. The enlightenment has not only given man new courage to think for himself, and liberated his reason and made it autonomous. At the same time it has given man an enlightened understanding of the limits of his own thinking and warned the autonomy of the reason against *hybris*. This was the great achievement of Kant, more than anyone else. Hegel added the perception that the reason is not an entity which is available and complete in itself from the first, ready at any time for any call, and unaffected by the course of human history. He saw that in its nature it is subject to historical conditions. But both the limits of reason and the historical limitations to which it is subject were then forgotten by positivism. This was why the individual specialized branches of knowledge were able to celebrate their great triumphs in the nineteenth and twentieth centuries, but at the same time lost their link with the totality of the universe, and ceased to extend their gaze to the universal

horizon in which they too stood. The consequence of this was that reality was fragmented into unrelated units. This led some to despair completely of the possibility of relating their specialist knowledge to any totality and of integrating it into any universal context. Others were lead to make an overweening attempt to comprehend totality by declaring partial aspects of individual specialisms to be of universal application. In this way scientific study was transformed into a philosophical world view, and knowledge was reconverted into faith – as though no one called Immanuel Kant ever lived in Königsberg and no one called Georg Friedrich Wilhelm Hegel ever lived in Berlin.

Even the student rebels of the present day mock the representatives of individual branches of scholarship as blinkered specialists. But with their optimistic and unqualified reliance on reason they betray themselves as pre-Kantians. They have not yet applied reason to a critique of itself, as Kant did. This may be one of the reasons why their chosen heroes – especially Adorno, Horkheimer and Habermas have, one after the other, and with considerable haste and disdain, been abandoned. For they were very well aware of the limits of reason as Kant defined them. But this uncritical attitude towards reason is certainly why they, the pure rationalists, have always lapsed too easily into irrationalism. For anyone who is ignorant of the limits of reason is an easy victim of every kind of irrationalism.

What we need today is not less enlightenment but more enlightenment. That is, man must continue to make his way out of the immaturity for which he was himself to blame, and which in part he has brought back down upon himself. This continuation of the enlightenment must consist at the present day above all in a deeper understanding of the limits of reason. This deeper understanding of reason within its own limits must be manifested in two ways. First of all, there must be a new recognition of the irrational. The expression 'irrational' itself shows that this recognition involves an act of self-limitation on the part of reason. It refers to what reason recognizes is inaccessible to reason alone, and therefore does not belong to it. Secondly, reason must show that it has a better understanding of its own limits by understanding that it is historically conditioned, and is not in absolute control of any moment of its own history. But everything which is historically conditioned is situated

within a universal horizon which it has not created itself, but
within which it finds itself. This is also true of reason. Consequently, no branch of rational study can delineate this universal horizon by its own means and methods. Its existence is
always a matter of belief, not in the sense of believing something
to be true, but in the sense of trust. But no branch of rational
study can endow man with this trust. Dorothee Sölle is right
when she says:

> That there is trust in the world, as necessarily as there is bread, and
> that love happens in the world, can neither be demonstrated nor refuted
> by science. Neither sputniks, the theory of evolution nor artificial rain
> have the slightest effect on this fact. It cannot be calculated and
> measured.[5]

We would add that it could well be that every branch of
rational study contains an element of trust, which it unconsciously assumes and by which it lives.

2. No science is without faith; it is of course without religious
faith, but not without any kind of trust at all. When we analysed the act of questioning, we established that man has an
unconscious trust in language. We must now go further and
affirm that man's *thinking* is also based upon an unconscious
act of trust. When I think, I am trusting that by thinking I will
gain a coherent understanding of reality and arrive at the truth.
There is no rationality without this element of trust. Carl
Friedrich von Weizsäcker explicitly stated that the rational
sciences displayed an ordered reality, though without enquiring
about its all embracing meaning, or about God. But then he
went so far as to assert: 'I believe that in the form of trust in
the consistent behaviour of the world, it in fact assumes the
presence of God.'[6]

This pre-condition of belief that is found in science applies
not only in a general sense, but also in detail. Belief is the
'logical *a priori*' of all human creative activity. There can be no
scientific investigation and technical planning without forecasts, programmes and prognoses. These forecasts, programmes
and prognoses are 'only believed' at first. This is true of the
plans for a projected dam, the search for a virus, and the flight
to the moon. 'Thus faith becomes the ferry-boat which carries
us to discovery. Only faith carries us across the open sea of the

universe to the new shores of knowledge.'[7]

'Faith' is an assumption in the most mundane everyday activities of physics. It is simply a 'matter of faith' that all quantitative measurements of physical conditions can be translated into numerical language. The reading of a needle on an ammeter or the rise and fall of a column of mercury in a thermometer – something that happens hundreds of times a day in every laboratory – only has a technical or scientific meaning when the point of the needle or the column of mercury coincides with a numerical symbol which can be interpreted as a mathematical entity. This seems so obvious to us that we no longer give it any thought. But in fact it assumes a 'belief that the world can be mathematicized'.

These examples show that instead of making a sharp distinction between belief and reason and regarding them as hostile, we must again recognize that they are related – not so much as brothers, but as cousins. There is no belief which has not sought to clarify itself and achieve self-awareness through rational thought, while on the other hand there is no rational thought in which belief is not implicit. Of course this assumes the acceptance of a distinction between different kinds of belief; belief as a condition of the natural sciences is something different from belief as the content of religion. What distinguishes one kind of belief from another is the way in which, and the degree to which, they can be verified. The belief that is always a primary assumption in science and technology can always be 'publicly' tested and precisely verified by instruments and the evidence of the senses – the dam holds, the virus is discovered, the flight to the moon ends with a landing.

This is not so with belief in God. Compared to a planned moon landing it is like firing a rocket off from the earth without knowing beforehand whether there is a moon or not. But that in spite of this it is not a leap into the cosmic vacuum depends solely on the fact of the revelation of God. This forms the sole 'reassurance' for faith, and therefore it plays a similar role in theology to the actual existence of nature in the natural sciences. But even the revelation of God has to be verified. In the first instance, since it concerns the assertion of historical facts, this verification can take place by the processes of historical criticism. But here as everywhere critical historical study only achieves 'approximation', a reasonably close approach, 'as good as there', to its object. Although the well-known distinction made by Luther between *securitas* and *certitudo*, between the certainty that relies on human evidence and the certainty that is the conviction of faith, may begin to sound rather hackneyed when uttered by Christians, it is applicable here. I can only achieve certainty of the revelation of God and therefore of belief in God through 'practice': by committing myself to its truth and trying to 'live it out in my life'.

Of course the verification obtained through this kind of experience is quite different from the verification of the belief assumed in science, but it is of no less value. On the contrary, it is of the utmost intensity. Someone brave enough can consider it worth dying because of it, or even for it, while Galileo did right to renounce his scientific discoveries on its account. But if faith is not to be soaked up into an unlimited subjectivity which brings an end to all dialogue, it must be ready to demonstrate its personal experience in the reality of the world, and to justify itself 'publicly' in the same way. This brings us back to what we have called the 'method of verification'. But it is not only Christian faith which rests upon such a practical, personal and irrational decision, and which accordingly needs verification.

3. The new humanism of recent years, with its interest and concern for society, declares itself in the same breath to be scientific, unbelieving and rational. But is it really so? Can one seriously claim that there is a scientific and rational basis, without faith, for a commitment on the part of one's fellow men, a struggle against inhumanity and injustice in the world, and the attempt to bring about a better ordering of society in which there is more humanity, justice and peace upon earth?

It is usual to justify the necessity of aid for developing countries on the grounds that without it the other two-thirds of the world would 'be on top of us' in twenty years, that social revolutions would break out which would sweep us up and carry us into general chaos. I sometimes wonder whether this rational consideration is not merely a secondary reason for us. Could one not advance the equally rational arguments that if we leave these nations to their fate, they will no longer have the strength in twenty years' time to be any threat to us? Is not the primary reason for the aid which we give at the present day, however selfish our motives and however inadequate it may be, that we simply cannot bring ourselves to leave these people to their own devices? But if we cannot bring ourselves to do otherwise, then our motive is no longer rational. That man is the 'ultimate', to which anything else is relative, and that he possesses 'infinite value', is a conviction which is incapable of rational justification. Although science can provide the means to bring this conviction to reality, it cannot itself provide a basis for it.

We should be warned by the fact that, of all people, the founder of psychoanalysis, Sigmund Freud, admitted:

> When I ask myself why I have always behaved honourably, ready to spare others and to be kind whenever possible, and why I did not give up doing so when I observed that in that way one harms oneself and becomes an anvil because other people are so untrustworthy, then, it is true, I have no answer.[8]

What Freud admitted about himself personally was expressed as a general principle by the sociologist Max Horkheimer when he said that 'no moral policy can be derived from the standpoint of positivism', and went on to say:

> From the scientific point of view, hatred, for all the difference in its social function, is no worse than love. There is no scientific reason why I should not hate, if it does not bring me any disadvantages in society. Everything that is connected with morality in the end derives logically from theology, or at least not from any secular basis, however hard one may try to be cautious about theology.[9]

Belief and unbelief have the same formal structure. Unbelief also rests on a decision, a choice, and cannot supply its own proof. For did not Marx, Nietzsche, Bloch and others not make a decision and a choice? Did their atheism or humanism have purely rational roots, or did it draw its strength from greater depths of existence, which cannot be plumbed by rational means? Is it really possible, we must ask, to make a simple distinction between 'belief' and 'unbelief', and accordingly present world history as nothing more than the feel of battle between the two. The consequence is that so-called 'unbelief' must also be verified in the reality of the world in the same way as belief, and that the arguments it advances must be just as much the systematic development of what is immanent in the experience underlying it as is the case with theology when it turns belief into rational thought.

And thus the conflict between belief and unbelief is about the world, about which of the two perceives the reality of the world in the right way. But this 'perception' must not be understood purely in a rational sense, as an act of the understanding, but also in the practical sense of 'realization', as when one speaks of realizing a plan or an opportunity.[10] Anyone who realizes a plan or opportunity does not only realize the possibilities implicit in this plan or in this opportunity, but brings them to reality by making use of them. This kind of 'verification' never takes place without a total personal commitment on the part of the believers or unbelievers concerned. Both have to produce their 'demonstration of the Spirit and of power' – this is the only proof for or against God which is still admissible in a world that has become worldly – if indeed any other were ever admissible.

4. *Verification in Concrete Terms*

If we are not to be open to the charge of making abstract assertions, we must now give some concrete and practical examples of what we have so far described in a theoretical and general way as the 'method of verification'. In this way we hope to verify it in its turn. To this end we shall take a number of key phrases from the bible and translate them into present-day terms. This we shall do with the hope and the intention that the past experience of the reality of God which they express and contain may once again appear true and credible to us, even in the changed reality of our life and of the world we live in. In this respect we are convinced that the present-day task of theology is basically no different from that which Martin Buber once laid down for his own work:

> I testify on behalf of experience and appeal to experience ... I say to those who listen to me, 'It is your experience. Think about it, and what you cannot think about, try to attain to as experience' ... I have no doctrine. I only show something. I show reality, and I show in reality something which has not been seen or has not been seen enough. Whoever listens to me, I take by the hand and lead to the window. I open the window and point out. I have no doctrine, but I conduct a conversation.[11]

We shall practise the method of verification in the form of four concrete examples.

(a) 'Under the Law': Man in the World

In the bible the word 'law' mostly refers to the Jewish law, the *torah*, which is regarded as originating with Moses, but which tradition has greatly enriched with innumerable commandments and ordnances. For us the meaning of the concept of law has for a very long time had the wider meaning of a universal principle. By 'law' we do not nowadays mean simply a series of outward ordinances, a collection of moral, ritual and cultic provisions. For us, the word 'law' implies a total definition of man in his attitude to the world. 'Law' means the fact that we form an integral part of history, which has a claim upon us, and are similarly integrated into the world, which imposes its necessities upon us.

To be *under the law* means that we are born into this historical horizon, into this scientific and technical age, into this wholly unique situation, and have no way out of it. The consequences of this are that

- we have to live with the bomb, between Americans and Russians and with the Chinese;
- that we are firmly in the grip of the inherent laws of politics, economics and society, and are pushed, rather than pushing ourselves;
- that we are born of particular parents, have particular inherited tendencies and are limited to a particular social environment;
- that we have to eat, drink and clothe ourselves, and are threatened by hunger, thirst, the weather and disease. That we are tied to a particular profession, a particular company, a particular marriage, and work ourselves to the bone for them every day;
- that we have to look on impotently while the work to which we have devoted the best years and powers of our life is ruined by someone else's incompetence;
- that we would like to be good and yet do evil;
- that we are journeying towards death, that our powers decline every day, and as soon as we are born, we are old enough to die.

In short, to be under the law means that we are completely integrated into history and surrounded by the world – and there is no way out of either.

But all these restrictive limitations which we have listed contain not only a force to which we are subjected, but also a challenge which we have to hear, a demand which we have to fulfil. Every situation puts us to the test. The law demands obedience. Although rational science and technology are our fate, and we cannot avoid them, they also offer us possibilities and tasks which we have to face up to. Admittedly, we have to live with the bomb, but our task is to live with the bomb and not to die by it. Admittedly we have to feed ourselves and reproduce ourselves, but we must plan nourishment and reproduction in a responsible way. Admittedly, the state, economy and society have their own laws, but we have to recognize, formulate and operate these laws. Thus every situation contains both force and challenge, necessity and demand: 'This is how it is' and 'This is what you should do' – and this is what it means 'to be under the law'.

What the bible says about 'law' is an assertion that in every situation and reality which we encounter, God is already present, so that when we are spoken to about God, what we are hearing about is not something alien and additional, which does not originally belong to our life and now has to be added to it. Instead, we are being called towards something which has already affected us in our life and which we cannot escape – whether we listen to what is being said or not. To be under the law means that we have the information and should know what to do.

(b) Created and Sustained by God: Existence Owed to Another
That God creates and maintains the world is not something that can be preached from outside. Man must become inwardly aware of it himself. He must experience it in his existence in the world. We encounter the creator only in our 'feeling of creatureliness', in our experience that life is not wholly under our own control; that life at its most profound is not an act, an achievement and a work, but something that happens to us, a gift and a grace. Thus belief in God as the creator and sustainer of the world does not begin by repeating the biblical creation

narrative, but by pointing to man's own direct experience of 'total dependency'. It comes with the discovery of the experience that underlies all life, that man does not 'make' but 'receives' his life, and that it is not he who has made himself and his own world what they are. This he owes to another. Whenever fresh thought is given at the present day to the question of prayer, the starting point will probably have to be this experience of 'owing one's existence to another'.

Several times already we have come across the fact that man in the first instance does not 'make' but 'receives' his life. We have already established that man can only ask because he has already received answers; he can only speak because the world is presented to him in speech; he can only think because what exists makes itself perceptible to him in reason. We can go on to say, too, that he can only live because time is given to him. The well-known saying of Jesus in the Sermon on the Mount refers to this fact: 'And which of you by being anxious can add one cubit to his span of life?' (Matt. 6.27).

As in all precise verification of the biblical statement that man is created and maintained by God, we can point to two concrete experiences in addition to these more general experiences.

When we count up the periods in our life in which we can really say that during them we lived – that is, lived, not just vegetated – they will probably add up to no more than a short period of time, perhaps only a few months, weeks or even days. Everything else was mere preparation, routine or everyday existence. Let us then go on to ask what kind of periods these were in which we 'lived'. We shall see that for the most part they were periods in which we did not consciously achieve anything, but in which 'things happened to us' and we had the feeling that it was not we who had done this, but that there was a power present which was filling us. The most important thing is not what we call this power, whether we call it God, Spirit or Love, or whether we prefer at first not to give it a name at all. All that matters is the experience that this power is present and that we open ourselves to it.

Again, we know that there is no success in life without work. But we have also experienced the fact that our work and achievements are not directly translated into success and effect. Sometimes they succeed, sometimes they fail. The uncertainty whether they succeed or fail does not depend on how much we put into them, as though there was a direct relationship between quantity and quality. Something else is involved which is beyond our control, something incalculable, which cannot be assessed statistically. The bible speaks of the 'grace' and 'blessing' of God. And I repeat, it is a matter of indifference whether or not we wish to call this experience by the same name. All that matters is that we recognize in our work this element which is beyond our control, and that it arouses in us a thankful astonishment and induces in us that attitude of careless ease without which the vital impulse is absent from any work.

We must go on here to ask whether as Christians we often do not place too strong an emphasis on the way in which all life brings decisions. Does not our life consist much more in accepting decisions that have been taken about us, rather than in constantly making decisions on our own account? When is a more absolute decision ever taken about us than in the case of our birth and death? This is why Schleiermacher called being born and dying 'windows which have been hacked through' and look out on to the universe.

The experience that we owe our existence to another is also reflected in the unconscious trust which underlies and determines the existence of every human being, and without which he would be unable to live. Edward Schillebeeckx calls this the 'original trust' of man, and even says of it that all human existence is endowed with the 'promise of salvation'.[12] In fact, just as we showed that man's life in the world is 'under the law', so we must now affirm that it already contains within itself a longing for something which is whole and entire. And just as we said that wherever man feels himself enclosed and at the same time challenged by the law he is already exposed to the presence of God, so we must now go on to add that wherever he experiences his life as withheld from him, and at the same time as something received by him, he is likewise already seized in a hidden way by the reality of God. If man's belief in God had no foundation in such an experience of life, the suspicion that it was mere projection would be very difficult to refute.

(c) 'Exodus': the God of Life and History

Because God creates life and acts in history, in the bible the exodus forms one of the basic situations of all human existence. One might almost say that the people of Israel lived from one exodus to another. Historically this began with the exodus from Egypt. This forms the event which constitutes Yahweh's covenant with Israel, and is the whole foundation of the nation's history. When the history of salvation was later conceived of in a universal setting, the call of Abraham was introduced at the beginning, and this too was associated with an exodus. Abraham received from Yahweh the command: 'Go from your country and your kindred and your father's house to the land that I will show you' (Gen. 12.1).

At a later period came Israel's exodus into exile in Babylon, and then the return to Jerusalem, and finally, after the destruction of the Temple, the scattering of the nation throughout the world, until in our own times it has once again begun to draw together again.

When the early church took over the Old Testament, the exodus also provided the basic pattern for the Christian interpretation of existence and history. The apostle Paul draws an analogy between the transition brought about by Christ from the old to the new aeon, and Israel's exodus from Egypt, while because of his obedient exodus, Abraham becomes the father and pattern of faith. The New Testament says of him, almost echoing the passage quoted above from the Old Testament: 'By faith Abraham obeyed when he was called to go out to a place which he was to receive as an inheritance; and he went out, not knowing where he was to go' (Heb. 11.8).

In the bible the decisive acts of God always 'happen outside', that is, not in the inner realm of the cult, but in the outward realm of life and the world. The people of Israel received the law from Moses outside, before the camp; it was outside the house that the father awaited the return of the prodigal son; Jesus of Nazareth was crucified outside the walls of the city of Jerusalem. The Epistle to the Hebrews draws the consequences of this: 'Therefore let us go forth to him outside the camp, bearing abuse for him' (Heb. 13.13).

But what has the exodus of a nation which took place more than three thousand years ago to do with us at the present day, and what meaning for us is there in the exodus of a man and his clan, to which it is scarcely possible to give any historic dating? The process of verification can be carried out only by bringing the situation up to date: by showing how the exodus also forms a basic situation of our own existence and history, and how we can 'make visible' in the reality of our own life and history the experience of God once associated with it.

Exodus takes place within the course of individual lives at the present day in puberty, in the learning process, in retirement and in death; sociologically in the constant changes in the economic and social order, in which the only thing that is constant seems to be change; and in changing trains, changing jobs, changing schools, leaving home. It takes place in the history of thought in the bringing to completion of the enlightenment, which Kant described in as many words as the 'way out' taken by man out of the immaturity for which he was himself to blame. It takes place in politics in the form of the revolution, persecution and flight which seem to form a permanent element in the history of the world in the twentieth century. What we have already noted about man's life under the law and under the promise occurs in all these situations. In them man experiences both a harsh necessity, with the claim it makes on him, and the opening up of a new possibility of life which is offered to him apart from his own acts. We may say that exodus is a demonstration of faith, hope and love – faith as the experience of being protected on one's journey, hope as the active expectation of a future which is promised but not guaranteed, and love as mutual help on the journey towards the future.

(d) Repentance: Guilt – Judgment – Grace

The word 'repentance' plays an important role in the bible. The prophets of the Old Testament were constantly calling the people of Israel to repent and, according to the New Testament narrative, Jesus of Nazareth began his public ministry with the words: 'Repent, for the kingdom of heaven is at hand' (Matt. 4.17). In the bible 'repentance' means the 'conversion' of the individual, a turning away from his own perverse way by his turning back to God. But this is seen not only as an individual act, but is integrated into the whole context of the history of God's dealings with man. Both aspects have become alien and incomprehensible to our own age. The turning of an individual to God is seen as the characteristic of an out-of-date private 'religiosity', while the acceptance of a total divine structure of history is seen as the expression of 'theism' as a world view which is no longer tenable. But the question remains whether, just because this interpretative instrument is worn out, there has been an end to the reality which the biblical language of repentance, judgment and grace was trying to express. The main dividing line at the present day in this respect runs not between theists and atheists, far less between Christians and non-Christians. It lies between those who still pose the question of guilt and its consequences in the life of the individual and of society, and thereby remain open to the deeper mystery of life and history, and those who no longer ask this question and thereby reject any deeper meaning in life and history. Such a rejection means more than simply the end of a particular interpretation of history, which happens in this case to be derived from the bible. It means the end of all inquiry into the meaning of life and history, and is therefore a final 'farewell to history'.

Of course we can no longer interpret every turn that history takes, every victory and every defeat, simply as God's rewards and punishments. There is also a natural growth and decay in history; there are biological laws within it, birth and death, sickness and age, natural catastrophes, the products of blind chance, undeserved misfortune; and there is tragedy in history. The drama of history is too manifold and too complex for everything in it to be reduced to a simple equation of guilt and punishment, righteousness and reward. History is morally ambiguous, and God's acts in it are hidden. Yet history is not without all morality and righteousness, and sometimes we can even perceive something of the moral content contained in history. Even though it is veiled, and rarely recognizable, the ordering of history is nevertheless also an ordering of guilt and punishment. Paul Tillich, who has explored the reality of history more profoundly than most, does not hesitate to speak openly of sin and punishment in history. In a passage in his sermons in *The Shaking of the Foundations* he says:

We do not like words such as 'sin' and 'punishment'. They seem to us old-fashioned, barbaric, and invalid in the light of modern psychology. But whenever I have met exiles of high moral standards and insight, I have discovered that they feel responsible for what has happened within their own countries. And very often I have met citizens of democratic countries, citizens of this country, who have expressed a feeling of guilt for the situation of the world today. They were right, and the exiles were right: they are responsible, as are you and I. Whether or not we call it sin, whether or not we call it punishment, we are beaten by the consequences of our own failures. That is the order of history.[13]

'We are beaten by the consequences of our own failures' – this points the way in which guilt and punishment take effect in history. The ordering of guilt and punishment does not as it were break into the natural process of history from above, but comes about as part of that process; it is firmly woven into the texture of historical events. Just as God does not sustain the world by recreating it from nothing at every moment, but makes use of the process of nature itself as the means by which he sustains it, so his judgment comes about not by constantly interrupting the course of history, but by occurring 'as of itself' through the causal network that exists within the world. God does not punish by thinking up special measures which man can be expected to feel, as a father might have formerly considered whether to deprive his son of his pudding, send him to his room or beat him. Instead, the punishment takes place in the course of historical development as a necessary consequence of the guilt. Basically it consists simply of God letting man's existence continue on the basis which he himself has brought about, so that he is abandoned to the effects of his own misdeeds. God draws back from man and leaves him to the consequences of his own actions. 'God gave them up' – these words from the Epistle to the Romans describe in essence the whole mystery of divine judgment. Thus the punishment is already implicit in the misdeed; what happens in the course of our life or of history is only the working out of what was concealed in it from the first.

For example; God's judgment on the German people after the war consisted solely in God's abandoning the Germans to the consequences of their own political actions: 'He gave them up.' Everything that has happened to us has only been the consequences of our own guilt. 'The fathers have eaten sour grapes, and the children's teeth are set on edge' (Jer. 1.29; Ezek. 18.2) –

we have learnt the bitter truth of this saying of Old Testament prophecy. But no one can say that the German people have recognized this truth in their history. There has been no repentance. In this case 'repentance' would have meant admitting our own failure, accepting the defeat of a war which was our own fault, and so working the past productively into the political future. Because we have failed in this, a threatening 'too late' hangs over everything that we do nowadays in society or politics. There is no way out: the reality avoided yesterday is the reality of today and tomorrow. Our history does not lag behind of itself. We cannot simply leave it like a crumpled piece of paper, lying on the street, or take it off like a coat we have grown tired of. It goes with us, and is in us, whether we like it or not.

Again, someone may have set his heart on money or on glory, and what he has set his heart on becomes his god. All his efforts, regardless of the cost, are directed towards having this and possessing it forever. In this way his life becomes one of breathless haste and constant over-exertion. Completely devoted to money or fame, he does not notice how his substance is being wasted more and more quickly – until one day the crash comes. Either his physical resources are no longer up to it, or else he simply comes to a sudden realization of the dreariness and emptiness of his life, and yawns with dreadful weariness from pure boredom. But whatever form the crash takes, it is not an alien element from outside, but is a punishment which is a direct consequence of his actions. God carries out his judgment simply by abandoning the person to the consequences of his own actions; 'he has given him up'.

Again, take the case of a politician who is not interested in the well-being of his fellow citizens, but is driven only by the urge for power and the advancement of his career. Consequently he loses his balanced view of reality. Because he is arrogant, he takes an over-confident view of political and military realities. But this is where his destiny begins to be fulfilled. Abandoned to the consequences of his own actions, he is ruined. 'God has given him up.'

But with the gospel a new and different order of history appears on the horizon: the order of grace and love. Once again, we ask how this comes about within history. How is it realized in politics, in economics and in social life? How can there be

grace and love, a new beginning and a new future in these
fields? The answer is, only in the same way as the old order was
realized, the order of guilt and punishment. It does not happen
by magic, by an intervention of God from above, but in a
historical and human way. History takes a new course when
men who have freed themselves from the guilt of the past begin
to pray and to do what is right – that is, to carry out the practical
actions which are necessary at the present historical moment to
maintain in being the world and the human race. Whether such
prayer and right doing will really bring about a new beginning
in history is not ultimately in our hands. But if it succeeds, it is
not our achievement, but the grace of God.

The merciless judgment 'too late' hangs over the whole of
history. But it is the duty and right of a prophet alone to proclaim this. A theologian is not a prophet. For this reason we
ought at this point to break off our attempt to verify what the
bible says about repentance, grace and judgment in the reality
of our life and our work. But we cannot do so without making
a further point. Let us imagine two people discussing the
historical course taken by Germany after the war. One of them
says, 'We Germans have suffered the consequences of our own
guilt, but we have not been purified; and therefore all we have
done now runs the risk of being condemned as "too late".' But
he never once mentions the name of God. The other says,
'Certainly we Germans have brought terrible guilt upon ourselves, and God has punished us for it. But the guilt of the others
is at least as great.' And he begins to list them all: the guilt of
the Russians, the guilt of the Americans, the guilt of the British,
the guilt of the French, the guilt of the communists, the guilt
of the Jews – and he concludes by asking, 'When will God punish
them as well?' Which of these two has experienced God: the
one who mentions his name or the one who does not?

The concrete examples we have given are not intended to
provide a proof of belief in God, but only to show that it is
possible and a reality. The least and yet the greatest thing which
the method of verification can achieve is the reaction described
by Rabbi Levi-Isaac of Berdychev in these words: 'Perhaps
it is true ... Think of this, my son: Perhaps it is true!'

6

Empirical Theology

1. The Method of Induction

Men today are demanding an experience of reality. Whether they could bear this reality if they were to experience it is another question. At any rate, they would like to experience it for themselves and draw their own conclusions from it. The prototype of modern man is 'doubting Thomas', who said of the risen Jesus, 'Unless I see in his hands the print of the nails, and place my finger in the mark of the nails, and place my hand in his side, I will not believe' (John 20.25). As we know, Jesus did not reject Thomas's demand as improper, but satisfied it, and so Thomas believed.

This attitude of Thomas, apparently unbelieving, but in his very unbelief pressing for his own personal experience of the truth, is the way we must follow today in our experience of God. And so theology is obliged to verify in the reality of the world all the statements it makes about God. But this task has to be carried out by an appropriate procedure, by a method not of deduction, but of induction. In the present century, Karl Barth is the great exponent of an unrelieved theology of deduction. He could sum up his entire theological programme in a single sentence, consisting of only three words: 'God is God.' And he went on, in words which do not exactly explain this tautology: 'It is the doctrine of the Trinity which is the fundamental affirmation of this equation, which is not immediately obvious, and on which all theology is built.'[1] Then Barth, beginning 'up above', worked for forty years to deduce his whole theology, sentence by sentence, from this first premiss. It is this procedure which led to the well-known charge which Bonhoeffer made against Barth, of a 'positivism of revelation'. Barth, he said, was asking men to believe according to the principle of 'Take it or leave it'.

But because theology has a duty to verify Christian faith, the method it must follow at the present day is that of induction. A trivial but telling illustration of this change in the method theology has to follow can be found in a pun made by the leader of a bible study group in Swabia. He began a study hour by saying 'Today we shall consider a single word of holy scripture, the word "whereas (*sintemal*)".' And then the devout man continued: 'Where 'as your life been leading you (*Sinnt 'emal nach über euer leben!*)?' And this is the question: as with the incarnation, the way to belief in God leads through the door of the stable, the everyday experiences of our life and of ordinary human relationships. And theology must adapt itself to an experience of God which leads in this direction. It is this which brings it to the method of induction.

When theology speaks of God at the present day, it must not begin 'up above', not in a supernatural other world beyond this world, nor in any ideas, conceptions and doctrines about God, far less in a philosophical or religious world view which is assumed in advance. Neither a dualist metaphysics nor the acceptance of the authority of holy scripture can be posited in advance. Instead, theology must begin 'here below', in the world in which we live. It must take as a starting point our experiences and the things we know. All men need as it were to be loaded up with such experience and factual knowledge, which can then be collected and drawn into a common process of thinking and learning. This process must be carried on in a constant encounter with the historical facts of biblical tradition, but must not be confused by the philosophical and religious assumptions of the bible.

The task of verification has certain necessary consequences for the way in which we have to conduct theology at the present day. Basically, the process of induction signifies nothing more than the application of the method of verification to the daily practice of theological study.

2. *The Theory of Practice*

The age of great theological systems and system-builders is past, and indeed the day of systematic theology in the classical sense seems to be gone. Our contemporaries, whose life is no longer lived in a closed and unified social system, but in an open and pluralist society, have a deep mistrust of all dogmatic assertions, theological deductions and attempts to impose a systematic unity. The age of systematic theology, and of historical and exegetic theology, is now past. Today it is the turn of practical theology, not in the sense of a theology better adapted to the practical and technical functions of the pastoral ministry, but in the sense of a much clearer link between all theological thought and empirical facts.

What we need at the present day is an *empirical*, and indeed *experimental* theology. This means a theology in concrete terms, related to particular situations, and with a pragmatic impulse. This means that it is bound to be fragmentary and pluralist – but by the same token it will be a 'contemporary' theology in the best sense of the word, *ad hoc* theology, a theology which proceeds from one case to another.

The path of empirical theology does not lead from the abstract to the concrete, but in exactly the reverse direction, from the concrete to the abstract. Luther gave an exact description of this procedure when he laid down as a rule for all theology that it should begin *ab individuis*, with specific details, and should end with *universalia*, general principles – and not the reverse.[2] Empirical theology always works 'bit by bit'. It always starts with a single partial problem, and calmly refuses to fit this theological fragment into a total system, as though it were the one thing necessary to hold the lot together. Its purpose is not an enduring doctrinal construction meant to last for generations, but an introduction to life for a single generation. And therefore it is characterized not by a timeless systematization undertaken with a desire for perfection, but by a ready spontaneity, with the courage to leave questions unanswered. The final result can no longer be a closed system. In fact closed theological systems are something against which a warning has to be given, especially when they claim to contain

God. In such a system God is put in his place; he has been 'shown where he stands'.

The pattern for empirical theology is to be found in 'God's becoming man' in Jesus Christ. This provides not only the object of theology, but the field within which it operates and the methods it must follow. In everything that theology thinks, says and does it must follow God's movement towards man. The concern of empirical theology is that theology should 'become human' as God became man. When theology becomes human in this way, theologians cease to be fellows of their colleges and become our fellow men. What they say about human existence, which at present seems so abstract and formal, becomes filled with human life. There the pale phantom called 'man' which haunts theology once again becomes a living and concrete flesh and blood person, who possesses not just a head and a mind, but also a heart, a soul, and a body, and always lives in a particular social context. There the despised 'non-theological factors' are once again accorded their limited but proper place. There experience, religion, piety, tradition and history are no longer simply man's revolt against God, but at the same time the vessels of God's revelation. Such an empirical theology would also be more in accord with the way Jesus spoke of God. He always spoke of God in an 'up to the minute' way, in words suited to the situation of the moment. He aimed at an existential relevance and not at conceptual clarity, and every question, and any experience, however rudimentary, was of greater importance than a fixed conception of God or a detailed creed. Just think of what Jesus meant by faith!

There is the woman from the region of Tyre and Sidon, who came crying after Jesus to heal her sick daughter. She did not belong to the people of Israel – we would say, she was not in the church. Yet she did not stop crying after Jesus until he finally turned and fulfilled her wish. And Jesus explicitly adds, 'O woman, great is your faith!' (Matt. 15.21-28).

Again, there was the centurion of Capernaum, who came to Jesus because of his sick servant. He, too, was not a Jew, but a heathen, and to all appearances also an intellectually inflexible person, capable only of thinking in the categories of a non-commissioned officer. But Jesus also says of him: 'Truly, I say to you, not even in Israel have I found such faith' (Matt. 8.5-13).

Finally, there was the woman known throughout the city as a sinner, who came to Jesus and anointed his feet and dried them with her hair. Jesus also said to her: 'Your faith has saved you; go in peace' (Luke 7.36-50).

All these people were told by Jesus to their face that they believed, and yet he did not require any confession of faith of them, or ask them about their conception of God. This is a completely non-religious way of speaking of faith. The name of God is not even always mentioned. Naturally, faith here is always directed towards God, but in every case this faith in God is only present when it is expressed in concrete form in a particular situation in life and a particular experience of life.

In empirical theology the relationship between *theory and practice* has changed, and indeed is reversed. The well-known Marxist theory that practice comes before theory is also true of Christian theology at the present day. Theology can only exist as the theory of practice or, more precisely, as the reflective thought which accompanies practice. Nothing that cannot be transformed into appropriate action is of any use in theology.

But at the present day, theory and practice are still far apart in Christianity. The most scandalous example of this is the unworthy dispute which still remains unresolved between the churches about the eucharist. Why is intercommunion made dependent solely upon a theological consensus which must be agreed in advance? Why not take the reverse course, and begin with a common celebration? If, as everyone who takes part believes, the Lord is really – in whatever way – present at the 'Lord's Supper', then one must expect that experiences are being shared which will lead in due time to theological consequences, although they may not lead to the establishment of a theological consensus.

But at this point we must sound a strong note of warning. The requirement that the starting point of theology should always be an experience, and that in its form and method of work it must always be 'empirical theology', must be defended against possible misunderstandings. Three points must be made:

1. Empirical theology does not simply mean man's 'introspection,' as though, if man could only penetrate deeply enough into his own mind and heart, he would discover the

truth of God there. It means that man must consider himself and his world in the light of the revelation of God, and so recognize that his reality is a reality determined by God.

2. Empirical theology does not mean merely reproducing experiences, but clarifying them and working them into shape in the process of understanding. Only then do experiences become experience. 'Experience consists of direct experiences clarified by thought, expressed in words, and only then consciously apprehended.'[3]

3. Empirical theology does not simply mean the reproduction of subjective human feelings, but the perception of the voice of God, and it is this that gives coherent utterance to one's own unuttered feelings.

To sum up, one can say that empirical theology is the description, after rational consideration, of previous experiences.

Thus not even empirical theology can be conducted without systematic definitions and reflection. But every definition runs the risk of putting limits upon God; for 'to define' literally means 'to draw limits'. One cannot say that God 'exists', but only that God 'happens'. We explained this in setting out the method of verification. Anyone who defines God 'fixes him', and makes him a specific and limited external object. Here again, one of the 'Laconic Remarks' of Heinrich Wiesner is to the point: 'Dogma is a grammar of faith. Living language takes little notice of it.'

A theological concept must be nothing other than experience which has been submitted to the process of reflection. A relationship between a theological concept and the experienced reality of God is like that of a map to the country it portrays. Theology and its concepts are just like the manna which the Israelites ate in the desert: there was always just enough for one day; one could only enjoy it today, because tomorrow it would already be spoilt. And therefore existential experience must always come first, and conceptual reflection second. Theological statements are nothing more than the experience of God brought into order and summed up in conceptual terms. In this sense the 'Christian' always comes before the 'theologian'.

The literal meaning of empirical theology is 'the theology of experience'. This phrase reminds us of pietism. But we are not embarrassed by this reminder; on the contrary, we place a good deal of value upon it. For now as ever pietism provides an important source of Christian devotion – though only the pietism which first arose in reaction to orthodoxy, not to the enlightenment, and which has still retained a sense of this origin. It was the pietist Philipp Jakob Spener who replaced the concept 'dogmatics' which had hitherto been dominant by the expression 'the doctrine of faith', in order to ensure that theology too gave due place to the element of personal experience and certainty. This was a reaction against the itemization of objective theological tenets by tradition Protestant orthodoxy. Since then, however, German pietism has forgotten its historical origins and has made an alliance with the established provincial churches and with theological orthodoxy. This took place in the nineteenth century in opposition to liberal theology. In our own time, the alliance with orthodoxy has been renewed in the attack against the existentialist theology of Rudolf Bultmann and his school. In so doing, pietism has failed to realize that it is running the risk of losing what is best in it, its awareness that what matters is not pure doctrine, but faith and life, that it is not the head but the heart which makes a theologian and a Christian.

It is because of this important spiritual inheritance that we are concerned to defend pietism from the orthodox functionaries of the confessional movement whose slogan is 'No Other Gospel' (*Kein anderes Evangelium*). Of course the pietism we are calling for must be of a higher order, just as Schleiermacher called himself 'one of the Herrnhut Brethren, but of a higher order'. The experience of God, which is of such great value to pietism, must be a *present-day* experience of God, that is, it must be contemporary and therefore not anti-intellectual, but reflective and rational.

In taking the part of pietism, we naturally wish at the same time to give a warning against placing too high a value on correct theological statements, and therefore against any kind of dogmatic 'orthodoxy'. An excessive concern for purity of doctrine brings an element of joylessness, fear and constant over-exertion into theology – just like the claim of the 'theology since the death of God' that it has to take the place of God in the world. The God-is-dead theologians and the orthodox seem

equally ignorant that the wisdom of God *rejoices* in the in-
habited world and *delights* in the sons of men. That is, both are
purists and remain 'under the law'. What the counsel for the
defence in Camus' story *The Fall* says, with Jesus in mind, is
true of all the 'orthodox':

> They have hoisted him on to a judge's bench, in the secret of their
> hearts, and they smite, above all they judge, they judge in his name. He
> spoke softly to the adulteress: 'Neither do I condemn thee!' but that
> doesn't matter; they condemn without absolving anyone.... Whether
> they are atheists or church-goers, Muscovites or Bostonians, ... they
> invent dreadful rules, they rush out to build piles of faggots to replace
> churches. Savonarola, I tell you. But they believe solely in sin, never in
> grace.[4]

We have certainty about God only in faith; whereas in
theology we have only conjectures about God. That is why it
makes no sense to me that when someone comes and says 'I
believe in the love of God, even though the world is as it is', he
should first be set an examination in the faith and asked what
he thinks about the virgin birth, the divine sonship of Jesus, the
empty tomb, the historical value of the Gospel of John, the
resurrection of the body or the Trinity. Why, instead, do we
not say to him, 'What, you believe in the love of God, even
though the world is as it is? Friend, how great and fine your
faith is! Show me it so that I can share it!' Our theological
squabbles can come later.

When at the last supper Jesus told the disciples that one of
them would betray him, they did not ask him, 'Who is it?'
Each of them asked him, 'Lord, is it I?' So, when it is a matter
of judging what is right belief, no one should loudly proclaim,
Lord, it is I! Everyone should ask quietly, Lord, is it I? If all
who have the name of Christ could put their own name in
Judas' place in the list of the disciples, our ears and eyes would
be opened, and we would forgo all judgments.

3. *Theology for Non-Theologians*

What we have said about empirical theology leaves no room
for a great deal of the theology that is practised at the present
day. At the same time, it establishes a new relationship between
theologians and non-theologians.

Kierkegaard once asked: What is a professor of theology? His answer was, 'He is a professor whose subject is somebody else being crucified'. This is a very biting reply, in Kierkegaard's fashion, admitting no qualification, and therefore exaggerated. It is not meant to have a practical application, but to wound. And yet, woe to the theologian who is no longer wounded by it: Somebody else has been crucified – and he preaches and teaches about it!

There is a constant risk in theology of God becoming the special province of academics and specialists. Naturally, theologians, like all scholars, must conduct their specialist discussions, in which they can raise their problems without disturbance and exchange their opinions. The well-known saying of Horace: *Odi profanum vulgus et arceo* – I hate the common crowd and keep away from it – which all faculties and academic disciplines rightly make their own, also draws its magic circle round theology. But the result of this is that all the narrow-mindedness, bad manners and scandals which pullulate inside academic ivory towers, also infect theology. As early as 1922 Karl Barth wrote from Göttingen to his friend Eduard Thurneysen:

I am quite certain that one must attribute much of the distress of theology not to the stupidity and ill nature of theologians but simply to the inevitable disorder of the academic occupation. Even an archangel would become banal if he were occupied with this endless drawing out of sticky threads.[5]

What Barth calls the 'drawing out of sticky threads' is largely the result of the *historicizing* of theology. But in this respect theology is only sharing in the whole intellectual history of the West. In the West everything has already been thought, believed, said and written; it seems that for us there is nothing new under the sun, no truth that can astonish us. We drag ourselves wearily back to our own history. Whatever the challenges and questions with which we are faced at the present day, we first work through the whole of our past to its origins in Eastern and Western history. And when we get back to the present, we are out of breath, and have lost the strength to say anything for ourselves. *Ad fontes* – back to the sources! For the Renaissance and humanism this call meant a liberation from a worn-out past, by renewing it with the aid of its historical sources. But all it does for us is to weigh us down with the whole burden of our history. In the justification for the choice of subject in his inaugural lecture, which we have already quoted, Rolf Schäfer said of the present-day student of theology:

He is an expert in the exegetical subjects, in the history of doctrine and in contemporary dogmatic systems, he is a master of the fine distinction between orthodox belief and the heresies, he composes sermons which proclaim the word of God most accurately – but at heart he is not involved with the substance they contain.[6]

The application of the methods of historical criticism to the biblical testimonies and the tradition of the church at one time meant the liberation and the renewal of theology. But these days are past; since then, historical knowledge and critical research in theology have themselves become a tradition and a burden. In this respect, however, theology has merely shared the fate of most of the other humanities. This 'historicizing of the intellect' is nowadays a cause of distress not only to theologians, but also to philosophers, students of language and literature, historians and lawyers. Anyone who still calls for a knowledge of Latin, Greek and Hebrew as a requirement for the study of theology should ask himself whether this does not in fact make theology the prisoner of the sub-culture of a vanished humanism.

When Barth made his new departure in theology, it was to a considerable degree a protest against this one-sided historicizing of theology, against the 'reverence for history'. It was born from the 'difficulty in preaching' felt by the clergy. But the result was that from the first Barth's theology came to have the character of a theology for clergymen. This theology for clergymen served us quite well in enduring the church struggle in the 1930s, but it could scarcely have succeeded even in this if it had not been nourished by the iron rations of the pietist religious feeling amongst the laity which this theology had condemned so scornfully and mercilessly.

Again, it is difficult to assert that the existentialist theology of Rudolf Bultmann and his school has succeeded in breaking out of the frontiers of a small group of scholars and making its mark amongst the 'fellow men' which it looks for so passionately and refers to so often. It made a serious effort to do this, more serious than any other theology, and used Heidegger's categories of thought and language as an instrument for this purpose. But it was this very instrument which gave it the appearance of abstract intellectualism which makes it so alien and incomprehensible to many people.

Thus Protestant theology is once again threatening to become an affair of experts, almost the stock in trade of a guild which exists to hand down its knowledge by methods which are as correct and accurate as possible. The same seems to be true of Catholic theology. The Catholic layman Ingo Hermann laments:

Anyone who, with an awareness of the urgent political, social and ideological problems of the world, reads through the programme of lectures in the theological faculties at the universities and theological colleges, the lists of theological publishers or the titles on the shelves of booksellers who deal with theology – and particularly, anyone who glances through theological textbooks – will be struck by the apparent unconcern and untroubled preoccupation with its own affairs in what is put forward at the present day as theology.[7]

And the Catholic pastoral theologian Norbert Greinacher writes in the same collection of essays that contains the above quotation, almost echoing the above words:

When one looks at the themes of theses and inaugural dissertations, and studies the publications of professors of theology, one is tempted to ask whether all this is not a 'theology for theology's sake', in which the reality of the faith of modern man is forgotten.[8]

One is involuntarily reminded by present-day theology of a cathedral, with two men working on a scaffold at the top of its highest spire. They are having a violent quarrel about whether the last bit of carving should twist to the right or to the left, and they seem about to throw each other down to the ground. But down below on the street the people are looking up and cannot understand what the two men on the spire are quarrelling about. And because they do not understand, they shake their heads and pass on. The tendency which threatens every branch of scholarship, to ply its art for art's sake, and to turn its back on the rest of the world, is more dangerous for theology than for any other academic discipline. This is because of its object. Theology claims that its object is universal, that God is the concern of all men. If the faculty of theology still holds a primacy of honour within some universities, this is only because its object is universal. But it must put this universality into practice. Horace's *Odi profanum vulgus* is a claim which it is entitled to make only within strict limits. For theology can never be a scholar's subject in the same way as may be possible for other disciplines. In its academic discussion, it must always have contemporary man in mind, and he must constantly be present as a silent listener.

Empirical theology calls for *a new relationship between theologians and non-theologians.* Because it represents the description, on recollection and reflection, of a previous experience of God, empirical theology is on principle 'public'.

Hitherto theologians have sat apart from each other, singly or divided into schools, under the tree of knowledge and have shown each other the fruits they have plucked, good to look at and good to eat. While this has been going on, Adam and Eve have been gathering fruit for the market in the sweat of their brow. But empirical theology requires that we make the idea of the priesthood of all believers a reality in the field of theological thought – not only when ethical questions of work and society are at issue, but also when theology is considering God, Christ, the bible, the creeds, the resurrection and the Trinity.

This means that 'the title of baptism must take precedence over the title of any other office'.[9] A happy definition by Schleiermacher describes laymen as Christians who have power and authority 'for the independent practice of Christianity in the world'. Out of their own thought and experience non-theologians can be expected to make an important contribution to a future theology. Of course no progress will be made without the 'courage to be wrong'. If we are not willing to turn a blind eye to certain theological weaknesses, we cannot expect the laity to produce any theology of their own. Theology, too, can make its motto *Fiat theologia, pereat mundus*, but this destroys all life.

We do not despise academic theology, nor do we share the suspicion with which many devout laymen regard it. We believe that there must be academic theology in the sense of the methodical and structured consideration of the revelation of God to which the bible bears witness. We are also of the opinion that there must be in the church a body specifically trained to exercise it on behalf of the others, and not to please themselves! It is at this point that we take issue with modern theology, regardless of the school or opinion it represents.

We cannot imagine that the question of God is as complicated as theologians sometimes make it. God may be concealed, and he can even be very profoundly concealed, but he is never complicated. The complication of our theology is in flat contradiction to divine revelation. It thereby contradicts the clear will of God to which every page of the bible bears witness, that God wishes to seek men out, then reveal himself, impart himself and make himself known to men. God has left his concealment and entered the manifold variety of life, and has revealed himself in *one* human life, in the man Jesus of Nazareth. Through this revelation the concealed and manifold God has become 'simple' on our behalf. The incarnation of God in Jesus Christ implies both the simplification of God and the simplification of theology.

Just as Switzerland possesses only a small professional army, whose task it is to set up a large territorial army, so theologians, too, ought to form only a small professional army with the sole task of building up a large territorial army. And therefore Christian dogmas and doctrines must be brought down from heaven to earth for Adam and Eve, on to the same earth on which Jesus of Nazareth and the whole bible stand. What we say about God can no longer be uttered 'from above', in an authoritarian fashion and in the form of a monologue. We must now speak about him 'here below', at ground level, on the level of those who listen to us – that is, we must speak of him democratically in the form of a dialogue. This is in accordance with God's own coming down from heaven.

7

God Comes Down from Heaven

1. Immanent Transcendence

Everything we have said hitherto about the possibility of the experience of God at the present day, and of the way in which the language of theology can be both credible and in accordance with this experience, has been determined by two factors.

On the one hand, we have constantly kept our feet on the ground, and have never allowed ourselves to be carried away into another world. We have strictly maintained that the field within which the reality of God must be experienced is the reality of the world. Either we experience God here in the world, or we do not experience him at all.

On the other hand, we have never simply equated the reality of the world with the reality of God. We have strictly maintained that all experience of God is only an indirect experience of God. That is, it is contrary to the outward appearance of the world, and its watchword is always 'nevertheless'. A God who was nothing more than a rubber stamp of approval on the tangled confusion of what actually exists in the world would be a wholly superfluous addition to it, a kind of icing on a cake that has gone very wrong in the cooking. If the word 'God' is to have any meaning, then it must have a meaning which is not already evident in the facts themselves. This meaning, however, must not be something over and above the facts, but must be concealed within the facts.

Here, then, we have bid a final farewell to *supranaturalism*. Supranaturalism is not an essential element in Christian faith, but is a world view which belongs to antiquity – although it is the mode of thought in which Christian faith has been dressed up for many centuries. But this world view has now finally collapsed, and is no longer a possible mode of thought. Since the end of the enlightenment we no longer think of two separate and opposed worlds, a supernatural world above and a natural world here below. We think only of the single undivided world, and we see no way of getting away from it.

But although supranaturalism has been overcome, this does not mean that transcendence has been abandoned. We have left supranaturalism behind us as an outdated pattern of human thought – but we cling all the more firmly to transcendence. Of course, the concept of transcendence has changed as a result of being separated from that of supranaturalism. To express this change, we shall use the term *immanent transcendence*.

The expression 'immanent transcendence' shows where and how the experience of transcendence takes place. It implies a transcendence which we experience in immanence, that is, within our own world. If we are to sum this up in a single statement, we may paraphrase Rudolf Bultmann and define it by saying that immanent transcendence asserts the paradoxical identity of what happens within the world and the actions in space and time of the God who is beyond the world; and in this way it maintains a simultaneous relationship of faith to God and to the world.[1]

In plain language, the meaning of this is as follows: We are faced by the reality of the world with its natural data and historical facts, accessible to scientific study and technological planning. It is evident that nothing divine can be perceived in them by our eyes and ears. A believer, however, recognizes in them the hidden presence of God. But the way in which he perceives this presence is by understanding himself and his own existence in the world in a new way, as an existence given and determined by God.

The replacement of the thought-pattern of supranaturalism by the concept of 'immanent transcendence' does justice both to the revelation of God and also to the completion of the process of the enlightenment. It does justice to the revelation of God, in so far as it leads to an understanding of God as coming down from heaven to be immanent in the world. It is in accordance with the final outcome of the enlightenment, in so far as it represents the 'transition' of God in which the 'death of God' is understood not as an end which man has brought upon him, but as an impulse in the godhead himself – that is, it accepts that he 'changes'. What this change consists of is not the loss of God's transcendence, but the fact that his transcendence is encountered from now on only in immanence.

Instead of speaking of immanent transcendence we can also speak of *transparence*. Immanence means that we do not encounter God in a world other than this world, but solely in the reality of this world. Transcendence means that God is not identical with this world, that he is not simply a part of the reality of the world. Both these truths are contained in the concept of transparence: the reality of God who is beyond and above the world is only manifested in the reality of this world.

The meaning of transparence is clear in the parables of Jesus. Jesus's parables are not a crib for those who want their theology made easy. They are much more: they contain a new interpretation of the world. Jesus portrays to his audience perfectly ordinary events from their everyday surroundings, from home life, work, dealings with the authorities, nature and history – from things and events which everyone knows and experiences daily. But he presents them in such a way that they become transparent, so that his hearers can perceive the reality of God in them. Of course one must not overlook the fact that it is Jesus who is doing this. For his interpretation of the reality of the world as transparent is intimately related to his authority, to his promise that God who was distant has now come close to man.

To describe the place where God is to be found the theology of biblical times used the expression 'height'. Paul Tillich, as is well known, has replaced the expression 'height' by that of 'depth'. In our view, both conceptions have their own limited and proper place – provided, of course, that both conceptions are understood not spatially but symbolically. The expression 'height' points to the transcendence of God, as do such terms as 'above', 'beyond'. The expression 'depth', however, shows where this transcendence can be experienced, and indeed, shows that it can only be experienced by a man in his existential life, that is in immanence, in the reality of his life and the world. Thus the two concepts uphold and correct each other. Of course at the present day I would prefer the symbolism of 'depth' to that of 'height', because it demonstrates more clearly that the revelation of God is not a matter of adding a second, separate divine reality, but of manifesting the reality of the world as the reality of God. The transcendence of God cannot be experienced in any other way. Rudolf Bultmann expressed this decisive point when he wrote:

> The only idea of God which is possible for modern man is that which can find, can seek and find the *unconditional in the conditional*, the beyond in this world, the transcendent in the here and now.[2]

But how and where can we experience transcendence in immanence? We experience transcendence in immanence in the following ways:
– in man's desire for openness and wholeness, and his consequent inability to avoid asking questions which go beyond himself;
– in the fact that man attains to his true self only by getting outside himself and excelling himself; so that he is the less human, the more he remains enclosed within himself, and the more human, the more he reaches out beyond himself;
– in the fact that man seeks the fulfilment of his life in a face to face encounter with another person, but only finds his fulfilment in letting go of himself in his involvement with this other person;
– in man's dissatisfaction with the use of his reason alone in order to act reasonably; so that when he wants to act reasonably, he must always act in accordance with what his heart tells him as well;
– in the fact that man is by nature free, but possesses freedom only in being released from harmful restrictions and limitations;
– in the fact that we possess nothing which we have not received, our own selves least of all;
– that we have always to step forward anew into the future; so that not only our own lives, but the whole history of mankind is a constant exodus, and anyone who does not take this step forward at the right moment always remains stuck where he is;
– in the fact that our belief in God is contrary to the outward appearance of the world, and that there is a note of defiance, of 'nevertheless' in all trust;

– in the fact that we ourselves have always to leave behind the belief in God we have at any time and have to break down our own images of God.

In all these examples the movement is in the same direction: it is that of an 'immanent exaggeration',[3] a reaching beyond ourselves as we are at any time, a process of being led out of ourselves to be more than we are, of being drawn forward, of going beyond the present stage, of openness towards something new. This shows that the experience of transcendence is directly related to what the bible calls *metanoia*, a turning round, a changing of one's mind. This experience of transcendence is not a matter of reason, and does not require any sacrifice of the reason. It is more than this, and its demand is greater: it is the transformation of a whole person. In other words, transcendence is not something which can be conceived of intellectually. It must be experienced existentially, and even suffered.

We wish to stress two of the examples we have given, because they play a special role in theology as evidence of man's experience of the transcendent. The first is man's encounter with his fellow men, and the second is man's openness towards the future.

First of all, *man's encounter with his fellow men.* The idea of man's relationship with his fellow man is one of the favourite and most important concepts of contemporary theology. In particular, it plays a dominant role in the 'theology after the death of God'. In this theology, man's relationship with his fellow man is the principal point at which God happens at the present day, or, more precisely, it is the event, possibly the only event, in which God dwells. For this interpretation of man's relations with his fellow men as an experience of transcendence, an appeal is usually made to Dietrich Bonhoeffer, who described Jesus as the 'man for others', and accordingly described man's relationship to God as 'a new life in "existence for others"'.[4]

We are in agreement with the 'theology after the death of God' when it answers the question where and when man can experience the transcendence of God at the present day by pointing to his fellow men. In fact, how can God come to us 'from outside' otherwise than from our fellow men? Manfred Mezger is right when he says that 'love which serves and understands is "transcendent"', and explicitly adds, 'but its transcendence does not lead to the next world, but to one's neighbour'.[5] But we disagree with the 'theology after the death of God' when it equates the existence of God and man's relationship with his fellow men, so that the experience of transcendence is once again reduced to nothing.

The fact that God and our relationship to our fellow men are not identical is evident from the example of love between two people. Our feeling that inability to make contact with one's fellow men is a deficiency, or at least a disadvantage, testifies to the fact that a relationship to others – we may even use the term 'dialogue' – is the basic pattern of all human life. Every person reaches out of his solitude towards an encounter with some other person. But if he makes this encounter, and experiences it as a dialogue which involves mind, heart and body and brings him happiness, his feeling of solitude nevertheless remains. Even after the highest and most intimate act of love, and indeed then most of all, we are seized by an inconsolable sadness, the desire to be totally absorbed in the other person, and for a union and fellowship which is ultimate, at the deepest level, and unending. But where the other person who is loved is not transparent in the sense that beyond him can be perceived an absolute and total encounter on this profound level, the lover seeks fulfilment in endless games of love, without ever finding it. He practises exotic techniques of love-making, but all of them lack the one decisive condition for their success: the knowledge of the transparence of the other person in the encounter, through which can be perceived the ultimate impossibility of fulfilling all our desire for a perfect encounter and union. Only where one is aware of transcendence in the sense of a transparence which reveals beyond the person in an encounter, an encounter which is absolute and all embracing, can love go beyond mere technique and succeed, as far as love between two human beings ever can succeed.

But what happens when no encounter with a fellow man is possible? This question points to the fact that the question of God is always implicit in the experience of immanent transcendence. But we cannot go into this here. We shall have several other criticisms to make of the concept of our relationship with our fellow men, which is so overworked by the 'theology after the death of God'.

The other example of the possibility of experiencing transcendence, which we stress particularly because it plays an
important part in present-day Protestant theology, is *man's
openness towards the future*.

Here again, we must first express our agreement. It is a fact
that at the present day, the beyond of God is no longer heaven,
but the future. To confirm that this idea is a proper one, we
need only point to the significance of the word 'new' in the
bible: the 'new wine', for which the old wine skins are no longer
suitable, the 'new covenant', promised in the Old Testament
and established in the New Testament, and the 'new heaven'
and 'new earth', which are the dwelling of righteousness. God
here is shown to be 'he who comes', and whose transcendence
man experiences not by looking back into the past like Lot's
wife, and turning into a pillar of salt, or by clinging to his
possessions like the rich farmer in the parable, so becoming
imprisoned in the present, but by 'setting out' like Abraham
and looking towards the future.

But it is not sufficient simply to understand transcendence
in terms of time, as it was formerly understood in terms of
space, and to remove God from heaven above and put him in
the future. This is simply to change a vertical image for a horizontal one: instead of being 'above', God is now 'in front'. But
to look for God in the future in this way is just as much a
human conception as the old idea of supranaturalism. The coming of God has to be experienced in the present time, or else
it is not experienced at all. Naturally, these theologians are
aware of this difficulty. In order to escape it, and to bring the
future of God into the present, they identify the future of God
with the course of world history:

> Either the place of God is in the 'secular' future, 'under our control',
> and God's future is the future of natural and technical development,
> at which man is at work and for which he is responsible – or else we
> can leave God where he was in the world beyond.[6]

Here again, the transcendence of God has disappeared, just
as it did with those who looked for it in a relationship with
our fellow men, while here he is equated with the destiny of
the world. Just as we asked in the first case what happens when
no encounter with one's fellow man is possible, we must now

ask what happens when my endeavours with regard to the future of the world come to nothing? Has God, too, come to nothing? We must not abandon the distinction between God and the world, any more than that between God and our fellow-men. Even *immanent* transcendence always remains transcendent.

This criticism of the excessive emphasis placed on the future, as almost the sole experience of transcendence which man has at the present day, is likewise only provisional. We shall return to it several times.

2. *The Indestructible Nature of the Question of God*

We have discussed in positive terms the possibility of experiencing transcendence in immanence. We shall now make use of the *via negationis,* that is, we shall point out the negative consequences which result from the absence of such an experience of transcendence.

It has become almost the fashion today to explain almost every possible state of consciousness in psychoanalytical terms as 'repression'. May not modern man's loss of transcendence, so much discussed, and sometimes even proudly asserted, be nothing more than such a process of repression? May not the sadness, dreariness, fear and boredom with life, and also the insatiable appetite for work and the exaggerated impulse to achieve something, result from the fact that man has either forgotten or repressed within himself his inherent reaching out for the absolute? And may not this repression now be taking its revenge on his mind and even on his body? Here the psychiatrist can teach the theologian. He can draw from his clinical experience examples of the way in which someone who no longer asks about the meaning of life and the world, and breaks off man's relationship with the transcendent which is expressed in this question, often develops neuroses, and consequently takes refuge in substitute satisfaction such as sex, a craving for approval and drugs.

Is not the assertion that life is meaningless secretly nourished by the desire for a meaning? Is not even suicide a demonstration, a final despairing protest that there really ought to be a meaning? Finally, why are most atheists so rarely capable of expressing their assertion that there is no God in sober and objective terms? Why have they usually to argue their case so vehemently, emotionally and polemically? Why have they still to fight against God, when they do not believe that there is a God?

All these observations show that whether man wishes or not, he lives very close to the absolute, the eternal, and that he is disturbed by this proximity – and is quite incapable of suppressing this disturbance by force or silencing it with 'comforting reinterpretations'.[7] Either way, the obtrusive presence of transcendence remains, and with it, the questions it poses. When man closes his ears to these questions, transcendence does not cease to exist – but one must ask whether man does not then cease to be human.

There are two texts which support this suspicion. With a surprising degree of agreement, they affirm the fact that man's humanity is dependent upon his asking about the absolute, and is therefore related to the transcendent. This agreement is all the more striking in that the intellectual background of the two writers is very different. One is the Catholic theologian Karl Rahner, and the other the social scientist and philosopher Max Horkheimer, who cannot be suspected of any Christian prejudice.

Karl Rahner poses a 'hypothesis of the future' in order to test it:

> Let the word 'God' disappear, without any trace, and without leaving any visible gap behind, and without being replaced by any other word which makes a similar appeal to us.

What would be the consequences? Man would no longer be brought face to face with the whole of reality and of his own being. The consequence of this would be a complete breaking down of the world and of man into isolated fragments. Man would experience the world broken up into nothing but individual entities, and his existence would be reduced to single moments. He himself would become an individual entity engulfed in the world. But he would no longer be aware of this, and would no longer be confused and troubled by it. For if man was no longer even capable of using the word 'God' in order to deny him, this would be the 'sign that man was dead'. But no one would be there to perceive this sign. And therefore the result of Karl Rahner's test of this 'hypothesis of the future' is that 'man would cease to be a man. He would have regressed back to being an ingenious animal.'[8]

In a dialogue with the magazine *Spiegel*[9] Max Horkheimer came in a different way to a conclusion expressed in almost the same words as Karl Rahner. For Horkheimer, as for Kant and Schopenhauer, the world is mere phenomenon, and therefore 'not absolute', or 'at least, not the ultimate'. When asked what was the ultimate for him, Horkheimer did not reply: God. On the contrary, he explicitly rejected belief in an almighty and benevolent God as a 'scarcely credible dogma'. He would not have any 'proof of God' – and yet wanted 'a theological postulate'. And when asked what remained as the ultimate, he answered, 'Longing'; More precisely, this was 'longing for the other', the 'idea of the absolute': 'This longing is an essential attribute of a person who really thinks.'

Because this longing is no longer present in a world which is totally under man's control, Horkheimer is worried for man's future. Its characteristic will be boredom. When asked why the future would be boring, Horkheimer replied:

> The concerns of theology will be abolished. This will mean the disappearance from the world of what we call 'meaning'. There will be plenty of bustling activity, but it will be quite without meaning. One day philosophy will also come to be regarded as a childish concern on the part of mankind. People will agree with the positivists that it is childish to speculate about the connections between the relative and the transcendent.

The editor of *Spiegel* interjected here: 'It could be that when men have satisfied their material needs, including their sexual needs, they will turn to games.' Whereupon Horkheimer concluded the interview with a statement which is in almost verbal agreement with the outcome of the 'hypothesis of the future' which Karl Rahner posed, albeit only experimentally: 'Animals play games, too. I can quite well imagine this coming about with men.'

The comparison between these two statements by Rahner and Horkheimer shows that at the present day the decisive boundary lies not between Christians and non-Christians, but between those who still ask about God, and those who no longer do so. A secret alliance between Christians and atheists is becoming increasingly noticeable – at least with those atheists who consciously deny God, and by that very fact are still asking about him. And may not even the language of the 'death of God' used at the present day by both Christians and non-Christians, simply be a new expression of the 'indestructible nature' of the question of God? The question of God still holds the attention of both Christians and atheists, although they approach it from different angles. By the debate in which they are involved with each other, for or against God, they are drawn very close together. Both are asking, beyond all details, and beyond all fragmentary elements, about the totality of the world. In this way, they are keeping alive the question of the truth, beyond and above transitory needs and purposes. And at the present day this is an achievement. With this situation in mind, we recall the well known saying of Augustine: 'Many are within, who seem to be without, and many are without who seem to be within.' What divides Christians and atheists is not the question, but the answer.

8

Jesus of Nazareth — A Divine Revealer or Our Fellow Man?

1. A Critical Acceptance of Revelation

Anyone who asks about God at the present day still poses the question within the framework of the Christian language and tradition defended by the church. This language and tradition goes back to certain words, events and persons in history, and ultimately and principally to Jesus of Nazareth. The American theologian Paul van Buren has expressed this situation in a single brief sentence: 'We were "saved" some nineteen centuries ago.'[1]

In all theology, in whatever way it may speak of God, the figure and message of Jesus of Nazareth has an irrevocable 'priority', in both time and importance. Jesus of Nazareth is the *datum* from which all Christian thinking takes its bearings, and in both meanings of the word. On the one hand the figure of Jesus is something given. Secondly, this 'something given' is a datable event in history, which happened 'under Pontius Pilate'. This is the only reason why the Roman procurator has found his way into the creed.

All theology has to take account of this basic fact. It must always look back to it as a historical event, while at the same time this historical event furnishes the basic idea and content of all theology says. The divine Aeneid, as Luther calls the biblical history of the revelation of God in the last notes he ever made, must always be taken into account in this way; otherwise there can be no experience of God in the present time. All Christian opinion is in agreement about this, be it Karl Barth, Rudolf Bultmann, Wolfhart Pannenberg, or even Herbert Braun and Dorothee Sölle.

Thus anyone who wants to know what the name 'God' signifies cannot begin with general statements about his nature, and conceptual definitions. He must start with the history in which God himself 'made a name for himself'. It is because of this memory of the past that Christianity gives the appearance at the present day of being an 'affair of yesterday'. For a race which has turned its face so decisively towards the future, and takes scarcely any account of the past, which speaks in the future tense in preference to the past, and whose life seems to take its tempo from this fact, this recalling of the past, like every other kind of looking back, seems an unreasonable requirement. But it is a requirement which no Christian can avoid. And thus all Christians who seek to give an honest account of their cause come to the point where they have to recount this history. And the history that they have to recount is not the history of their own 'pilgrimage of the soul', but the history of Jesus of Nazareth. And yet they have to tell this story a different way every time; they always have to tell it in such a way that it answers the questions of their own age, so that 'the affair of yesterday' becomes 'an affair of today'. We are not going to discuss here *how* the story of the Jesus of Nazareth has to be told at the present day. Our only concern here is that on principle, if anything is to be said about God at the present day, the story of Jesus of Nazareth has to be told. Thus, faced with the general dismissal of 'metaphysics' at the present day, Christians can confidently reply: It doesn't matter what has happened to metaphysics – we do not offer metaphysics, but a history.

The Christian 'memory' of history brings with it the question of the *authority of the bible*. The bible is the history book of God's dealings with men. This history of God's dealings with men is set out in stories of men's dealings with God. But this means that we only possess the history of God's dealings with men in the form of human reactions to it, and therefore as an indirect testimony. The bible is not the document of God's revelation, composed by God himself. It is only the document, written down and handed on by men, of their belief in the divine revelation. Indeed, we are not ashamed to give due honour once again to an expression long despised by a fearful and therefore narrow theology, and to call the bible one of the greatest 'religious documents' of humanity. Why we regard it as the greatest, we shall explain elsewhere in this book.

It is true that the claim is often made about the bible that 'God has spoken', an expression which in fact frequently occurs in the bible itself. But when God speaks he always does so through men. And therefore, because many different men were involved, and the reasons and situations which led to their speaking changed so much, the forms in which their testimony is given are also very various: stories, prayers, songs, hymns, creeds, proverbs, letters, laws, statutes, prophecies and visions. To this extent one can say that the bible contains 'the broken pieces of a great confession of faith', and is therefore a fragmentary book.

Associated with the biblical tradition is the claim that it also contains the revelation of God for our own time: what happened once, happened once for all, so that it can go on happening again and again. Thus the problem of the authority of the bible takes the form of the question how a revelation of God which has happened once can be given again, and appropriated in such a way that it arouses faith in God once again at the present day. The principle on which this is possible is known as the *point of contact*. A point of contact implies the revelation of God, as a prior condition, but not the prior acceptance of it.

Adolf Schlatter once said that Christians are not above but under the scripture. In these words he expressed the fundamental conviction of many generations of Protestant theologians. We would answer this statement with the thesis that the Christian is neither above nor under the scripture, but is faced with the scripture. The age of the 'authoritarian use of the biblical text' is past;[2] that is, the age of obedience based on a heteronomous traditional authority, which was acknowledged simply because it was traditionally regarded as an authority, and not because one had tested its basis and content and become convinced that it was accurate and true. 'It is written' – and that's that! This attitude to the 'holy scripture' is similar to the view of late Judaism. One of the rabbis summed it up at the end of the first century in these words: 'It is not a dead body which defiles, and it is not water which makes clean, but an ordinance of the king of all kings.'

Nowadays, the authority of the bible is not seen as an outside authority imposed on us, but as the final outcome of an encounter in which the hearer reaches a personal conviction. In practical terms, this means that we follow the bible, but we do not begin with the assertion that the bible is the book of divine truth, and that you start by believing that! Rather, without requiring any prior acceptance, we interpret the texts of the bible in the same way as we interpret other texts, with the same instruments and methods, and without any sixth sense, so that other people can understand it and realize that it concerns them, happens in their lives, and is true. Thus a dialogue takes place in which the bible poses questions to us and we give our answers, but at the same time put our questions to the bible and test the answers it gives us. In so doing we are not being narrow-minded, but we are keeping the ninth commandment. This commandment also applies to the way we speak of the bible, and we should remember how Luther interpreted the commandment: we should forgive it, speak well of it and make the best of everything. If the weaknesses of the bible are shaded out in this way – just as with a human being – its true colours and strength are seen all the more clearly.

If a person then assents to what the bible says, and the truth of the biblical text becomes clear and convincing to him as only truth can, he may from then on be able to profess his belief that the bible is the book of divine truth. The only way to the acceptance of the authority of scripture is through free assent to its *content*. That the understanding and acceptance of the bible is the work of the Holy Spirit is not a requirement to be made in advance, but a subsequent experience of the faith when it comes to reflect upon itself.

What is true of the bible is also true of *Jesus of Nazareth*. We may accept him, but we do not begin with the assertion that Jesus is the Messiah or the Son of God, and that this has to be believed first. Once again, we have to interpret the texts which tell of Jesus in such a way that our contemporaries can see that this Jesus of Nazareth is right, that what he says is important for us, that we cannot manage without him. And then they may perhaps subsequently agree with the church's profession of faith: Jesus is Lord. This is exactly how the gospels describe the process, when they show those who heard Jesus saying in their astonishment: 'He taught them as one who had authority' (Matt. 7.29).

The process by which Jesus of Nazareth, a man who lived almost two thousand years ago, can become the revelation of God to someone at the present day, has been described by Eugen Rosenstock-Huessy in the following way. He calls Jesus the person who 'humbly lowered himself to the level of an uncompleted phrase'. 'Without you, without me,' he goes on, 'he is never Christ. He is still looking for his name ... The half phrase, the first half of the phrase, is Jesus; the other half is the believer. Only the two together can bear witness to Jesus Christ. For he is only truly risen because you speak his name in full.'[3]

What matters here is not the adoption and acceptance of the late Jewish and Hellenistic titles which the first Christian churches bestowed on Jesus of Nazareth, in order to express the distinctive nature of his mission and authority. The words one uses to express this are not a matter of dogmatic precision, but of the way one is affected personally. The following words are not those of a modern social theologian, but of Dietrich Bonhoeffer in his lectures on theology in 1933:

> What does it mean when, in his world of suspicion and distrust, the worker says, 'Jesus was a good man'? It means that there is no need to distrust *him*. The worker does not say, 'Jesus is God'. But when he says, 'Jesus was a good man', he is at any rate saying more than when the bourgeois says, 'Jesus is God'.[4]

There is no advance certainty of the truth of the revelation of God, no more than there is any advance certainty of the existence of God, or indeed of any love, any friendship or any truth. I can only be certain of the revelation of God as truth by coming to grips with it and testing it. The writer of the fourth gospel portrays Jesus as laying down the rule for this. Freely translated, it reads: 'Come to terms with the will of him who sent me – then you will know whether this teaching is from God' (John 7.17). Elsewhere the same evangelist describes this process, in terms which are wholly foreign to the Greek language, as 'doing the truth' (3.21).

But what if for some people the guarantee of truth is not Jesus of Nazareth, but Socrates, Goethe and Kant, or Karl Marx, Lenin and Mao? Honest Christians can only advise them to test

Socrates, Goethe and Kant or Karl Marx, Lenin and Mao, and
see for themselves what they make of one of them. When they
have done that we can see where it gets them.

Whether what we are involved with in this way is right, good
and true, and whether the revelation of God takes place through
it so that a new experience of God comes about, can only be
shown by the way it works out in practice and takes effect. It is
measured not by outward success, but by the way in which
it changes men and their lives, lightens their way, gives them
hope and helps them to live their lives by opening up a new
future to them – in short, by bringing men salvation. And no
one escapes this independent proof of the truth of God. In it
the point of contact between the present and the past links the
two, so that the past revelation of God becomes a new experience
of God in the present.

The following scene from the bible is a model for the process
by which revelation is personally appropriated: Jesus had discussed the life of a Samaritan woman with her at the well. In
the course of this conversation the woman realized that Jesus
was the Messiah. She ran into her village to tell her people, and
they believed her. They came out in order to bring Jesus into
their village. But when they themselves had heard him, they
declared to the woman, 'It is no longer because of your words
that we believe, for we have heard for ourselves, and we know
that this is indeed the Saviour of the world' (John 4).

The personal acceptance of the revelation of God always takes
place in this way. First of all we encounter an existing tradition which claims to contain the revelation of God. This tradition we accept, not thoughtlessly and *en bloc*, but testing it
critically, selecting it carefully and taking it on trial. When
this testing, selection and trial convince us of the content of the
tradition we have received, we then recognize it as the truth,
and it takes on for us the authority and quality of divine revelation. In this way we pass on from the historical mediation of
revelation to a direct existential experience of it, and are no
longer secondhand hearers, but firsthand hearers. There is no
other way for us to receive and accept the revelation of God at
the present day.

2. *Christology without God*

In the early years after the second world war almost every other objection put forward in religious and theological discussions amounted to the question: God, of course – but why Christ? Since then, the question has been almost reversed. The form it takes nowadays, more and more often, is: Jesus of Nazareth, of course – but why God as well?

At that period, in the immediate post-war years, a Christmas sermon might begin as follows: 'That God created the world and the people in it, that he rules over the nations and guides their paths, that he has given his commandments and watches over good and evil – this and much else we already know about God, even without Christ. This is found in other religions, and we can even read about it nowadays in the papers. But at Christmas we learn something new about God, something quite different....' Then follows the account of the revelation of God in Jesus Christ.

But at the present day I can imagine that a Christmas sermon might proceed in exactly the opposite direction, rather as follows: 'That God created the world and the people in it, that he rules over the nations and guides their paths, that he has given his commandments and watches over good and evil – that and much else, which our fathers once thought they could take for granted about God, has become wholly incredible to us. We can understand what people mean when they speak nowadays of the "death of God". But it is precisely because of the death of God that Christmas has taken on a new meaning for us. He tells us that even though God is dead, yet we still have someone to whom we can cling, and to whom we can turn: the man Jesus of Nazareth...' And then the sermon would go on to describe the message and figure of the man who came from Nazareth.

An American student at Yale University neatly, if somewhat superficially, summed up this shift of emphasis in the relationship between God and Jesus when she said to her student chaplain: 'I don't know whether I believe in God. Jesus is really more my type.' It was reasonable enough to reduce the attempt to go on speaking of Jesus even without God, or in spite of the death of God, to the ironical formula: 'God is dead, and Jesus is his Son.' In fact, instead of speaking of 'theology after the death of God', it would be more correct to speak of 'Christology after the death of God'.

Theologians themselves are not without blame for this break-down in the connection between God and Christ. The way in which apologetics have been conducted for several decades is now rebounding upon them like a boomerang. For half a century, from the early dialectical theology of Karl Barth to the later stages of Rudolf Bultmann's programme of demythologization, theology has withdrawn without resistance from the whole field of the preliminary approaches to religion, in the face of the attacks of modern atheism, and has retreated on to the absolute and unique nature of the revelation in Christ. Just as in ice-hockey, a player will try to relieve the pressure on his own goal by hitting the puck as far forward as possible – against the rules – so theology has tried to relieve the pressure on belief in God in the modern age by using christology as a kind of 'clearing shot'. All the objections which were advanced from various quarters against belief in God were accepted wholesale, and even gratefully, but at the same time diverted by being attributed to 'religion'. It was admitted without hesitation that religion was in fact of purely human origin, the invention of man's desires and thoughts. But for Christian belief in God an appeal was made to God's own revelation in Jesus Christ. The theological rule of thumb, which it was hoped would do the trick, was: 'Religion from below – revelation from above.' Thus theology, with its 'christological positivism' as it were played into the hands of secularization, by giving God less and less foothold in the world. All that was left to God in the end was the revelation in Christ, no bigger than the point of a pin.

This christological clearing shot on the part of theology was not without its ironical element. It could only succeed, so long as it was still rooted in a world view generally accepted as valid, that is, in the universal theism, or 'religious pantheism of history', which could still assume that the human mind and cultural life were imbued with a general religious outlook. But it was this which the advocates of a christocentric theology would not allow, but violently resisted. To the extent to which they exhausted the reserves of the world view which had been characteristic of the Christian West, their 'christological positivism' itself was threatened, and the death of God began to corrode away the revelation of Christ which they were guarding so closely. Thus theology at length found the puck back again in its own area, and had its work cut out to defend its goal.

The decisive issue in the present dispute about Jesus is basic-ally the old problem which has preoccupied all christology: how God and man are associated in Jesus of Nazareth, and how, as a result, this event can be regarded as the revelation of God. But anyone who questions whether and to what extent one can still speak of God has made the basic problem of all christology more acute to a hitherto unknown degree. Strictly speaking, he has actually resolved it, by removing half of it completely, so that one can no longer talk meaningfully about the revelation of God at all.

The consequence which the theologians draw from this situa-tion, more radically in America, and in a more moderate form in Germany, is not that they should stop speaking about Jesus altogether. On the contrary, they do so more one-sidedly and more emphatically than before. But in the way in which they do it, they partially or wholly ignore the particular relationship which, according to the testimony of the whole New Testament, Jesus has to God as his 'Father'. For nowadays, since the 'death of God', this relationship seems to them to have become in-comprehensible and meaningless. One sometimes even has the impression that these theologians are aware of this gap in their 'godless' discussion of Jesus, and are unconsciously trying to compensate for it by raising their voices.

Thus the issue is posed and the task set out. The issue is the same for everyone: it is the problem of how we can still believe in Jesus Christ, and speak about this belief, in the face of the event that we have called 'the death of God'. The task with which this issue presents us varies according to our theological standpoint. The 'God is dead' theologians have to demonstrate how far they are remaining faithful to the overriding purpose of the biblical tradition about Jesus, when they take no account of God, and how far they are able to carry it out anew for our own age. Moreover, they have an obligation to show why they place so much weight on this person Jesus of Nazareth, and how far the figure and message of Jesus does not immediately lose its unique significance once it is cut off from its connection with God. The others, who continue as before to speak about

Jesus precisely on account of his special relationship to God, have exactly the opposite task. They must interpret the biblical testimonies to Jesus Christ in such a way that the statements they contain about God can become important, comprehensible, meaningful and significant in a new way to their contemporaries, in the face of their experience of the 'death of God'.

3. The Deity of God and a World from which Divinity has Departed

The thing that forces both Christian theists and Christian atheists to take account of the *datum* provided by Jesus of Nazareth is the profound theological dilemma, the apparently hopeless puzzle, with which everyone is faced with regard to the knowledge of God. Like every act of knowing, the knowledge of God requires an analogy, a kind of 'affinity' between subject and object, between the one who knows and that which is to be known. This is in accordance with the epistemological principle that only like can know like. This fact is at the root of the theological dilemma.

This dilemma is twofold. It results in the first place from the *deity of God*. If God is God, and no other being in the world is like him, then no being other than God can know about him. But if only God knows about himself, then it is up to him to establish the 'affinity' which is the condition of all mutual knowledge. That is, an act of self-revelation is necessary on God's part, so that other beings can share in his knowledge of himself. This act of making himself known, in which God imparts himself to man, and at the same time enables man to accept his imparting of himself, is what we call 'revelation'. God himself must speak of himself as 'God', if men are to recognize him as God.

That God is God, and man is man, and that there is no way from man to God, only a way from God to man, but that it has pleased God in the absolute freedom of his love to impart himself to man, and that he has done this in Jesus Christ – this is the fundamental note which has sounded through everything Christians have ever said about God, and has turned theology almost entirely into christology.

In the works of Karl Barth, this way of speaking about God

has retained its splendour. In his theology this basic christological melody became a unique hymn to the freedom and the
greatness of the love of God, and the universality of the 'free
choice of his grace'. But in many of his theological successors,
at least in the second and third generations, all that is left of
man's wonder at the deity of God is the fear that God may be
reduced to human terms. In Barth the powerful positivism of
revelation was still to be found, but in his followers this had
turned into a narrow-minded *ecclesiastical* positivism. From
fear of the danger of allowing the revelation of God to be no
longer conceived on the basis of the act of God, but determined
by human experience, Friedrich Mildenberger, almost in despair, throws himself upon the authority of the church:

> The church must vindicate the word of God, and must dare to speak
> with an authority whose basis cannot be called into question.

From this it follows that the task of theology is that of the
servant of the church:

> It can and must be satisfied with making the claim of the word of God
> comprehensible. It can consequently leave on one side the question of
> whether or not it is true, and can rest content with pointing out that
> the statements it subjects to critical examination are those held by the
> church.[5]

How a contemporary theologian can think such thoughts, let
alone commit them to paper, is beyond our comprehension. We
would not be surprised to find statements like this in the works
of late mediaeval nominalism, when there was a place for them.
But in our age they are completely out of place.

We do not deny that the theological basis of the revelation
in Christ may properly be sought in the divinity of God; in fact,
this is a necessary consequence of the inner logic of the idea
of God. But it is almost impossible for us to regard considera-
tions of this kind as anything more than correct statements of
theological abstractions; existentially, they mean virtually nothing to us. In this theology the shoe no longer pinches – on the
contrary, this theological shoe has become too big for us!

At the present day, the fact that *divinity has departed from
the world* causes us much greater embarrassment. This brings
us to the other aspect of the theological dilemma with which
we are faced in respect of all knowledge of God. We can know

precious little about God from the world in which we live; it
gives us very little help towards any kind of experience of God.
We no longer discover, like the psalmist, the marks of God in
nature, and we no longer see, like the prophets, the great acts of
God in history. For this reason, it is such writings as the book
of Job, Ecclesiastes or the psalms of lamentation which we are
able to accept as prophecies of Christ, rather than the mighty
prophetic oracles which are read in church at Advent and
Christmas. When we look at the reality round about us, our
first impression is of a world which is obscure and opaque; we
sense an irreconcilable discord in existence, in which the scales
are tilted towards the darkness.

This is also the reason why the sceptical observations of
Ecclesiastes have once become so relevant. Although the
Preacher lived more than two thousand years ago, he seems to
us almost like a contemporary. When he looks at the world,
he, too, perceives little in it which tells him of God. All he finds
in it is contradictions, which do not fit in with God. He cannot
pile up enough contradictory concepts to describe the ambiguity
of existence:

> A time to be born, and a time to die; a time to plant, and a time to
> pluck up what is planted; a time to kill, and a time to heal; a time to
> break down, and a time to build up; a time to weep, and a time to
> laugh; a time to mourn, and a time to dance; ... a time to love, and a
> time to hate; a time for war, and a time for peace.

All these contradictions he finds not following each other or
acompanying each other, providing a meaningful solution to one
or complementing each other, but confused and entangled with
each other, entwined with each other in a meaningless way, cutting across and destroying each other in mutual hostility,
apparently without end. The world he describes is enigmatic, discordant and contradictory – it is the world in which we live. But
where is God in it? At the very least, he seems to have the two
faces of Janus. We dare not assert that we have never discovered
anything of God in the world; but neither can we say that we
have found God in the world. The utmost that we can say with
confidence is, in the words of Pascal:

> All appearances indicate neither a total exclusion nor a manifest

presence of divinity, but the presence of a God who hides Himself. Everything bears this character.[6]

Whether this kind of experience, or lack of experience, leads
us to speak only of the 'concealment' of God, of his 'absence', or
even of his 'death', no one can deny that atheism has good
grounds for claiming that it can find a factual starting point
for its claims in the reality of the world. Dorothee Sölle and
Helmut Gollwitzer, two theologians who in other respects disagree violently about the question of God, are in complete agreement about this. Dorothee Sölle has made a statement which has
often been recalled in recent years, and which we have already
quoted: 'How, after Auschwitz, anyone can praise the God who
o'er all things so wondrously reigneth, I cannot understand.'
And Helmut Gollwitzer advances a similar argument against
the Anglican Bishop John A. T. Robinson, who, when he looks
into the depths of reality, believes that he can perceive divine
love as the personal basis of all being:

Our harassed contemporary of 1964 looks pensively into the bishop's
kindly face. Whatever depths he plumbs, he certainly does find there
the demonic abysses occasionally mentioned by Robinson, he finds the
loneliness and lostness of the person amid the horrifying indifference
of nature towards it, but of love he finds at the ground of being not a
trace ... neither by looking around nor by looking deep does he find
any reason at all to trust in the ground of being. That, however, in the
age of Auschwitz and Hiroshima, is his real question.[7]

This describes the theological dilemma in which we find
ourselves with regard to the knowledge of God. Our difficulties
arise not so much from the unknowability of God, which is due
to his deity, but from the unknowability which is due to the fact
that divinity has departed from the world. Our experience of
the world scarcely ever brings us any experience of God. On the
contrary, it seems to negate even the last scrap of knowledge of
God which we think we possess.

But in this context it has been traditional to point to man's
'sin', and to attribute to this his inability to know God. His
unbelief, it is suggested, is the reason why man is incapable of
knowing God in the world. This is certainly true. But we can
only agree with it in the qualified way in which the counsel

for the defence speaks of man and his situation in the world in Camus' story *The Fall*:

I'm like that beggar who wouldn't let go of my hand one day on a café terrace: 'Oh sir!' he said, 'It's not just that I'm no good, but you lose track of the light.'[8]

This if nothing else should make us realize that we need to take account of the *datum* provided by Jesus of Nazareth, when we are discussing whether God can be known.

The objection that we are making what we can accept the standard of our knowledge of God, and in this way are trying to bring the revelation of God from the start within the grasp of our human questions, does not alarm us. In the history of Christianity it has never been otherwise. The revelation of God has always been spoken of within a particular historical situation; the truth of God has as it were always had its 'location in time'. Christianity is not a 'religion of the book', and the bible is not the Koran. And therefore, if its truth is to be made relevant to the present time, it has not got to be quoted, but 'reproduced'. Implicit in the concept of reproduction is the 'dialectic of "old" and "new" ';[9] the old message has always to be produced anew. Of course we have to say the same as the bible says, but we say the same as the bible says only by saying it differently. Thus, the message of the bible must constantly be sent on to our contemporaries like a readdressed letter. This 'change of address' undoubtedly implies a risk, this is the temptation to use our questions as a standard by which the revelation of God is measured, and so degrade the process of bringing the bible up to date into one of forcing it to fit our own ideas. On the other hand, the address must be the right one, otherwise the receiver never opens the letter. The message of the bible must always be uttered with 'a change of words' in every age. A Christian theologian can only agree with what the Jewish Rabbi Leo Baeck says of the bible:

Whenever a new view of the world was achieved, the bible had something else to say ... and therefore the bible progressed, and every period acquired its own bible.[10]

Why else are there four gospels in the New Testament and not only one? Not in order to display the manifold nature and the fulness of the gospel of Jesus – this was only a side effect, which took place incidentally. The real reason was the fact that new questions constantly occurred which necessitated a reinterpretation and further development of the unique source. The story of Jesus of Nazareth had constantly to be recounted in different places and at different times, in such a way as to give answers to the questions asked at that time and place. What had gone before was constantly revised by new material, and so the one gospel produced several different gospels.

Luther once said that we must make 'new decalogues', as Peter, Paul and Jesus did, and so we too must make 'new gospels'. Since the days of the early church, every generation is faced with the task of writing, on the basis of the four canonical gospels of the New Testament, its own fifth gospel, the gospel for its own time. And nothing should prevent us from doing the same for our age. If we did not do so, what we said about God would become timeless, and Jesus himself would never be spoken of. Without a change of address in the sense of a reproduction, the gospel would stop being 'good news', and would become an 'old newspaper', and people throw old newspapers away or do something else with them.

4. From the Majesty of Christ to the Humility of Jesus

For centuries the gospel story has been told in such a way that Jesus has seemed to be a shadowy, fabulous being, half man and half God, whose feet scarcely touched the ground. It is true that he was stated to be 'true man' and 'true God', and the history of christological dogma tells of an unceasing endeavour to maintain this dialectic and to maintain the right relationship between the two natures of Christ, without damaging either of them. This leads to profound speculations, for all of which there was good practical justification. Yet basically the problem of forcing an agreement where there was none was never solved. Wherever there was an attempt to maintain the doctrine of the two natures in a strict form, the final result was either blatant paradox or elaborate artificiality, if not absurdity. The history of the church is full of examples of this, not just at its lower levels, but amongst its greatest men.

Scarcely anyone has laid such simultaneous emphasis on both the two natures of Christ, and attempted to maintain the ten-

sion between them, as strictly as Martin Luther. This was an
important factor in the magnificent sweep of his theology. Yet
can we, at the present day, really repeat statements such as these
of Luther: 'Mary gives suck to God, the creator of heaven and
earth...; Mary rocks God...; when he is washed [the Christ
child], it is God who is washed and vice versa'? And can we still
say with Luther that during the storm on the Sea of Galilee
only the human nature of Jesus slept, but not the person itself,
not the Son of God?[11] The matter becomes even more tangled
in the case of the passion of Christ: how could Jesus in the
garden of Gethsemane sweat from fear of death, if his suffering
was the will and work of God, and he was bound to know this
because of his divine nature? Was he merely dissembling, or
did he not fully enter into 'God's school of suffering' – or was it
that he still knew nothing of the theory of his sacrificial death
which his apostle Paul was to proclaim? Finally, consider Jesus's
cry at his death on the Cross: 'My God, my God, why hast thou
forsaken me?' If one thinks strictly in the categories of the
doctrine of the two natures, either this statement becomes a
monologue conducted within the Trinity, and therefore a mere
show, a tasteless farce; or else, in order to maintain its deadly
seriousness, one must once again take refuge in dogmatic arti-
ficialities. The final result in the history of the church was
almost always a victory for monophysitism, and therefore for
docetism. That is, the veneration of the divine nature of Christ
gained the upper hand to such an extent that his human nature
threatened to become a mere apparition. And can we wonder
that this happened? If God is God and man is man, then the
divinity of Christ was bound to overshadow his humanity, and
ultimately to swallow it up. And therefore the story of Jesus
Christ, as it was told by the devout laity, if not always by
learned theologians, came to look something like this:

By a decision taken from eternity in heaven, foretold on the
earth by the prophets and foreshadowed by strange signs, Christ
was born of a virgin in a miraculous way. He was surrounded
from the first by angels, who accompanied him throughout his
life. At his very birth the heavens opened, and the angels came
down and proclaimed him as the redeemer of the world. Thereupon shepherds who were nearby hurried to proclaim their
future saviour, and wise men were lead by a star from a distant

land, to spread their precious treasures before the newly born royal child. All this fulfilled what had long been awaited, just as every individual event later fulfilled one passage of scripture after another. An angel warned the parents to flee with their new born child, in order to protect it against the machinations of the wicked king who feared for his throne, and their return also took place following a divine command. Even during his childhood he was distinguished by special gifts, which foreshadowed his future importance. When he was twelve years old, he disputed with the theologians in the temple, so that they marvelled at his divine understanding. At his baptism the heavens opened above him, and while the Holy Spirit came down upon him, God himself testified aloud that he was his Son. He resisted temptation by the devil, who was trying to divert him from his divine mission; instead, the angels served him. Then he went through the country preaching. His preaching was accompanied by manifest miracles. He healed all kinds of sick people: lepers, the possessed, the palsied, the lame, the blind, the deaf and the dumb. One only had to touch the hem of his garment to be healed. He changed water into wine and fed thousands of people with no more than a few loaves and fishes, and at the end more was left than was there at first. Both the wind and the waves obeyed him. He calmed the storm and walked on the water. He was even able to bring the dead back to life. By all these words and actions he showed that he was the long awaited Messiah and the Son of God. The evil spirits cried this out after him, one of his disciples declared it openly in the name of the others, and he finally admitted it himself when he was questioned. At the end of his ministry he went to the cross, and in this too he was only fulfilling the will of God as it was written in the scriptures. Three times he prophesied himself that he had to suffer and die, but also that he would rise again on the third day and come again at the end of time, in order finally to bring in the kingdom of God through the resurrection of the dead and the judgment. His death took place to redeem men from their sins. And so he died with the words: 'It is finished.' The tomb in which he was laid was sealed and closed with a heavy stone. Nevertheless, it was afterwards found empty. He appeared in bodily form to his disciples, came to them through closed doors, walked about, ate and drank with them. At the end he gathered them together,

once again on a mountain, and sent them forth from there with
the commandment to preach his gospel to all nations and to
baptize them in the name of the triune God. Then the clouds
lifted him up to heaven. So the story ended where it began, in
eternity with God in heaven.

When we hear this 'life of Jesus' our first impression is that
one who could know and do all this was a man of God! But it
is this, which attracted previous generations to him, which
makes him suspicious and incredible to us. Our protest is not
due to our historical and critical awareness. We do not object
in the first instance that it cannot all have happened like this.
Our mistrust is much more deeply rooted and existential. When
this Christ says to us: 'Come to me, all who labour and are
heavy laden,' we do not dare, because we do not trust him. That
is, this Christ is too great and too marvellous for us. Since we
no longer have an all-embracing closed picture of the world,
with heaven, earth and hell, with an above and a below firmly
fixed in their places, with reality divided into this world and the
world beyond, and with a constant coming and going between
the two, there is something in us which resists taking part in or
being drawn into so universal and objective a drama of salvation. We do not long for omnipotence and universal authority
but for support and solidarity. We do not want a man of God
who already knows and can do everything in advance, but a
real concrete human being, who, where he is concerned with
God, works without a safety net and a cabinet with false bottom, so that he has no possibility of taking refuge in another
world which is always accessible to him, or of retreating into a
divine nature which is his own. We can understand Heinrich
Heine when he writes of Jesus of Nazareth, with a characteristic
mixture of irony, sentimentality and genuine bewilderment:

He is the God whom I mostly love – not because he is a legitimate
God whose Father since time immemorial ruled the world, but because
he, though a born Dauphin of Heaven, is democratically-minded, loving
no courtly splendour; because he is not a God of shaven and shorn
bookish pedants and laced men-at-arms; and because he is a modest
God of the People, a citizen God, *un bon dieu citoyen*. Truly, if Christ
were no God, I would vote that he should be such, and much rather
than an absolute God who has forced himself to power would I obey
him, the elected God, the God of my choice.[12]

Consequently, we read the New Testament gospels at the present day with other eyes than those of our fathers, and therefore the fifth gospel, which we have to draw up for our own age on the basis of the four canonical gospels, will also look different. It might go as follows:

A person was once born in emergency accommodation, in the corner in a bundle of straw, and the first people to take any interest in him were agricultural workers, the proletarians of the time. He and his family soon had to emigrate. There was nothing exceptional about his childhood. Before he began his public ministry, he explicitly denounced all the devices and attributes which promise success to a political leader or a social revolutionary: power, food and publicity gimmicks. But when they later wanted to make him their leader, he withdrew from them. Without claiming any title or office, he sought only to advance the cause of God in the world – and he believed that it was now 'high time' for this. But it was inevitable from the very beginning that he should come to grief. His very first appearance in his own home town ended in a fiasco: the people drove him out of the town and tried to kill him. He then became a wandering preacher, going throughout the country, without a pass and with no fixed abode. He preached to those who found it difficult to believe in God and had no idea of theology. He was free of all prejudices. He associated with those who were excluded from society, with people of doubtful morals or who were politically unreliable, and sat down with them at the same table. But he also went into the houses of respectable citizens, theologians and devout people. He was interested in them only as human beings. For this reason he was basically indifferent to the current church regulations; sometimes he carried them out, and sometimes he regarded himself as above them. He associated with children, not with lawyers. His own very devout family declared him to be mad, which for them meant that he was possessed by the devil. He came into conflict with the political and ecclesiastical authorities, who very successfully co-operated in an attempt to liquidate him. For a time he withdrew abroad. But then he consciously sought a decision in the capital. At first it seemed that he had succeeded, and the crowds followed him with enthusiasm – but then the fatal destiny which had followed him from the first was fulfilled. One of his immediate circle denounced him, popular opinion turned against him overnight, and his followers abandoned him to the last man. Dropped by everyone, he was afraid to die. By the usual methods of clerical and political justice his trial was rushed through. The charge was blasphemy and high treason, and the sentence was death. Completely abandoned, he went to the gallows, very quiet, very obedient, but nevertheless to the gallows. He was executed together with two criminals and died with the words: 'My God, why have you forsaken me'?

There are some people who will be as alienated by this 'life of Jesus' as others are by the one we outlined above. But their objections clash – for one group, our sketch of the life story of Jesus is too unhistorical, while for others it is not sufficiently divine. We take leave to disagree with both charges.

We do not dispute that in our description of the course of Jesus' life we have used numerous biographical details which are regarded by critical historians as 'legendary'. We would reply that the most critical theologian does not base his Christianity on a reconstruction of the 'historical Jesus', but on a picture of Christ which is rich in unhistorical features. Anyone who nourishes his belief and religious practice solely on the historical Jesus is like someone who takes in all the calories he needs in tablet form, instead of enjoying a varied diet of well prepared and well cooked food.

When the story of Jesus Christ is retold, what matters is not accuracy in detail, but the general direction. Of course the direction must be the right one! The clearest description of the direction taken by Jesus in the course of his life is described by Paul in his famous hymn to Christ, once one realizes that the pre-existence of Christ accepted in it is to be understood as a symbol, and the humiliation which follows it is taken not in a special metaphysical sense, but as a historical process within the world:

Have this mind among yourselves, which you have in Christ Jesus, who, though he was in the form of God, did not count equality with God a thing to be grasped, but emptied himself, taking the form of a servant, being born in the likeness of men. And being found in human form he humbled himself and became obedient unto death, even death on a cross (Phil. 2.5ff.).

The direction taken by the course of Jesus's life, which is

described in this hymn, is confirmed by the results of historical research. In all four gospels, the piece of traditional material which has most firmly retained its original shape is the narrative of Jesus's passion. This historical conclusion suggests that the starting point for a general theological interpretation of Jesus's life should be not above, in eternity, in heaven, but below, on the earth, in the depths of Jesus's humanity. Martin Kähler has summed up this historical and theological conclusion about the gospels in the statement that they are not biographies with a tragic conclusion, but passion narratives with extensive introductions. We have done no more than verify this statement.

But for this very reason the portrait of Jesus we have sketched seems to many people to have turned out not sufficiently divine. Whereas the objection to the first portrait was that this Christ is too great and too marvellous, the objection is now that this Jesus is too small and too insignificant. We do not deny that in our sketch of the life of Jesus we have consciously emphasized his 'humanity'. For this is the point in which theology and the church at the present day are decisively in need of revision. Consequently, the tendency of the fifth gospel, which our generation has to write, must also point in this direction. Anyone who complains that the Jesus described in this way is 'not divine enough' might like to answer the question, whether he is prepared to stoop as low as God himself stooped.

But the same question must be answered by the theologians who think it possible to say something about Jesus without taking account of his relationship to God.

5. *The Life of Jesus – the History of God's Dealing with Men*

For the 'God is dead' theologians, Jesus of Nazareth has not simply dropped into the mass grave of the past, into which so much else, even God, is nowadays dumped. In spite of the death of God, they continue 'Jesus's enterprise', and regard 'Jesus's affair' as continuing. In fact, in their eyes, the 'miracle of Jesus' only really stands out against the background of the absence of God. Thus for many people, at the very moment they experience the death of God, Jesus of Nazareth takes on new life. His figure inspires them with fresh hope.

As is usually the case with theological movements, each in-

dividual gives his own highly personal ideas and reasons; but
when they are gathered together, they reveal a single outlook, a
common trend. The whole stream flows in the same direction.
We might define this tendency in the case of the 'theology after
the death of God' by saying that the watchword of its christology
is 'fellow man'. This almost stands previous christology on its
head – though whether it is being stood on its head or stood
back on its feet remains to be seen. Hitherto, the principal
significance of Jesus was seen in the fact that he brought man
into a new, right relationship to God. The underlying assumption of this was that he himself stood in a special relationship to
God, and the consequence was that men's relationship to one
another was also renewed by it. Now the principal significance
of Jesus is seen in the fact that he brings men into a new, right
relationship with each other; the assumption on which this is
based is that he himself stands in a special relationship to men.
What the relationship of Jesus to God is in these circumstances,
and how far men's relationship to God is exercised in their
relationships to one another, remains in the background, and
this question is interpreted differently, depending upon whether
one is an atheist or an a-theist.

Thus 'common humanity' becomes the event in which God
dwells, whatever that may mean, and Jesus becomes the person
who sparks off this common humanity, however one may conceive of this process. He is the 'representative', the 'teacher', the
'example', the 'man for others', 'altogether man', the 'free man'.
He interpreted love for God as love for one's neighbour and by
his attitude gave men the courage and ability to love their
neighbours in this way. His own completely unprejudiced association with all men inspired his disciples and made them
capable of the same freedom. This has remained true down to
the present day. Wherever men practise a common humanity,
Jesus is a hidden presence – and God only ever exists between
men.

Here the theological deficit which arose in christology as the
result of the 'death of God' is made good in anthropological
terms. Its concrete content is left open. Anyone can bring in
what according to his own convictions is the best for humanity.
At the present day, this deficit is made good principally in a
social or even in part a social revolutionary direction. Jesus's

faith, his preaching of the 'kingdom' is interpreted as 'Utopia', as a 'world transforming theory', the content of which is a 'real humanism'. And therefore at the present day 'Christ' is present 'in disguise' wherever men are struggling and suffering for justice, freedom and humanity, for food, peace and the future.

Because its tendencies are simultaneously towards christocentrism and anthropocentrism, the theology after the 'death of God' represents itself as a *christological atheism.* In order to save at least the figure of Jesus, it is ready to sacrifice the person of God. But the question is whether this sacrifice is worth it, whether the gradual run-down can be halted, or whether Jesus of Nazareth himself may not rapidly become redundant. A short time ago the question was: God, yes – but why Christ? Today it is already: Jesus of Nazareth, yes – but why is God still necessary? How long will it be before people ask: Why is Jesus of Nazareth still necessary?

We agree with the 'theology after the death of God' where it takes the humanity of Jesus so seriously, and therefore follows Luther's advice, that one cannot ever draw the Son of God deep enough down into the flesh. In this way it fulfils the urgent need for revision which we too have asserted is necessary for christology. But against the 'theology after the death of God' we would object that it wholly eliminates the other aspect of Jesus of Nazareth: his openness towards God, his direct relationship to the Father. And this is in flat contradiction to the results of historical exegesis.

Every critical historical study of the New Testament sources shows that Jesus's relationship to God was the essential and decisive element in his self-consciousness. If we know anything at all about the 'historical Jesus' it is the fact that he knew that he had a unique relationship to God, and that this is the basis of everything that he said and did, and of his preaching of the 'kingdom'. Whatever we like to reject from the story of Jesus as later legendary additions or theological interpretations: his pre-existence, the virgin birth, miracles, statements about himself, titles, the empty tomb, the ascension, we cannot do this with his relationship to God, with his profession of faith in him whom he called his 'Father'. Anyone who rejects this is not just rejecting a later addition or interpretation, nor something that is only an element of the world view of the time. He is taking away the basis of the whole structure. Edward Schillebeeckx is right when he describes the saying of the Christ of the Gospel of John: 'I am not alone, but I and the Father who sent me' (John 8.16, Vulg.) as a 'precise interpretation of the life of Jesus'.[13]

The gospels contain a testimony to this intimate relationship between Jesus and his Father which is not given with that purpose, but for that very reason is better evidence. This is the simple fact that Jesus prayed. Of course, at that time, as today, every devout Jew prayed. But in the life of Jesus prayer plays a particular role, over and above what was required by ritual. The gospels tell on several occasions that Jesus withdrew to some distant place to pray, that in the morning, before the break of day, he left his disciples and withdrew to pray, that he spent a whole night alone in prayer on a mountain, and that he prayed even on the Cross. No special emphasis is placed on Jesus's prayer, and it does not give the impression of having been specially introduced, but is something that fits naturally into his actions. In this way, it points to the source of these actions. When the God-is-dead theologians describe Jesus as the 'free man', they forget the source of his freedom from all prejudice: his obedient submission to the task given him by God. Or when they call him the 'man for others' they overlook the fact that the basis of his common humanity with us is in his immediate and direct relationship to his Father. Urs von Balthasar relates the two aspects to each other in the right way when he says of Jesus: 'If he had not withdrawn so far into loneliness with God, he would never have been able to go out so far in fellowship with men'.[14] By contrast to the God-is-dead theologians of the present day, Jesus's opponents recognized this. They regarded his assertion of a common humanity with all of us, his free and unprejudiced association with men, as a blasphemy against *God*, and that is why they sought his life.

To express Jesus's unique link with God, the New Testament describes him as the *Son*. It is of no importance whether or not Jesus himself claimed the title of Son. Whatever may be the case, this title expresses the decisive facts of Jesus's special link with God and the attitude that resulted from it. Now at the present day, after the enlightenment, it is not possible for us to interpret Jesus's sonship as the early church did, in terms of his 'natures', but only in 'historical' terms. Jesus shows himself to be the Son by letting God be his Father. We could say that he completely fulfilled the first commandment, and feared, loved and trusted God above all things. But no one becomes a son by his own achievement, but only by an act of the father, either by conception or by adoption. Both ideas have been repeatedly used as symbols to describe the basis of Jesus's sonship. Nowadays these symbols have nothing to say to us. But they remain of significance to us because of the idea they represent: one only becomes a son through the father, so that the title of Son points back to the will and work of God – though only in the way in which the 'Son' has understood the will and the work of the 'Father'.

Thus the opposite of what is asserted by the 'theology after the death of God' is in fact true. It is not that, because God does not intervene and vindicate his cause, Christ appears in his place. Rather, because Christ comes on the scene, God intervenes and vindicates his cause. In the theology after the death of God the revelation of God is turned into a deposing of God, in which God is robbed of his power. He is not represented by God, but replaced, as one owner of a business succeeds another. According to this view, the event which we describe in symbolic language as God's 'becoming man' signifies not the coming but the going of God. But this idea is derived not from the New Testament, but from Ernst Bloch, the most recent of the Protestant church fathers.

But the picture in the bible is exactly the reverse. There Jesus has nothing of himself and does not wish to be anything of himself; but by having nothing of himself and not wishing to be anything of himself, he becomes constantly more transparent with regard to God. Dorothee Sölle's expression 'God's actor' is inadequate to express this transparence of Jesus with regard to God. With this expression she comes dangerously close to the docetism which she is so right to fear. The actor takes on his role, but he does not identify himself with it, or at least not to the uttermost degree. Otherwise, he would really have to die at the end of the play like its hero and remain dead on the stage. Instead of which, he gets up after the curtain has fallen, goes into his dressing room, takes off his costume, goes home and eats steak. But Jesus of Nazareth identifies himself even unto death. With whom? With God? With men? Or with both?

He identifies himself with both, with God as with men. But this may no longer be understood in supra-natural or magical terms. Rather, it takes place quite 'naturally'. What happens here is history, nothing but history. A rabbi appears with a message. For all the variety and lack of connection between the individual parts of this message, a unified basis underlies the whole of it. This unified basis consists in the paradox of two basic truths.

The first basic truth of Jesus's message is that at its most profound level the world is not in order, and that man is not what he should be. For Jesus this is so obvious that he takes it for granted without specially mentioning it. By contrast to every tendency and school in modern existentialism, the fallen nature of man does not form an independent theme in the preaching of Jesus, but is no more than the background to the other truth, which is the one that matters.

The truth that really matters in the message of Jesus is that the same world which at its most profound level is not in order, and the same man, who is assumed in his present condition to be other than what he ought to be, are surrounded, maintained, upheld, determined and guided towards their goal by the *love of* God. But this is not declared as a general truth, valid for ever and ever, but is uttered to those who hear it as a new, concrete and momentary truth: that the remote God has *now* come close to man and seeks fellowship with man. Jesus of Nazareth brought this truth into the world, and vouched for this truth with his preaching. But he did not only preach it, he lived it in the whole course of his life; he 'lived it out' in the fullest sense of the expression – he pledged his life for the truth of this love and lost his life for it. In this sense we can say that Jesus of Nazareth died 'for us'. In reality, as the Gospel of John says, he 'loved his own to the end', and the end was his death.

By staking himself, his very existence, on the word of love, Jesus brought about an identity between his existence and his words, his person and his work. It is this which gave his life story the shape and direction we outlined above. It is in fact like the fate of any one of the multitudes who have been persecuted in our own century, like the biography of a Jew under

Hitler. But above this human fate the bible sets up the inscription: 'Behold your God!' The New Testament asserts of this particular persecuted Jew that whoever sees him sees the Father.

That is, this life history of Jesus is the 'exegesis' of God. 'Exegesis' means explanation, interpretation; implicit in the word is the idea of a process, a movement. In the life of Jesus of Nazareth God gave an explanation of himself: Look, this is what I am like! In this way he made manifest the fact that the deepest ground and meaning of all history, and his own very self, his person, is love. But he did this not by teaching, but by demonstration. He verified his love, he 'realized' it, by giving his own self as the guarantee and by identifying himself with the destiny of men, down to the utmost depths of human existence, to death itself. This self-interpretation of God in Jesus of Nazareth signifies his self-identification with men, the union of omnipotence and impotence.

The heathen also know the God who is almighty, for he figures in all religions. But the God of the Christians shares the sufferings of mankind. In Christianity, for the first time in the history of religion, and indeed in the whole of human thought, a positive link is made between God and suffering. With this, the history of religion was brought to its conclusion, or more properly, to its fulfilment. For all religion means 'law'. But love is the fulfilment of the law. God himself fulfilled the law through his love, and thereby brought about the end of religion. This also means that the 'death of God' as a phenomenon of the history of religion goes back ultimately to God himself: ' "God", once he is conceived of as dead, can no longer be thought of as the world thinks of him.'[15] From this point on heaven may be empty, but in the whole universe there is no longer a place where God is not present.

6. *The Light Cast on God as a Light Cast on the World*

In the light of the revelation of Christ we are not shown a new world, we only see the world anew – as it were with the eyes of God, so that we recognize his presence in it. The revelation in Christ does not add to the reality of the world in which we live a second, distinct, divine reality, but only shows that the reality of the world in which we live is the reality of God. As a

light cast on God, it enlightens the world: God casts a light
on himself in Jesus of Nazareth, and the whole of existence is
illuminated for us. The light of God is of course always there,
but in his revelation it 'rises upon us' – just as the sun is always
there, and yet has to 'arise' for us to see. Anyone who regards
this as an inadequate presentation of the revelation in Christ,
and who misses in it 'the miracle of the new creation' and sees in
it only 'variations within the same identity',[16] still has in mind,
even if he is unaware of it or is consciously trying to reject it,
the supranaturalist pattern of thought, and is still following the
former practice of dividing the one reality beyond which one
cannot go into two separate, opposed worlds.

The prologue of the Gospel of John reads 'the word became
flesh' (1.14). In four words and in the categories of Greek
thought, this is the content of the revelation in Christ and the
fundamental dogma of Christianity. It states that the universal
logos, the divine mind which pervades the reality of the whole
universe, was manifested in a concrete historical person, in the
man Jesus of Nazareth. If this is true, it follows that the experience we have of the reality of the world and the experience
which we have of the reality of revelation are not mutually
exclusive, but are parallel and contain each other. Let us see
whether this is true, and in what way.

Once again, we shall begin with the experience of the world,
with the decisive theological dilemma with which we found
ourselves faced with regard to the knowledge of God: God is
unknowable not so much because of his deity as because the
divinity has departed from the world. Looking at the 'discord'
in existence, we said that we dare not assert that we have never
discovered anything of God in the world, but neither can we say
that we have found God in the world. This discord in existence
is something which we do not meet only in extreme situations;
we already encounter it daily in the fact that there is a constant
tension in our lives between what incomprehensibly slips away
from us and what is incomprehensibly given to us. We experience life slipping away from us in all the darkness, puzzles,
pain and lovelessness which we encounter, in every quarrel and
every farewell – in all these things life slips away from us like an
outgoing tide. But life is granted to us in all the brightness, joy,
happiness and abundance of love which we meet, in every

reconciliation and new encounter – in all this, life is given to us like a rising tide. This ambivalence of existence is something we cannot resolve. We cannot overcome it by drawing a line under the whole sum and offsetting the minus and plus sides of life against each other, to find out which is the greatest in the end. We shall never get any result by this method – or at most, a negative result. The Apostle Paul writes: 'I consider that the sufferings of this present time are not worth comparing with the glory that is to be revealed to us' (Rom. 8.18). Setting aside for the moment the question of our future glory, we can say of the present that we consider that the joys of this present time are not worth comparing with the sufferings that men must tolerate at the same time. In the world's calculation, the few entries on the side of joy add up to less than the total of suffering. A single person suffering from cancer, in the midst of the much vaunted beauty of nature, contradicts the whole of the beauty of nature. And therefore we shall abandon this train of thought at this point and go on to the other aspect, to the reality of revelation.

If we look at both experiences together, our experience of the reality of the world and our experience when we encounter the reality of revelation, can we then recognize that there is a 'surplus' contained in the truth of the revelation of God? This surplus consists in the manifestation of the fact, which it is simply impossible to derive from any experience of the world, that the final and absolute power over our existence is that of love. If we now consider in the light of this realization the 'discord' of existence which we have already established, and the tension within our lives which we are unable of ourselves to resolve, we may perhaps be able to see that even in what incomprehensibly slips away from us, God is close to us. And if, as the bible puts it, this knowledge comes into our hearts, perhaps we may also profess it with our voices, with the words: 'Yes, Lord!' or 'Thank you!', or with no more than a deep sigh. But in this 'Yes, Lord!' or 'Thank you!', or mere sigh, we are responding to the affirmation which God has uttered in Jesus of Nazareth. In this affirmation of God lies the ultimate basis of what we have called 'existence owed to another'. Ernst Fuchs gives the true meaning of the prologue to the Gospel of John when he translates it: 'In the beginning was the Yes, and the

Yes was with Love, and the Yes was Love ... and the Yes became flesh ... and we saw his glory.'[17]

We do not encounter this Yes of the love of God by climbing up into an imaginary heaven or carrying ourselves back to the years AD 1-33, but by reading and expounding the texts which tell of Jesus of Nazareth to our own time and to our own place. From the methodological point of view, it does not matter whether we start with the 'text' and end up with a contemporary and existential relationship to the life of society, or whether we proceed in the reverse direction from a contemporary and existential relationship to the life of society and arrive at the 'text'. For, as we have made clear, we are dealing with two spheres of experience which interpenetrate, modify and sustain each other.

But the method which I would recommend is not that of confronting our contemporaries in the 1970s with what a shepherd looked like at the time of the Old Testament, what the Pharisees were like and what the tax collectors did, how agriculture was carried on in Galilee and the lay-out of Jerusalem at the time of Jesus – going on with the familiar cliché: 'And what has this text to tell us nowadays?', leaping head over heels back into the present. Once we have wandered into the past time of the beginning of the Christian era, it is hard work to bring our contemporaries back into their own age and to prepare them for a new era. Historical fact makes things clear, but it does not bring salvation! We described the life of Jesus of Nazareth as the 'exegesis' of God. Exegesis always involves 'drawing out' what happened yesterday into the present day, and always implies 'bringing up to date': 'Today the scripture has been fulfilled in your hearing.' Where this bringing up to date is absent, there is no serious revelation.

As far as the expression of historical fact in dogmatic terms is concerned, we should be content with the Pauline statement 'God was in Christ', and allow each other complete liberty with regard to theological speculations on *how* God was present in Christ. In the New Testament itself, the testimony to the same revelation of the love of God in Jesus Christ is given in many, often contradictory and disparate ways. We can say that in the New Testament there may be only *one* Christ, but there are many christologies. All have the same Christ, but everyone has his own christology. If we could recognize this, we could save ourselves a great deal of time, energy and disagreement in the church. Theology might be caused offence, but would not give so much.

At this final point, many may perhaps ask what now remains of the *resurrection* of Christ. Our answer is that in everything we have said about the revelation of Christ, the resurrection was already present in a hidden way. The very fact that we interpreted the life of Jesus of Nazareth as the history of *God's* dealings with men assumed the event which we call the 'resurrection of Jesus'. The resurrection is not a miracle or a separate saving act on the part of God, but like the death of Jesus must be taken together with the whole of his life, teaching and ministry. Resurrection means that the revelation of the love of God in Jesus of Nazareth is stronger than death, that it is even not interrupted by what happened on Good Friday, but continues and will always continue until it has reached its final goal.

Through the idea of resurrection, the love of God receives its eschatological perspective. This protects it from the most dangerous misunderstanding to which it can be subjected. This is the suspicion that there is an attempt to camouflage the 'discord' of existence, the absurdity of the world, all the darkness, puzzles and contradictions in it, with the mantle of love. But the assertion of the love of God as self-evident has become incomprehensible to our age. The 'love of God' in this sense is dead; it fell in action, not at Stalingrad, but at the latest at Verdun.

The love of God is not like a mantle which can be cast over everything that is discordant, puzzling and contradictory in the world. It is the movement of God in history through which, on the principle of the opposite, he creates new life. It is this eschatological and dynamic view of the love of God which matters; it is a powerful, creative, forming love, the aim of which is to draw the whole world into the 'divine sphere' and to bring it to the fulfilment to which it is destined by its creation. And therefore this love, by the very fact that it is the love of *God*, is always in the first instance a love *against* us, before it can be a love *for* us. And so too all experience of God is against the outward appearance of the world, and is always marked with the sign 'nevertheless'.

But we should not suppose that by pointing to the principle of the opposite, we shall always be able to recognize the love of God. Even when his love is revealed, God's concealment does not stop for us; on the contrary, it grows even more profound. At the present time the tension between the revealed and the hidden God has risen to the point where it is intolerable. In the face of the revelation of the love of God in Jesus Christ, Hiroshima, Auschwitz, Stalingrad, Dresden, Vietnam, Biafra and South America become a greater enigma than they ever were. This is the enigma of the conflict between the omnipotence and the love of God, the dialectic between 'ground' and 'abyss' in the deity. We cannot resolve the enigma posed by this conflict and this dialectic; we can scarcely even bear it.

Consequently 'atheism', as an experience of the absence of God, has a place in all belief in God. We have always to endure tension between the revealed and the hidden God, between the absent and the present God. And we do not say: This is the tension which we have to endure, but: It is precisely at this point that we believe in God. On our lips the word 'God' is only an interjection, an appeal, a cry when we are sickened, a confession of faith, a prayer; but whatever it is, it is always in the vocative. And therefore one can only ever speak of God in personal terms.

9

The Personality of God

1. The Basic Theme of the Bible: The Encounter with God

The fact remains that the God who as a completely personal being is enthroned over the universe and mankind and rules it from above has ceased to exist for us – this is the outcome both of the revelation in Christ and the enlightenment. Atheists and a-theists are right to protest against this kind of 'theism'.

But there is no question that the bible speaks of God in such theist conceptions. The question is whether the common assertion at the present day of the 'end of theism' really strikes at the root of Christian faith in God. This is the central problem of all present-day discussion about God. The question, 'What sense is there in speaking of God?' must strictly speaking read, 'What sense is there in speaking of a *personal* God?'. The precise point at issue is whether God can still be understood as another person whom we actually encounter, and if this is what he is, how one has to speak of this person, encountered in this way.

We shall discuss the question of the personality of God by beginning with the content of the biblical tradition.

The first impression that we get when we glance at the bible, however casually, is that it is a *personal* book through and through. Helmut Gollwitzer calls it 'the "most personal" book in the history of religion', and quite rightly continues, 'It is the bible which first taught man what personality in the strict sense is'.[1] The basis of this wholly personal character of the bible lies in the fact that man's belief in God in the bible is experienced as an existential relationship; but in its turn, this existential relationship is experienced as a relationship between one person

What Kind of God?

and another. In the bible man speaks not only about God, but always speaks to and with God at the same time. Even where the bible speaks about God in the third person, it never does so neutrally, as from a distance, but always in an existential way, that is, always in the consciousness of a relationship, perhaps even a negative relationship to God – and therefore implicitly in the second person. In the bible belief in God always includes the idea that man encounters, works with and deals with God. Even someone who hates God speaks to him face to face.

The form in which belief in God is exercised in the bible is in the strict sense of the word a 'dialogue', and therefore a process which takes place between two partners. But a dialogue is always constituted by the personal categories of speaking, listening and answering. From God's side, therefore, this personal partnership is expressed in statements, commands, promises, anger, seeking, pursuing and forgiving, while on man's side they are expressed in listening, answers, questions, trust, obedience, prayer, praise and thanksgiving, or else in disobedience, estrangement, flight and cursing and then in repentance, atonement, sorrow and obedience. Although this often may be expressed in mythological or symbolic terms, or in the images of poetry, it is always conceived in a strictly personal way and in terms of historical facts.

The reason why belief in God in the bible is conceived of in such strict personal and historical terms is not that men first of all worked out a neutral and general concept of God, from which they then derived all kinds of individual conceptions of God. Exactly the reverse process took place. At first, individual persons and groups, or even a whole people, had particular historical experiences, in which they believed they were undergoing an encounter with God. They then recounted these in personal categories, images and concepts. The history of the encounter between God and man forms the content of the bible; and in it God is discovered as a person. This discovery is the great achievement of Israel in the history of religion. But at the same time Israel also discovered the 'world as history'.

According to the bible the first impulse in the history of the encounter between God and man was given by God, and by God alone. To this extent one must concede to the 'theology after the death of God' that the bible contains a prior assumption. But this assumption does not take the form of an underlying world view, consisting of a theist and personalist concept of God, which one must first accept intellectually before one can believe in God. Rather, it consists of the experience of God as a personal force, taking the initiative in the encounter with man, and in this way setting into motion and maintaining in motion the history which the bible narrates, though in a very varied and contradictory way. And the 'theology after the death of God' is also right in resisting all metaphysical 'worlds beyond' and 'underlying worlds' and looking for God in immanence alone – for the God of the bible moves constantly towards immanence.

The impulse of biblical belief in God towards expression in personal terms extends as far as grammar itself. The bible speaks of God in sentences in which God as the subject is associated with a predicate which in the form of a verb makes statements about his being or actions. This is an example of what Hamann and Rosenstock-Huessy have often emphasized: that God has something to do with grammar. Naturally the result of this process is what can be called 'anthropomorphic' statements about God. But the basis of this anthropomorphism is not a naïve, unreflective, primitive way of speaking about God in excessively human terms. The decisive reason for it is that on his own initiative God has entered into dealings with man, and therefore has to be spoken of by men in human terms. Apart from this, a crude religious anthropomorphism often does more justice to the reality of God than subtle philosophical speculation.

Now Herbert Braun tells us that we always encounter the word of God through the medium of human words, *secundum hominem recipientem*, and that consequently, in the bible itself, a process of 'interpretative correction' has already begun to take place. There is a movement from an understanding of God which is massively objective and expressed in terms of a personal anthropomorphism, towards a constantly increasing spiritual realization of the concept of God. Braun sees the content of this spiritual realization in an increasing departure from 'theism', which according to his view makes it clear that in the bible a personal encounter with God is fundamentally superfluous and can therefore be eliminated.

No one who understands the matter can deny that such a process of development and correction is in fact already recognizable in the bible. It is a long way from the demon which falls upon Moses in the lodging place (Ex. 4.24 ff), and Balaam's talking donkey to the Father of Jesus of Nazareth. This shows that man's knowledge of God grew step by step, through different stages and different levels. This is why we spoke of 'transformations of God', and expressed the view that it is beyond belief that anyone can understand and maintain the truth of the bible as the truth of God without historical research and understanding.

But the goal of this process of interpretative correction is not, as Braun asserts, the abandonment of theism in the sense of a gradual depersonalization of God. On the contrary, its tendency is always towards the ever greater extension of the personality of God: the personal encounter of God and man is always understood more and more as a universal reality, which concerns the whole existence of the world and of man.

There is an example of this extension which demonstrates it very convincingly – so far as one shares the view that the epistles to the Colossians and Ephesians are written not by the Apostle Paul, but belong to a later period. A number of valid arguments can in fact be adduced for this late dating: both epistles reflect a doctrinal development in the direction of 'early catholicism', and this shows that they come at the end of the process of literary tradition of which the New Testament is our record. Amongst the 'early catholic' themes present in both epistles, two are of particular importance: on the one hand, a powerful development of Christian revelation into the message of an organized church, and on the other hand its extension into a doctrine of cosmic significance. Now one would imagine that both developments, the ecclesiological and the cosmological, would have brought with them a certain depersonalization of the Christian message. But the reverse is the case: not only do both epistles firmly maintain the personality of God and Jesus Christ, but actually extend these to the realm of the whole cosmos. There is nothing more cosmic and yet more personal than these epistles.

Thus the personality of God, or more precisely the personal experience of God as a face to face encounter with another person, is a fundamental theological element in the content of the bible. If we were to go through the whole bible from beginning to end, we would never find a passage in it where this I-Thou relationship is absent from belief in God. Thus the personal encounter of man with the personal God is an essential structural element in Christian belief. In the bible it is part of the human condition that man cannot be conceived of without his encounter with the personal God.

How we are to express this basic theological element in the bible, whether in theistic, metaphysical, mythological, anthropomorphic, poetic or other terms, is almost a matter of indifference. For all our images, concepts, symbols and conceptions of God are too narrow for the reality of God, and this is true even of the category of the 'person'. All that matters is that we hold firm to the basic biblical teaching of the personal encounter between God and man. Then, of course, we can distinguish from this point of view between categories which are more or less appropriate. The keyword is demythologization, not depersonalization!

But it is not enough just to go back to the bible. Consequently, for all that is correct and of importance in Gollwitzer's arguments against the 'theology after the death of God', they are not adequate. Basically, Gollwitzer is only repeating what the bible says, simply affirming and asserting it, and therefore is guilty of the positivism of revelation of which Barth has been accused. But we are faced today with 'the end of theism', which has not been proclaimed without good reason; and the important question is how we can present to our contemporaries the basic biblical teaching of a personal encounter between God and man in such a way that they can understand and if possible even believe it. Here Heinrich Ott, Barth's successor at Bâle, has gone a good deal further than Gollwitzer in the theological discussion concerning the personality of God.

2. Man in the In Between

Here again, with regard to the personality of God, only an existential interpretation can help us – that is, an attempt to interpret and understand the personal being of God in relation to our human existential life. We shall begin on the human side.

Personality is the basic experience of all human existential life, and indeed there is a personal element in an encounter with any kind of reality. Scholasticism already perceived this in the assertion that all being in the world consisted in being in a relationship, and that no other form of being existed. Heidegger expressed the same view in other words: 'All existence is co-existence.' Two prepositions serve to illustrate the *basic personal content of all human existential life.*

The first is the Latin preposition *coram.* As Gerhard Ebeling has shown[2], it is the 'keyword' to Luther's whole understanding of being. *Coram* can be translated as 'before', 'in the presence of', or, in more concrete terms, 'in the sight of'. It therefore expresses a fundamental structural element in human existential life. Our life does not take place within ourselves, but always in such a way that we stand in a relationship, a relationship which is both our relationship to others, and that of others to us. The meaning of this mutual relationship, which is the situation of all human existence, can be clearly seen either in the German word *Ansehen*, or in the English word which can sometimes be used to translate it, 'regard'. It has a double meaning: an active meaning – I regard others; and it also has a passive meaning – I am regarded by others, and therefore possess their *Ansehen*, their regard. The double meaning of these two words expresses the fact that we never live for ourselves alone but always in a personal relationship, always 'from person to person'.

The situation which Martin Luther describes with the aid of the preposition *coram* is described by Martin Buber by means of the relational preposition *zwischen*, 'between'. He too has in mind the personality of man, the 'reciprocity' of all personal being. A person never exists in 'himself' but only in the 'in between' of a relationship with another person. Thus for example we say of two people who have a good or bad relationship between them that there is something 'between' them. This always implies that they affect each other in some way: love, loyalty, trust, friendship, enmity, hatred or mistrust are always a process between two people. If I love a person and trust him, or if I hate him and mistrust him, then not only does something pass from me to the other person, or from the other person to me, but something goes on between the two of us.

This points to the fact that all human personality involves something 'going on'. Something is going on not in the sense of events which follow one another, but always in a sense of events which affect each other as they take place. Thus I do not first experience myself as a person and then conclude that someone else is also a person; rather, my experience of myself as 'I' and my experience of the other as 'you' bring each other about in one and the same moment.

This personality, or more precisely, man's situation in a personal relationship, which Martin Luther expresses by the preposition *coram* and Martin Buber with the preposition *between*, is more than merely a category of human thought. It is part of the fundamental structure of being, which consequently is conceived of and practised by men, of course, in corresponding categories and bonds of relationship. Let us give another concrete example of this situation. A father has a son; but he scarcely takes any notice of him, and neglects his duty as a father in an 'irresponsible' way. But the father-son relationship remains as a structural element between the two, regardless of whether the father is aware of it and of the attitude he adopts to it. And its purpose is always for the father to take it up, respond to it and bring it to realization.

Thus personality is a basic experience, an original element in all human existence, and moreover human personality always exists in the form of inter-personality, a mutual relationship between one person and another. How does this understanding of the personal being of man help us to understand the personality of God?

3. God Personally

We are not afraid to draw a conclusion from the lesser to the greater: If a human existence always has a personal form, that of a reciprocal relationship between one man and another, how much more must this be true of the existence of God, and consequently of the relationship between God and man! Here we are not demonstrating the personality of God by analogy to the personal being of man. What we are doing is to assert that if there is to be any belief in God at all, it can only take place in personal form, and can therefore only be described in personal categories. Anyone who does not speak of God as a person, is still placing him on a lower level than man; he is making him smaller than himself. And Heinrich Ott is right when he states: 'A non-reciprocal relationship to God would be a sub-personal relationship, on a lower "level" than relationship with animals, and comparable to man's relationship to things'.[3]

The familiar objection, which originates in mysticism, was taken over by agnosticism, and which people like to repeat at the present day because it sounds very sophisticated and intellectual, that God is 'infinite' and 'ineffable', and that anyone who names him or goes so far as to call him a 'person' is enclosing him within the limits of finite humanity, is an objection which misses the point. This suspicion of 'anthropomorphism' is suspicious in itself. To renounce the idea of the personal being of God actually represents nothing more than an even more drastic anthropomorphism. The overt intention is to preserve the idea that God is infinite and unlimited, and for this reason to cling so firmly to the view that he is a-personal. But in fact it amounts to a covert attempt to make one's own limited powers of understanding the standard for God. Because one cannot understand God, one declares him 'incomprehensible'; but the very statement is an attempt to say something about God which one can still understand oneself.

But we could not have a personal experience of God if he had not revealed himself to us personally. Only because he who previously was disguised as something impersonal, an 'it', has made himself known to us as a person, as 'you', can we encounter him as another person, as 'you'. Here again we must go back to what we described in our account of the basic theological content of the bible as 'history of the encounter' between God and man. Above all, we must recall what we said about the life of Jesus of Nazareth as the history of God's dealings with men: in the history of Jesus of Nazareth God has interpreted himself and so revealed love as the final and unconditional power over our existence. We called this the 'light cast by God', which at the same time casts for us a light on the world, so that in the face of all the contradictions of life, and in the midst of the discord manifested by all existence, we are still able to show trust.

But we can only experience love and trust in a personal way.

And therefore we oppose to the thesis so widely proclaimed since the time of Nietzsche, that the mature man of the modern age cannot tolerate God as a person, because this degrades man into being an object and a slave, the contrary thesis: the mature man of the modern age can only experience God personally, as someone else whom he meets in a face to face encounter, and cannot tolerate him in any other way, because this is the only way in which he is preserved from being an object and the slave of God.

Of course we cannot express this thesis without at once adding a warning that we are not simply conceiving of God as an individual person and restricting ourselves to this conception. After all, the devil was once thought of as a person! Paul Tillich has expressed this warning for us in the following distinction: ' "Personal God" does not mean that God is *a* person. It means that God is the ground of everything personal ... he is not a person, but he is no less than a person.'[4]

Of course there is no way for us to avoid speaking of God as 'a person' if we are to express our experience of belief in words. But as always in theology, the direction to be taken here is from the experience to the concept, and not from the concept to the experience. The personal experience of God as another person, as 'you', is always prior to the personified conception of the divine 'you' who has previously been experienced. With regard to God, the concept of a person can never be more than an interpretative instrument, and can never become an aim in itself. That is, we can only use the concept of personality as an explanatory term, in order with its help to describe man's belief in God as a *personal process*. As soon as we 'fix' in logical terms the process which is constantly 'going on' between God and man, and turn our experience of God as an encounter with another person into a 'conception', this conception of God as a person turns into nothing more than a code. But like all other codes, this code has to be solved. What happens in this case is that the code-word 'person', applied to God, is either broken by the reality of God or filled in with our experience of his reality.

Whenever our conception of God as a person is not backed by our personal experience of faith, and still more, where our conception of God as a person is not constantly broken down, set in motion and made fluid by our personal experience, God is in

fact degraded to an object and a tyrant, while at the same time
man is degraded into a thing and a slave. In this respect all
warnings against objectivizing God are justified. Manfred
Mezger is right when he says 'Lake Constance exists, the
Himalaya exists, but God does not exist'.[5] And this wisdom
is not as new and original as it sometimes pretends. More than
thirty years ago Dietrich Bonhoeffer said in his inaugural thesis,
in almost the same words as Manfred Mezger: 'A God "who
exists" does not exist.' Eugen Rosenstock-Huessy expresses the
same fact in positive terms when he says that in reality one
can only speak of God in the vocative. Heinrich Ott is saying the
same thing when he puts the intransitive concept 'exist' into the
transitive and says that we must 'exist the You (of God)'; 'The
divine You, the person whom our existence encounters in its
totality, is found by us as we "exist" it.'[6]

But what is it like 'to exist the divine You'? If God is experienced in faith as one encountered face to face, then this
'personalizes' the whole of existence. But this also means that
the personal link between God and man, which the bible
describes in such words as 'faith, hope and love' does not take
place in a separate domain reserved or built on especially for
our dealings with God, separated from everything else that is
carried out in our lives. Faith, hope and love are exercised solely
in our everyday relations with our fellow men.

This brings us back once again to the concept referred to so
often at the present day of our 'fellow men' as the place in
which God happens, or more precisely, to our relations with our
fellow men as the event in which God dwells. We have already
commented critically on this expression, when dealing with the
more general problem of 'immanent transcendence'. We must
now take up this critical examination once again from the point
of view of the more specific question of the personality of God.

'Our common humanity' is the positive answer of the theology
after the death of God to its negative statement of the 'end of
theism'. It is attempting to express the fact that we can no longer
speak of God at the present day as 'a person', that consequently
a direct personal relationship between man and God is no longer
conceivable, and that the centre of gravity of all personality has
moved towards relationships between human beings, which

must now bear the whole weight of the former relationship between man and God. If God 'happens' any longer anywhere in the world, this is the place and this alone.

Once again we must begin by agreeing with the 'theology after the death of God' when it places such great value on relationships between man and his fellow men, even with regard to the relationship with God. Consider: How did we first learn of God? From our fellow man. How do we experience the love of God in our daily life? From our fellow man. How do we receive the daily bread for which we ask in the Lord's Prayer? From our fellow man. But we take issue with the theology after the death of God when it allows the personal relationship between man and God to be replaced completely by men's relationships with each other, and in this way transforms theology into anthropology. The 'theology after the death of God' does everything in order to have and preserve the personal being of man – only God is not allowed to be a person! But this is a contradiction in itself.

Of course theology cannot speak of God without at the same time speaking of man. But it is certain that theology also cannot speak of man, without at the same time speaking of God. Moreover, it speaks of him in an 'elevated' way. An example of a relationship between men illustrates the 'elevation' of the way theology speaks of God. When we have received a present from someone we love, we are naturally pleased with the object we have been given. But the origin of our joy goes deeper, and lies in what the present expresses about the relationship of the other person to us: that he loves us, shares in our life, and gives us a share in his life. But this means that although the giver is expressed for us in the gift, at the same time he far overshadows it. In the same way, our relationship to God is expressed in our relationships with our fellow men, and yet far overshadows them.

This becomes even clearer if we are cut off from all fellow human beings and completely dependent upon ourselves. Does God then cease to exist for us, so that we are quite alone and completely unloved? Here there is nothing but an absolute alternative: either we allow no place to the personality of God and to a direct relationship between man and God – in such a situation we would then be really alone, abandoned and unloved, unless we still could remember the days gone by in which we were once aware of being loved by a human being. Or else our personal existential life is not exhausted in our relationships to other human beings, but is rooted in personal relationship which, while it is realized in our relationships with our fellow men, is not completely identical with them. In the latter case, the personal relationship between God and us is retained, even if all our relationships with other human beings come to an end.

Once again this ultimate non-identity between God and our common humanity, or more precisely between our relationship to God and our relationships to our fellow human beings, can be illustrated by a concrete example. A prisoner sits in solitary confinement in a concentration camp, completely alone in the darkness, cut off from all his fellow men. The only sign of common humanity which he experiences is the tin bowl with the watery soup which is thrust into his cell once a day. Is this tin bowl, the only sign of any relationship with other human beings, the only way in which God's love presents itself to him? Of course the love of God must already have been imparted to him previously in some way, and not in a vertical line from heaven, but through one of his fellow men, if he is now to be certain of it. But at this moment his certainty depends precisely on the fact that God and the humanity he shares with others are not identical, but the love of God is prior to and above all common humanity.

This ultimate non-identity between man's relationship with God and men's relationships to one another can be seen in its most obvious form in the most extreme boundary situation of all human life: man's death. It is suspicious that the theology after the death of God has so little to say about human death. Even when another person is dying we can go part of the way with him. We can sit at his bedside or we can hold his hand, we can give injections to alleviate his pain or even to send him to sleep, and wipe the sweat of death from his brow. But the last part of the way he has to go alone. If it is not the end of his course – and hitherto, it has been part of Christian belief that it is not – this is only because God and his common humanity are not identical, but God's love was already there *before* his birth and will still be there *after* his death.

We can draw the theological consequences from the examples

we have given by turning again to Martin Buber's concept of the 'in between'; and by following Heinrich Ott in distinguishing a 'great in between' from a 'lesser in between'.[7] The 'great in between' refers to the personal relationship between God and ourselves experienced in faith, while the 'lesser in between' refers to our relationships with our fellow men, which we experience every day and everywhere. It is not the case that we follow a kind of processional way from the lesser to the greater in between, from our relationships with other human beings to our relationship to God. Both in between, the greater and the lesser, have a mutual relationship. The 'great in between', our relationship to God, is the basis of the many 'lesser in betweens', our relationships with other human beings – it describes the horizon within which they take place. On the other hand, the 'lesser in betweens', our relationships with other human beings, help us to illustrate and make concrete the 'great in between', our relationship to God.

This is what we mean when we affirm the personality of God in the face of the 'end of theism' as it is proclaimed at the present day. We are referring not to a dogmatic concept, but to a living experience in faith.

That the personality of God is not a dogmatic concept, but a living experience in faith, is nowhere so clear as in prayer. Thus wherever the personality of God is discussed, amongst friends or opponents, the question of prayer is always raised at the present day.

4. Prayer

As an introduction to the theological problems surrounding prayer at the present day, we shall begin with the personal testimony of a pastor from East Germany:

Yes, I pray too ... I pray too for everything I really care about, and I give thanks for everything that life brings me. These are not mere words, because I am writing these lines two days after the death of a person who was one of the dearest in the world to me. And yet I do not believe that anyone heard my prayer anywhere, and this concept seems to me to be utterly fantastic. I do not believe in a God who, after hearing my prayer, decides to help me and thereupon intervenes in natural laws, and by a supranatural act alters the circumstances at a stroke ... Nor do I wish with any greater longing that there was a God who would

hear my prayer directly and by an intervention of his omnipotence
would alter the situation ... Let us honestly take account of the fact that
for us Christians our destiny is just as unalterable as for all other
people. This may be painful, but it is honest ... Why then do we still
believe in God, why do we pray regardless of this? Because in prayer a
power can be given to us, with the help of which we can bear even the
hardest things ... I receive this comfort not from a supranatural higher
being, and yet it is quite real. It takes place in a much more profound
and mysterious way, if you like as a self-purification, but which at the
same time I do not carry out myself, but receive as a gift.[8]

These words seem to sum up all the problems of prayer at the
present day: no personal God who listens – no God above, who
intervenes – and yet we pray. How is this possible? Is it
possible at all? These are the questions we have to answer. We
shall do so cautiously and tentatively, not in the style of a confession of faith, but of a thoughtful weighing of different views,
and therefore step by step.

In the first place we begin with a personal testimony, taken
this time from a youthful recollection of Elly Heuss-Knapp.
She tells of her years in Strasbourg:

We helped the builders and understood something of their work.
And we built a castle with firm foundations and walls which stood two
feet above the ground. To protect it from the rain, we took some
guttering. The next day we read in the local news in the paper that 30
marks worth of gutters had been stolen from the building site near the
University. Our little group gathered in the makeshift den, and the
boldest boy said: 'All we can do is pray.'

This suggestion on the boy's part seems to me to be typical
of the prevailing conventional view of what prayer is, not only
as a caricature amongst non-Christians, but also in the religious
practice of Christians.

There are two objections to this view of prayer:

1. Here prayer is misinterpreted as *magic*. Someone hopes by
the aid of prayer to bring about a direct intervention of God in
the course of the world. In seven theses addressed to the
ecumenical working group *Politisches Nachtgebet* in Cologne
('Political Evening Prayers'), Fulbert Steffensky guards against
such a magical misunderstanding of prayer in the following
words: 'Christian prayer has renounced miracles; it does not
seek a magical change in the situation.'[9]

2. Here prayer is reduced to one element amongst others. I do all I can in my life, and besides this I pray. For example I plan a journey, take all possible measures to ensure that it succeeds, decide where I am going, sketch out a route, book hotels and insure the luggage, and to these measures I add at the end, or while I am doing it, something extra in the form of a prayer for success. This view of prayer as one element amongst others likewise misunderstands it as magic.

Secondly, let us suppose that a heathen is praying to his God and asking him to heal him of an illness, while somewhere else a Christian is praying to his God and also asking him to heal him from an illness. What is the difference between the two as they pray? Both are praying to their God and expect him to heal their illness by a direct intervention. If anyone says there is a difference here, the onus is on them to prove it. We at least cannot see any difference here, and believe that there is none, if prayer is understood in such a one-sided way as mere petition, and if we expect it to be heard in the form of a direct intervention on the part of God.

But it cannot be denied that in the bible, not only in the Old Testament, but in the New Testament as well, prayer is largely understood in this way. It is clearly related to religious conceptions which are no longer our own, and firmly rooted in a world view which we no longer hold. The consequences of this affect not only theology, but also belief. We can no longer allow prayer to remain as the last supranatural island in the ocean of reality. We can no longer speak on the one hand of overcoming supranaturalism and of immanent transcendence, and on the other hand still go on expecting direct interventions of God from above. And we cannot on the one hand criticize biblical texts such as the miracle stories, or interpret them existentially, and on the other hand continue uncritically a form of prayer which derives from the assumptions of the same world view. Anyone who still does so, and regards it as real Christian piety, ought to have Friedrich Nietzsche read a lesson on real Christian piety to him!

However small an amount of loving piety we might possess, a God who cured us in time of a cold in the nose, or who arranged for us to enter into a carriage when a cloud burst over our heads, would be such an absurd God that he would have to be abolished even if he existed. God as a domestic servant, as a postman, as a general provider – in short merely as a word for the most foolish kind of accidents ... 'Divine Providence', as it is believed in today by almost every third man in 'cultured Germany', would be an argument against God, in fact it would be the strongest argument against God that could be imagined.[10]

This brings us to the question of the intervention of God in the course of the world, and in particular to *miracles*.

Our third point is that the concept of miracle is not a scientific but a religious category; it does not propose any break in the causal nexus, but shows what love is capable of. Let us demonstrate this theme by looking at what happens when someone is saved from a disaster. A team of specialists, with all the technical data available to them, would be quite capable of reconstructing the way a person was saved second by second and step by step, without any gaps – we mean by without any gaps, without showing that the causal nexus was broken in any way. What combines the many individual technical facts and human activities into a whole, in which meaningless happenings are brought under control and turned into a meaningful event, is the intervention of the rescue team, the power of their love, which sets their reason and their hands in motion. If one of the people saved afterwards described their rescue as a 'miracle' he would be doing so *in statu confessionis*, that is, as a personal testimony of faith in God before other men. But he would be doing so against the outward appearance of the world, that is, against the fact that other unfortunate persons were not rescued, while others who were could not join in his testimony.

But did Jesus himself not say that all the hairs of our head are numbered, and that no sparrow falls to the ground without God's will? A God who counts the hairs on the head of men and lets sparrows fall from the roof on to the street is a mythological conception. But this mythological conception has to be interpreted, because it contains a profound meaning. In this saying Jesus is not trying to give a mathematical proof of the omnipotence of God, but is trying to bring us to trust God's love. He explicitly concludes with the statement: 'Fear not, therefore' (Matt. 10.29f.).

But this brings us to the question: Why should we still pray? What is the meaning of prayer today?

In our fourth consideration, in an attempt to answer this question, we shall once again begin by looking at the New Testament. We saw above that in many parts of the New Testament the statements about the theory and practice of prayer are so linked to contemporary assumptions about religion and about the world that it is no longer possible for us to share them. We must now add that certain passages in the New Testament provide the starting point for a new, more profound and wider understanding of prayer. Here are some examples. In the Sermon on the Mount, a few general instructions from Jesus on the right way to pray precede the Lord's Prayer. The last of these instructions, which leads directly to the text of the Lord's Prayer, reads: 'And in praying do not heap up empty phrases as the Gentiles do; for they think that they will be heard for their many words ... Your father knows what you need before you ask him' (Matt. 6.7 f.). Again, the apostle Paul exhorts the church in Thessalonica: 'Pray constantly' (1 Thess. 5.17). This is in accordance with the introduction to the parable of the importunate widow in the Gospel of Luke: 'He told them a parable, to the effect that they ought always to pray and not lose heart' (18.1).

These examples show that the limits are removed from prayer. First of all, prayer is separated from the cultic context and given a setting in the world. Secondly, it ceases to be something which man does at one particular time, and is made a constant attitude on the part of man. Both these processes take away from prayer any magical character, and make it the expression of man's existence in dialogue.

The basis of prayer as the expression of *man's existence in dialogue* is that God has revealed himself to men in a face to face encounter. Here we must once again recall what we said about the personality of man, and particularly about the way he exists 'in between'. There is a connection between this and the fact that man possesses speech, or indeed that he 'is' speech, he cannot have any personality without words, and therefore his existence 'in between', his direct encounter with his fellow men, must constantly be realized in the form of speech. But then the same is also true of man's relationship to God. If man experiences God as another person in a direct encounter, then all he can do is speak to this other person whom he encounters, and prayer automatically results as a conversation of man with God. The basis of man's existence as dialogue is clearly expressed as early as the Old Testament creation narrative. All other creatures are dismissed to their existence without words, with the mere 'Let there be ...'. Only to man does God begin immediately to speak, addressing him as 'you'. This shows that God sought man as a partner, which in its turn points back to the reason why God created man at all. The traditional dogmatic answer to this question is that God created the world to his glory, and man to be the one who should give him this glory. But does an artist really create his work only for his own glory? Did Beethoven, for example, compose the Ninth Symphony for his glory? Or was he not rather simply bringing to expression what was a living sound within him? The same is true of God. Because God is love, and because love cannot remain alone, but requires a partner, God created man. The glory naturally follows from this, but it is a by-product, not an end in itself.

It is the character of his love which brings God into dialogue with man. The object of the dialogue between God and man is the world. God honours man as his partner, by speaking with him about his creation, and man shows himself worthy of this partnership by listening to what God has to say to him about the world: God speaks, and man answers, and man asks back, and God answers in his turn. We must see Christian prayer within the broad horizon of this existence 'for which we owe a response to someone else', if we are to understand it aright. Perhaps the finest thing that has ever been said about prayer in the sense of man's existence in dialogue, and there as an expression of a continuous human attitude, is found in the words of Schleiermacher in a sermon:

> To be a religious man and to pray are really one and the same thing. To join the thought of God with every thought of importance that occurs to us ... and even in our most mirthful hours to remember His all seeing eye – this is the prayer without ceasing.[11]

Our fifth consideration once again concerns the *prayer of petition*. As surely as prayer is an expression of man's existence in dialogue, petition must form part of it. Otherwise it is not really the dialogue of a *man* with God. For a 'full human life' always includes 'imperfection', that is poverty, need, deficiencies and weakness, with the corresponding longing, desire, wishes and wants. There is a well known biblical truth: 'To give is more blessed than to receive', but sometimes to receive may well be more blessed than to give. Perhaps the test of perfect love is not a readiness to give to others, but the courage to confess to another person what one needs oneself, and to ask him for help, spreading out one's own wishes and desires before him. Where this openness is lacking, a person is still keeping something back to himself and is not giving himself wholly to another.

The same is also true of man's relationship to God, and therefore petition is an essential part of the dialogue with God. Rolf Schäfer is right when he says:

> People may well turn up their noses ..., saying that the prayer of petition is the lowest form of relationship to transcendence, because it is concerned with everyday things. All the same, the life of a thinker devoted to abstractions still contains everyday matters with the cares, desires and wishes that they bring with them, and it is in respect of these that his concept of transcendence has to show whether it extends down to concrete things.[12]

Dorothee Sölle goes even further:

> Poverty and longing form part of prayer ... When Jesus prayed for his life in Gethsemane, and when he prayed in despair on the cross for the presence of him who abandons us, he is a true man through this asking and despair. A prayer which has nothing more to ask may represent a religious ideal, but it is also inhuman, because it is unworldly.[13]

The ultimate intention of the prayer of petition is not to seek help from above by a direct intervention of God, but a longing for the certainty and assurance in which one can tell everything to another person – and behold, it is good. God hears and answers, but he does not work magic. The favourite objection here: 'Nothing is impossible with God' at once provokes the opposite objection: For this reason not everything is possible for God. It is not the will of God but the will of man which is altered in the prayer of petition, so that man submits himself with his wishes to the will of God. But this submission only concerns one's own wishes, not the need of others and the situation that exists in the world. This leads us to our sixth and final consideration.

Let us begin once again with one of Elly Heuss-Knapp's reminiscences of her youth, with which we began our step by step consideration of prayer. We did not tell how that experience concluded, and this we must now do. After Elly Heuss-Knapp has told how the boy said, 'All we can do is pray', she continues, 'After this prayer I realized that we had to take back what we had stolen. None of the boys dared to do so. My sister and I made the difficult journey alone in the darkness. For a long time afterwards I always curtseyed to night watchmen.'

What this continuation of the story reveals is the right relationship between *prayer and action*, between considering a situation in speaking to God and carrying out what we come to realize in this consideration. At the present day the main value is laid on this connection between prayer and action; in all recent consideration of prayer it is this which is emphasized. Contemporary attempts to reinterpret prayer and to make it possible in our own age ultimately share the same aim: prayer is seen as a responsible consideration of the world.

The best example of this is the seven familiar theses put forward by Fulbert Steffensky for the group in Cologne called *Politisches Nachtgebet*. The statements made there include the following:

Prayer prepares man to take over responsibility for his world. Thus it does not replace the activity of man by the activity of God. In prayer man takes on responsibility for the condition of this world ... Prayer makes us conscious of what does not yet exist, but has to be brought about by us ... In petition man takes on the cause of God as his own.[14]

No one can deny that what is said here about prayer is right. Of course prayer as petition for the world is not the unique discovery of the ecumenical working group *Politisches Nachtgebet* in Cologne. Yet we must not ignore the danger of a one-sided presentation. If prayer is directed in a thorough-going way towards political action, there is a risk of its being depersonalized. Where the aim of prayer is political action in such a one-sided sense, so that information and discussion have a dominant role in it, people run the risk of speaking no longer with God, but only to one another.

We do not agree with the criticism made by church authorities that the Cologne group *Politisches Nachtgebet* has fallen victim to this danger. There is still a personal relationship to God, even though it is not always consciously retained. One of the published addresses states explicitly: 'In prayer man expresses himself in the sight of God.'[15] In accordance with this, God is sometimes *addressed* in the various prayers. Nevertheless there is a risk that the one-sided political concern with the world, with the three stages of information, discussion and action, may fall short of prayer as dialogue with God. There is no question that prayer as dialogue with God concerns our whole life, and to this extent one who prays must always have in mind the world with its concrete political and social circumstances. But prayer is not simply a consideration of the world. Of its nature it is a dialogue with God, and only as such is it also a consideration of the world. The attack on a devout quietism which hands over responsibility for the state of the world to God, and which, because it has its hands together and its eyes closed, never gets to grips with anything, is a justified and timely one. But the will to action must never forget the sense in which life is 'beyond our control', the basic experience of all human life which we have called 'existence owed to another', from which alone, in fact, man's existence as dialogue derives and lives. Where the consideration of the world no longer takes place before the sight of God, so that man no longer has anything to ask, the dialogue has turned into a monologue, and prayer has ceased to exist.

Let us sum up what we have said about the personality of God in the form of an image, or more precisely in the form of a change of image. Paul Tillich in his discussion of God undertook a change of spatial conception, talking of 'depth' instead of 'height'. We would like to suggest a change of name, and speak of 'friend' instead of 'father'. The image of God as a father comes from the age of the patriarchal ordering of society, which is now coming to an end, and is no longer very convincing to us who live in a 'fatherless society'. It has no 'social context' in our life, and is therefore open to the suspicion of being imposed by an outside ideology. But perhaps the personality of God may be revealed to us anew if we call God our 'friend'.

We consciously use the word 'friend' and not 'brother', even though many believe that matriarchal and patriarchal society, the 'world of the mother' and the 'world of the father', will now be followed by the 'world of the brother'. To speak of God as 'brother' sounds too free and easy; and if one tries to avoid this free and easy impression by speaking of a 'big brother', the associations are unpleasant. Moreover, at the present day a friend is more important than a brother. That we have a brother is a fact we accept – or do not accept. On the other hand, friendship is something which is aroused and activated and as a personal fellowship. Even a brother only becomes a brother to us when he has become our friend. The bible provides a justification for calling God a friend rather than a father. We are told of Moses that God spoke with him as a man speaks with his friend (Ex. 33.11), and Jesus said to his disciples: 'You are my friends' (John 15.14). The expression 'friend' keeps a balance between closeness and distance, between heteronomy and autonomy, and is like theonomy in this respect.

IO

The Fifth Gospel

A Contribution to a Society whose Goal is Achievement

1. The Crisis of Identity and the Problem of Theodicy

The question which for centuries dominated the system of answers provided by the church and theology was that posed by Luther: How can I get a gracious God? This was not just a personal question asked by a single Augustinian monk who had to endure the inner struggle of his own soul. It was the universal question of an age which as a whole was impelled by fear for the eternal salvation of the soul. At that time, the end of the Middle Ages, 'everyone wanted to go to heaven', as a contemporary chronicler expressed it. What mattered at that time was the justification of man in the sight of God.

Rudolf Stadelmann describes the atmosphere of those times as follows: 'It is indisputable that the mass of those who believed that they had heard the trumpets of the last day has never been so touchingly large at any other time.'[1] No one could say that this was the atmosphere and hope of our own age. When we get up in the morning we do not hear the trumpet of the judgment of God and ask ourselves how we shall endure at the last day. When we get up in the morning all we hear is our alarm clock, and we ask how we are going to get through the next day.

The gospel of the justification of man in the sight of God was once a revolutionary and liberating message for men. At that time it transformed the world, or at least the West. But for most of our contemporaries, and even for many Christians, it has become boring, incomprehensible and meaningless. They no longer see what this message has to do with them, how far it is still relevant to the situation of their own lives, or how it helps them to overcome their conflicts and endure their life in the world. We are not saying that the question of man's justification is concerned with something which is no longer of importance to us. What we are saying is that when it is discussed, the question must be posed in a different way from the end of the Middle Ages, when Martin Luther was alive, and that this change in the question necessarily brings with it a change in the form of the answer.

This is the reason why our generation has to write, with the aid of the four canonical gospels of the New Testament, its own 'fifth gospel', the gospel for its own time. If it did not do so, the gospel would no longer give an answer to the questions of our time. This would mean that it would cease to be the gospel, and would become a religious law which had to be carried out. When we speak of the 'fifth gospel' we do so not because we are interested in being modern at any price, but so that the gospel can remain the gospel at any price.

But what is the question which the gospel has to answer at the present day in order to become the 'fifth gospel', and by this means remain the gospel?

Two attempts to save the gospel for our own age must be excluded, because they do not offer a satisfactory answer to our questions. The first is the attempt to persuade our contemporaries by enticements or threats that the question which still concerns them is, Where can I get a gracious God?, and that their trouble is simply that they will not recognize and realize this. Present-day man will respond to such attempts neither with friendly agreement nor with hostile rejection. His attitude will be simply to show no interest, or at best to be surprised. In short, he will behave as if he was not affected. For the question of the grace of God assumes an unchallenged belief in the existence of God. But the decisive religious characteristic of our times is that the existence of God is doubted and the death of God asserted. Man at the present day suffers not because of sin, but because his existence is meaningless; he is terrified not by the anger but by the absence of God; he does not desire forgiveness, but assurance; and therefore he does not ask for a gracious God, but for a real God.

The other inadequate attempt to write the 'fifth gospel' for

our own time consists of replacing the search for a gracious God
by the search for a gracious neighbour. Contemporary man
takes more notice of this. Every day, on the street, in his family
and in his work, he experiences the fact that he is dependent
upon gracious neighbours. But he does not find the search for a
gracious neighbour to be adequate. For it is his daily experience
not only that some of his neighbours are ungracious, but also
that some circumstances are without grace, and perhaps even
that the whole of existence is without grace. And therefore the
question of the justification of man in the sight of God becomes
for him the question of the justification of God in the sight of
man. To pious ears this sounds monstrous, even blasphemous.
But what use would it be even to rebuke, crush or punish men
because of it? It is the most thoughtful amongst our contemporaries who find the world absurd, and require of God, if they
ask anything of him at all, that he should guarantee the meaning of the world. But he does not find the meaning of the world
is guaranteed by God, and therefore he requires God to justify
himself before him with regard to the absurdity of the world.

Both these attempts to write the 'fifth gospel' for our own age
are inadequate, because neither of the two questions which they
seek to answer – neither the question of the gracious God nor
that of the gracious neighbour – are in themselves sufficient to
give an account of man's situation in our own age. One might
say that the question, Where can I get a gracious God? goes too
far, while the question, Where can I get a gracious neighbour?
does not go far enough.

But both questions agree in their ultimate aim, which is man's
search for a meaning for his activity and life in the world. The
experience of the absence of God, with the transformation of
the search for a gracious God into a search for a real God, points
to this. So, too, does the experience that existence is without
grace – so that the search for a gracious neighbour is turned into
a search for grace in the whole of being. Now the question of
meaning is not posed here, as it tends to be, in abstract and
general terms. It contains within itself two specific individual
questions; in the sphere of the life of the individual, that of
his *crisis of identity*; and in the historical and cosmic sphere,
the *problem of theodicy*. We shall see what these two questions

signify, and the way in which they are related, when we give
them a concrete content.

When man asks the meaning of his activity and his life in
the world, his aim is not a logical system into which he can fit
everything that happens in the world and that happens to him.
The search for meaning comes not so much from his head as
from his heart; it is not so much an intellectual as an existential
question. This is true even of intellectuals in their ivory towers.

What man is asking for when he asks about the meaning of
the world is the *certainty of his own existence*. In every man
there is an elementary longing to be able to trust. But a man
can only trust when the world seems trustworthy to him. And
therefore in the question of the meaning of the world, his desire
for certainty about his own existence is linked with a *longing
for the world to be reliable*. It is already becoming clear how
man's crisis of identity and the problem of theodicy are related.
Both questions, What is it which gives certainty to my life?
and, What is the basis of my trust in the world? are connected
and reinforce each other. It is quite astonishing that in spite of
living his life in a scientific and technological world, man still
poses these questions, because the world of science and
technology affords him an incomparably greater degree of
certainty than earlier ages. It is even more astonishing that it is
the scientific and technical world and the society formed by it
which provokes man's search for certainty about his life and for
reliability in the world. This shows that his search for certainty
in his existence and for reliability in the world is actuated by
more than a mere concern for external security. It comes from
his wish to be able to be himself, from the desire for identity
which is present in every human being.

Man would like to be 'somebody'; he longs to be indispensable
and to be approved. And according to Christian judgment he has
every right to this longing and desire; for he is a creature of
God. The animals, too, are creatures of God, but they have been
left to exist without words, and do not live in an existence which
is a dialogue, but only according to instinct. But Martin Buber
says of man:

Brought out of nature, where he is one of a species, into the adventure
of being a solitary individual, surrounded by the chaos which came into

being with him, he keeps a secret shy watch for the affirmation of his right to exist which can only be given by one human person to another. Men offer one another the heavenly manna of selfhood.[2]

This brings us back to what we described, following Martin Luther, as the *coram* relationship of all human existential life: the life of man face to face with others. We would like to have the 'regard' of our fellow men, we would like to be worth something to them, we would like to be 'somebody' in their eyes. This gives our life a 'forensic' character. Nowadays God's seat of judgment may be empty for us; but instead we live from morning till night, and sometimes even from night till morning, in front of judgment seats on which human beings sit. We find ourselves relying on others' judgments, and long for them to be favourable, and we are afraid that they may convict us. We may overlook, but cannot ignore, our husband or wife; we may keep out of the way of our superior, but cannot get away from him. And this gives us an unending need to achieve.

Whilst we no longer feel that we need to justify ourselves in the sight of God, we feel obliged to justify ourselves in the sight of our fellow men. For no one can live without 'justification'. The 'death of God' has not brought with it the end of the longing to 'be someone' and to 'count for something'. This, too, is a pointer to the 'indestructible character' of the question of God. However much we imagine we can free ourselves from God, we can never get away from him. And as a result we now have to bring about and achieve for ourselves what as creatures of God we would regard as 'vain': reputation, approval, standing and, within all this, our own selves. We now have to 'earn' our life. From now on a person is only worth as much as he achieves, on the principle that you are what you make of yourself. This leads to the cult of success, and there is no limit to our achievements.

But the result of all our achievements is the exact opposite of what we expected from them. Our achievements themselves do not bring us the ultimate approval and understanding we long for, because through these very achievements we have become the replaceable cog in the machine which we were trying to avoid becoming; for every achievement is replaceable. This brings about the failure of our existence as individuals which is usually known at the present day as 'crisis of identity'.

Let us first illustrate what we mean by 'crisis of identity' by means of a simple, everyday experience. When we come home in the evening after a strenuous exhausting day's work, we say involuntarily. 'I never had a moment to myself all day'. In this complaint we express the idea that we have scarcely had any opportunity to be ourselves for the whole day, but have simply had to adopt certain roles. But this personal and individual experience only reflects the total situation of modern techno-logical and rational society, with its requirement to achieve. Its characteristic feature is that in it not only do individuals simply play roles; in any particular role they are also exchange-able.

The image drawn from the ancient world, and used in the New Testament, of the body with its individual limbs, which is meant to show the mutual dependency of one limb upon another, and therefore the importance of every individual limb to the whole, is scarcely comprehensible in our present-day society. It assumes that every individual is irreplaceable – but every day we experience the replaceability of the individual. Anyone may just as well be someone else, and no one is himself.

It is this which lies at the root of the questions asked by contemporary man about his identity, and, in association with his identity, about the meaning of his life. He sees himself simply playing roles. He has to act as husband, wife, mother, father, colleague, superior, employee, householder, member of one sex or another, parishioner, taxpayer, elector, citizen in or out of uniform, warrior for peace, armed or unarmed – and he sees that in all these holes he is exchangeable, so that in reality he does not play any role, but is only a tiny cog in a huge machine. And therefore he asks himself who he really is.

This experience of a loss of identity is increased by the anonymity of life in modern society. This anonymity is not necessarily an evil in itself, and in fact provides a certain pro-tection for the individual. He does not have to enter into an I-thou relationship, in the whole profundity of existence as dialogue in Martin Buber's sense, with every ticket-collector or postman. These are functional relationships in which each plays his own part, without reducing the other to the level of an object, but at the same time without experiencing him as another individual. But the other side of this anonymity is the constant threat of a loss of identity. In this anonymous world, man increasingly has to ask himself what role he plays in it, whether he has any role in it at all; and once again, he asks who he really is.

He is back where he began, and at once has to begin again. Once again he is overcome with fear at the meaninglessness of existence; once again he asks whether his life contains any certainty and whether the world can be trusted; once again, he tries to create this certainty and reliability through his own achievements.

To use an old-fashioned theological concept, we can call this 'the righteousness of works' on the part of man. It is the mistake of trying to earn life, which is beyond our control, through our own achievements, instead of receiving it as a gift. The theological concept may be out of date, but what it signifies has remained. It is just that in our modern society, based on techno-logical and rational achievement, it does not have the same appearance as in the world of religious achievement in biblical times, or in the time of Martin Luther. But we always have to expound the message of the bible in such a way that it becomes an answer to the questions of our own time.

2. *Prometheus, Sisyphus and Jesus*

The symbolic figure of the beginning of the modern age, of its first great upsurge and constant driving emotion, is Prometheus, who according to the ancient myth made men and brought them fire from heaven. He represents the decisive change which has taken place in the modern age – man has now replaced God. This brought with it a new image of man: *an ideal* of man, the ideal of the autonomous personality. In his poem 'Prometheus' the young Goethe expressed it in terms of complete maturity:

Did you not bring everything to perfection yourself, O holy, burning heart? Should I honour you? Why? ... Here I sit, and form men accord-ing to my own image, a race that is like me ...

This 'Promethean defiance' sounds hollow and antiquated to us today. Present-day man no longer thinks of trying to equal God. How can he want to be like someone in whom he no longer believes, who no longer exists for him? For Prometheus God still existed; there was still a higher world above this lower world, the world of ideals, of the true, the good and the beautiful – and belief in it was the underlying assumption of his crime. But what still existed for Prometheus, and against which, therefore, he could still offend, has passed away for twentieth century man, and has become meaningless. The typical figure of our own age is no longer Prometheus, but Sisyphus, as Albert Camus describes him to us in his essays *The Myth of Sisyphus.*

The ancient myth tells of Sisyphus that because he had offended, the gods condemned him to roll a rock unceasingly up a mountain. But as soon as the stone had reached the top, it rolled back down again of its own accord, and Sisyphus had to go after it to roll it back up again – and this went on endlessly.

Sisyphus, who denies the gods, but always takes hold of the stone again, is the figure who symbolizes the final condition of the modern age. In him, the exceptional has become normal, what was proper to a high holiday has become an everyday event, the ideals have grown faded or have turned into daily duties. Sisyphus does not strive, as Prometheus once did, for the 'ideal', but exists in the 'climate of absurdity'. The world is opaque to him. He has no hope, and scarcely even manages longing; he is quite on his own. For him destiny is a human affair, which must be regulated by men. When we think of Prometheus we think involuntarily of high rocky cliffs, but with Sisyphus we think of broad open deserts, even though he has to go up the mountain. But although Sisyphus has to go up the mountain, he never thinks of perfection, and does not ask what the ultimate meaning is. Instead, he asks whether life has any meaning at all, whether it is worth it. His problem is suicide: to accept or reject, to flee or to endure – this is the question for Sisyphus. And Sisyphus accepts and endures – unreconciled, but voluntarily. Prometheus sometimes boasted and bragged, but Sisyphus keeps quiet. Prometheus may have been on a grander scale, but Sisyphus is more solid. He looks the absurd straight in the eye. He no longer has great enthusiasm for freedom, but feels himself condemned to freedom. But every morning, as long as he survives, he puts his shoulder once again to his stone and rolls it.

Some may object that we have run Sisyphus down too much, and described him in too dismal terms. Are not the great symbols of progress in our time, the scientists, inventors, engineers and explorers, more like Prometheus? No, even though they climb into heaven, bring down fire and even plan to make men, they are not like Prometheus. They are not idealists who look into the heights, but technicians who are doing their duty. Idealism would only put them off, like the 'contamination effect' in a chemical experiment. It would divert them from their course and unnecessarily endanger their lives. They do not look up, but forward, and every step they take is carefully calculated in advance, worked out by the computer and tested in the simulator. They do not go beyond their own limits, but they fill up the limited space with their works.

Even Camus runs the risk of idealizing Sisyphus and turning him in the end to Prometheus. He concludes his essay on Sisyphus with the emphatic words: 'The struggle itself towards the heights is enough to fill a man's heart. One must imagine Sisyphus happy.'[3] I am convinced that our contemporaries are better than some moralizing preachers in the church and in the world usually portray them in their sermons, repentance-day messages, appeals and campaigns. They display a great seriousness, a strict discipline, a sharp vigilance and a high level of responsibility – but I do not believe that they are happy. Sisyphus is serious, bold and faithful, but he has no happiness and no joy. The most he has is distractions.

Where is the critical moment in the life of Sisyphus? As long as he is rolling the stone up the mountain, everything seems to be well. Then Sisyphus is doing something, and while he is doing something, there are even moments in which he can be happy. The critical moment in the life of Sisyphus comes when he is standing on the mountain top, looking at the stone rolling back down, and wondering whether he should go after it. What motivates Sisyphus at this moment to climb back down the mountain, take hold of the stone again and roll it back up the mountain? It is at this point that he is faced by the question of certainty in life and reliability in the world, the combined problem of identity and theodicy. The question is, how Sisyphus, the man of modern society, based on technological and rational achievement, can learn to trust.

Eduard Spranger has spoken of the 'silent assumptions' on which modern man, apparently godless, bases his life. Amongst these assumptions he includes the 'unconscious trust' on the basis of which everyone acts. In fact, when one thinks how people go faithfully to work morning after morning, how after two world wars they have built up again what has been destroyed, within a generation, and almost without question, how in Vietnam and Cambodia they immediately cultivate their devastated fields, and how with total commitment they carry out great achievements and create 'immortal works', although they know that the end of them will be death and destruction – in the face of all this, one may ask what really impels men to this kind of action, and whether it does not express a trust which they are not even conscious of, let alone aware of its origin.

It is therefore the task of Christian preaching, he holds, to start from this unconscious trust, and to make it conscious, by showing that its true basis is God, and in this way to confirm and strengthen it. It certainly provides an important point of contact for Christian preaching. But is this not too optimistic a view of our present religious situation? At the present day we encounter to an increasing degree people who remain consciously aware of the absurdity of the world, and yet do not flee from it, but accept and endure life, honestly, bravely and faithfully – and in the very face of death they show dignity, and even graciousness. Yet they do all this without any belief in God, and even without any trust. Paul Tillich is probably right when he describes stoicism as 'the only real alternative to Christianity'.[4] We are faced here with an alternative: renunciation or redemption. Renunciation is a moral achievement on the part of man, but redemption is an action which I am not able to carry out myself, but which comes to me from someone else. But what we need is not morality but love.

But in *The Myth of Sisyphus* Camus writes: 'If a man realized that the universe like him can love and suffer, he would be reconciled.'[5] This is a very acute perception; it is like the oracle of a prophet who has no faith himself. It contains a hidden accusation and a secret longing.

Camus' hidden *accusation* is based on the pain which we encounter in all religions, from the ancient world to the present day, and which can be uttered either in secret lamentation or in open defiance. It is the suffering of man at the thought of the God or gods who enjoy their eternal blessedness in heaven and exercise their power upon earth, while men endure their sorrow and burdens. The most compelling expressions of this pain at the infinite distance between the gods who dwell in everlasting peace and men, who are cast into history, is found in Hölderlin's poem 'Hyperion's Song of Destiny':

You walk above in the light,
On soft smooth ground, O blessed spirits!
. . . .
But our fate is
To have no resting place,
Away they vanish, down they fall,
Men in their suffering
Blindly from every
Hour to another,
Cast down from rock
To rock like a waterfall,
Down the years into uncertainty.

The secret *longing* contained in the sentence from Camus quoted above is for men's suffering at the knowledge that their gods do not suffer to be alleviated, for the silent apathy of the universe to be overcome, for men to be reconciled through love – but not through a love which simply remains suspended in heaven as an eternal idea or broods over the waters like a spirit, but by a love which becomes a reality here upon earth and is involved in history, which suffers with men and shares their fate. This offers a possibility of help for Sisyphus.

For Camus the condition for this remains unfulfilled, and it becomes an accusation and a longing. But Christian faith believes in it as a reality. For the truth of this reality, it points to a concrete history and person, to the life of Jesus of Nazareth.

By contrast to Prometheus and Sisyphus, Jesus of Nazareth is not a mythological figure who has become a symbol, but a real historical person, who lived through and suffered the whole fate of a human being in this world. In this concrete historical life, faith encounters the truth of God. In what Jesus of Nazareth did and what happened to him, we can perceive who God is for us and what he is like. What present-day man demands of God, in such an apparently blasphemous way, actually happened here: God himself went into the witness box and justified himself before men. The life history of Jesus of Nazareth is the justification of God before men, in the face of the absurdity of

the world. Love and suffering – what Camus demanded of the
universe, in order for man to be reconciled – happened here:
the God of the Christians has suffered with men. Thus God
himself has solved the problem of theodicy.

Does man from now on possess certainty about the meaning
of his life and the world? Clearly not in the same way as he is
certain of facts, dates and things, as about a motor, a date or
number in history, or a chemical compound; nor in such a way
that he now has at his disposal a logical system in which he
can co-ordinate in a meaningful fashion everything that happens
in the world and which he himself experiences. The age of
great logical systems has gone for ever with Prometheus. Universal knowledge of this kind is denied to man, nor would it
give him the certainty which he demands. Contemporary man
does not want universality, but longs for solidarity. The answer
to this question about the meaning of the world is given not by
knowledge, but by trust. But trust comes only from love. And
it is this which man experiences in the life of Jesus of Nazareth:
that the ultimate ground and meaning of all being is love. This
is his security within the meaninglessness of the world. In no
other way can he find any meaning in life or any meaning in the
world.

But when Camus asked me why God 'permits all this', why
God permits children in this world to be tortured, to suffer and
to die, I had no answer for him, or at least not the answer he
expected from me, nor did I know whether this answer would
be of any real use to either of us. I could only bear witness
to the view that even these children are in the hands of God,
and that he himself stands by them in their suffering. And when
Camus then asked me how I knew this, and what right I had to
claim such knowledge, I could only point to Jesus of Nazareth.
For me, Jesus of Nazareth illuminates the meaning of the world,
not by teaching me about the world – which is the job of science
– but by giving me trust in the ground of the world, either as
the 'theists' express this trust, by addressing 'our Father in
heaven', or as the a-theists express it, with the affirmation that
the ground of being is gracious. And Jesus of Nazareth tells
me to do something else: to share in the concern that fewer
children should be tortured, suffer and die in this world.

Our Father in heaven, gracious being – no statement gets us

beyond this. One person may offer prayers to this being with fear and trembling, and another may weave a great theological system from it; it may bring the smile of the saved to the face of one and simply prevent another from going away and blowing his brains out – there is not really a great deal of difference. The act of redemption comes from God, but the degree of the consciousness of redemption is a matter of human temperament and the age in which a person lives. Even the Holy Spirit will not make someone suffering from melancholia into the soul of happiness; all he can do is keep him alive in spite of his melancholy.

The toil does not cease for Sisyphus. He must still go on rolling the rock. But sometimes, when he is rolling the rock up the mountain or following it as it rolls back down, he can now open his mouth, which in his independent fashion he has kept shut, and utter the word 'God'. Perhaps it is only a sigh, spoken under his breath. But the man who says 'God', or even only sighs it from his heart, has ceased to be Sisyphus.

3. The Priority of Receiving over Action

During his imprisonment Dietrich Bonhoeffer composed a poem entitled 'Who am I?'[6] This title expresses what we call, following current usage, the 'crisis of identity'. That there is a close connection between this question and the 'problem of theodicy' is shown by the fact that this poem was written in a cell in a Gestapo prison at a time when the will of God in history seemed even more deeply hidden than ever. Certainty in existence and reliability in the world were both at stake.

In this poem Bonhoeffer begins by looking at others and asks what they tell him about who he is. To them he seems calm, cheerful and firm, like a squire in his country house; free, friendly and clear, as though it were his to command, and not up to his warders; equable, smiling and proud, like one accustomed to win. If one were to sum up the impression he makes upon others in a single phrase, one could say that he has their 'regard'.

But then Bonhoeffer looks at himself, and what he sees is the exact opposite; he is not calm, cheerful and firm, like a squire in his country house, but restless and longing and sick, like a

What Kind of God?

bird in a cage; not free and friendly and clear as though it were
his to command, but trembling with anger at other people's
wilfulness and wounding actions; not equable, smiling and
proud, like one accustomed to win, but struggling for breath,
thirsting for words of kindness, for neighbourliness, or else
trembling for friends, weary and empty at praying, at thinking,
at making faint, and ready to say farewell to it all. If one were
to sum up Bonhoeffer's view of himself in a phrase, it would be
that he is 'poorly regarded'.

One image contradicts the other – which of the two is the
right one?

Bonhoeffer once again places the two images side by side, and
asks which of the two he really is. Is he one or the other, or one
person today and tomorrow another, or both at once, and therefore a hypocrite before others and a weakling before himself?
But the comparison does not lead to any 'identification'. The
answer to man's question about his identity is only possible in
one way. Bonhoeffer gives it in a single line at the end of a
whole poem: 'Whoever I am, thou knowest, O God, I am thine.'

What takes place here at the end of the poem, in its last line,
is a surrender, not as the expression of ultimate resignation,
but as an act of total trust. Man surrenders the judgment about
who he is to God – and it is this which identifies him as the
person he is: one who is created, one who receives. But this is
his security within the world. Thus we do not succeed in becoming ourselves by realizing ourselves in our acts and successes, so
obtaining the 'regard' of our fellow men, but by receiving ourselves as creatures from the hand of God, and then, regardless
of the regard we obtain, doing for our fellow men what they
need. Certainty about our own existence is not based on achievement, but on trust. But trust is only aroused in us through love.

Let us once again illustrate this connection between identity,
love and trust by means of a human relationship, the love between two persons. True love is not shown by one person's trying
to assimilate the other to himself, but by each achieving his own
identity through mutual love, in a kind of echoing process. It
is not an achievement with which each has to present the other,
saying as it were, 'Look, this is what I am!' It is a gift in which
each receives himself from the other, 'Look, this is what I can
be like!' But there is no way in which I can obtain the other's

love; he must give it to me of his own free will. However much we strive and however much we do – courting, writing letters, sending flowers, telephoning, asking, begging, humbling ourselves – nothing is any use. Either the other person loves us, regardless of anything we do about it – or not, regardless of any thing we do about it. If the trust between two people depends only upon what the other has done to deserve it, then neither are escaping from the situation of mistrust.

But human love is only a parable and reflection of divine love. And thus the simple answer which Ernst Fuchs gives to the difficult question of how one comes to believe in God, is as follows:

> First you must live! And in your life you must take notice of the experiences which love brings you...; not the unhappy experiences, not those you find in novels, but the fortunate experiences. You must not observe human failure, but, in a word, the history of love itself ... This is the thing: love guarantees itself. Anyone who experiences this is a believer ... Now replace the word love by the word God. One instantly realizes that belief in God is the most natural thing in the world. And to a practical understanding it is immediately comprehensible.[7]

In Descartes, man's assurance of his own identity is given in the saying *Cogito ergo sum*: I think, therefore I am. We expressed this view of man's identity in even more radical terms above, in the words: *Interrogo ergo sum*: I ask, therefore I am. Now we have established the principle: *Amor ergo sum*: I am loved, therefore I am. Whoever understands this, has at a stroke understood the heart of the gospel and the true art of life. This is what we have already termed 'existence owed to another'.

If the certainty of our existence and reliability in the world is not based on our achievements, but on trust, and if trust comes only from love, then in theological terms this signifies the *priority of the gospel over the law*, and in practical terms the *priority of receiving over action*.

But this order of things is in flat contradiction to the prevailing view of life at the present day, not only our own personal attitude to life and the law of a society based on achievement, but also, to a large extent, to the attitude of the church. Because we live at the present day in a world in which it seems that everything 'can be done', we forget what first makes it possible for us to do anything. We are therefore misled into giving action priority over receiving. But the most decisive contribution that the church can make to present-day society, based as it is on achievement, is to remind it of the priority of receiving over action as the basic law of all human life. The first question which is usually asked at the present day is: 'What shall we do?' But this habitual question, 'What shall we do?' must be answered by another and less usual question: 'Where do we receive something from?' Once again we must learn to recognize that we cannot do or achieve anything until we have received something. But this has consequences for our life in society – and for the church.

If it is true that receiving has priority over action, then the rhythm of 'withdrawal and return' must be established in the course of our life, and there must be times in our lives in which we withdraw from distraction into recollection, and become individuals in the purely spatial sense as well. Thus opportunities for retreat and seclusion seem to us to be one of the most urgent requirements of our modern achievement-based society. But these periods of 'withdrawal' must serve not merely as a preparation for 'return', but must also have a meaning in themselves, just as surely as the meaning of human life is not exhausted in action alone.

This brings us to an important aspect of the church's contribution to a society based on achievement. Instead of simply playing its own part in keeping men constantly active and on the alert, the church should rather make it possible for them to stop and rest, and pause to take breath. In this respect theologians sometimes seem to estimate the needs of the age differently from those of their contemporaries who live daily under the pressure of society's urge to achieve. To his own understandable surprise, a student chaplain had the greatest success of the term amongst his students not with a social and political campaign, but with a simple meditation on the biblical phrase, 'Rest a while'. In the same way, a busy architect, heavily involved in modern society's urge to achieve, made the following suggestion to his parish minister in a letter:

Ministers, who concern themselves so much nowadays with parish administration, must concern themselves with the open spaces in the church. They ought to provide open spaces for meditation in services. Such a change of thought is not easy for us today. But there is something particularly humane about it … Perhaps ministers would have time for quiet and reflection, and reduce the danger of heart attacks. This is not a plea for inactivity. On the contrary, I believe that our activities would be better if they were prepared in more peace and quiet. Our life is pre-programmed, on working days by the compulsions of everyday life, and on Sunday morning by the compulsions of worship. Perhaps we would live in better control of our lives if we found the opportunity on Sunday mornings to think over the programme for our lives.

The prevailing tendency in the church, it must be admitted, seems to be pointing in exactly the opposite direction. Pursued by the fear that it is declining, Christianity at the present day is to an increasing extent threatening to become a single vast human endeavour, and the church a stereotype of modern society's devotion to achievement. In this respect there is an unintentional alliance between the radical 'right' and the radical 'left' in the church; Walter Künneth and Dorothee Sölle are in unconscious agreement here. That is, both sides are reducing the gospel to the law, and giving action precedence over receiving.

The 'right' wing' *makes* faith a human endeavour and achievement. The principal danger which threatens Christian faith at the present day seems to us to lie here. It is not that we can no longer believe in certain specific things in the same way as our fathers: the virgin birth, the empty tomb, Christ's descent into hell and ascent into heaven. Nor is it simply that it is difficult for us to maintain any belief in God at all when faced with the absurdity of the world. The danger is that we should make faith a human endeavour and achievement, regardless of whether it is our understanding or our will which is required to carry out this endeavour and achievement. But this is a flat contradiction to everything which the bible calls 'faith'. The result would be 'another gospel', or more properly, no longer the gospel.

Whether it suits these orthodox believers or not, Christian truth has a *goal*, and its goal is *man*. God made this plain once for all when he became man. Where the truth has no longer man in mind, there is an unhealthy perversion. The truth no longer exists for man, but man now has to exist for the truth; and the truth then becomes cruel and lights the fire at the stake. Truth for truth's sake is as terrible as justice for justice's sake. Only where truth walks with love does it bring life and freedom;

truth without love is like the law, it kills.

The radical left wing, on the other hand, makes *love* a human achievement and endeavour. Even where it speaks of the love of God, it usually does so in the sense of a human act: that man should love his fellow men. There is an almost total disregard of the 'passive' element in Christian love, the way in which it is an experience which is received: that man knows that he is loved and therefore protected by God. In the bible love is a reciprocal movement which cannot be divided into an active and passive aspect, into act and experience. But this division takes place when love is demanded in a one-sided way as a human achievement. The consequence is a strenuous moralism, not the Philistine moralism of petit-bourgeois Christianity, which was chiefly interested in the seventh commandment, but a lofty social moralism. But it is still a moralism, which ceaselessly compels man to action by issuing challenges, appeals and political programmes. In this way God falls under the suspicion of being no more than an ethical projection.

Basically, this is no more than a new kind of 'righteousness of works', except that the righteousness which is sought for is no longer in heaven, but on earth. As in the case of every moralism, the result is a profound melancholy. The assertion that Christ is closer to the hippies than to the provos[8] may be an exaggeration, but it makes a fair point, as surely as for the Christian faith the gospel has priority over the law, and, accordingly, receiving has priority over action. When the gospel is perverted into the law, Christianity drops back on to a lower level of religion. Something breathless, strained, fearful and hectic is introduced into Christianity, and this is the characteristic of all 'religion' in the world.

The ancient Christian images of 'heaven' and 'hell' have taken on a new significance in our own age. Hell is anywhere on earth where people think their life has to be earned, where people try to realize themselves in their own achievements and successes, where they put up a fence round what is their own, grudging life to others and disputing with them the living space which they have in common. But heaven is everywhere on earth where people receive life as a gift, where they thankfully receive their own existence and everything that belongs to it, when they live with open hearts, and where as a consequence they are open to others and give them with all their hearts what they themselves have only received as a gift.

The church should be on earth in the place where heaven is, and should play its part in seeing that there is more heaven on earth.

I I

Against the False Alternatives

1. Political Theology

In the hall of the old grammar school which I attended, the two end walls were each hung with a large painting by Anton von Werner. On the wall that you faced hung a scene from the wars of liberation of 1813-15: men, women and children were bringing their gifts, precious objects, silver plate, jewellery and money, to sacrifice on the altar of the fatherland; and beneath was a quotation from Schiller: 'Unworthy is the nation which does not joyfully stake its all on its honour.' The picture at the back of the hall showed Martin Luther at the Diet of Worms in front of the Emperor and the estates of the Empire, one hand laid as prescribed on his heart, and the other pointing to his writings; and beneath was the well known saying: 'Here I stand, I can no other, God help me. Amen.'

Every Monday morning we looked at these two pictures during the obligatory school service, and what was said to us in these services agreed with what the pictures showed. It was either 'inward', and consisted of the proclamation of the 'eternal', and sometimes only of the good, true and beautiful, with a corresponding exhortation to faith, love and hope, concluding with the promise of our own immortality; or else it was 'outward', and consisted of praise of the fatherland and the nation, and sometimes also of culture, with a corresponding appeal to obedience, loyalty, discipline and bravery, concluding with the assurance that it was sweet and honourable to die for one's country. There was virtually no connection between the 'inward' and the 'outward'. But whenever any connection was made between the two, the form it usually took was that the inward aspect provided the power for the outward, for proving oneself in one's life and calling, in the field of the nation and of culture. Thus the standard was provided by the outward aspect. The reverse relationship, where the inward aspect posed critical questions about the outward, was scarcely ever mentioned.

What was shown and proclaimed in that school hall at services was nothing exceptional, but was representative of the attitude not only of the greater part of German Protestantism, but of almost all Christian churches in the world. The concern was for man's eternal salvation, and his earthly well-being was forgotten; the emphasis was on the individual, and social relationships were forgotten; the gaze was fixed on heaven above, and the earth was overlooked. Individualization and spiritualization were the two great dangers which have constantly haunted Christian preaching in the modern age. The charge which Martin Buber made against the churches, in a personal conversation, as his main objection against Christianity, was at that time an accurate one: 'I refuse to go around with a redeemed soul in an unredeemed world.'[1]

The consequence of this 'a-political' attitude of the church was that with no more than a handful of exceptions it stood on the side of political conservatism. Just as the Church of England was once said to be the Conservative Party at prayer, so one could have said the same of the established Protestant churches in Germany, and not only of them, but equally of Methodists, Baptists and Catholics. Most ministers and their families voted solidly for one of the German nationalist parties. It may have been a rationalist slogan, that the church blessed guns; but certainly, when war broke out, governments could rely on the loyalty of the churches. The state rewarded the loyalty of the churches with appropriate privileges, which went far beyond that of the undisturbed practice of Christian worship and amounted to unequivocal encouragement.

Thus the church was one of the 'retaining forces' in society; it gazed at the incorrigibility of the world and contented itself with maintaining the world as far as possible in its political and social *status quo*. But those who were not prepared to rest content with the world as it was, but sought to change and improve it, so that men had a little more scope for their lives, were left abandoned by the church, and their efforts to better the lot of mankind were suspected as idealism, a naïve belief in progress, and an attempt on man's part to redeem himself. And when, instead of the church, other forces and groups tried to alter and improve social circumstances, churchmen complained at these groups trying to do under the red flag what churchmen in their black or violet robes had omitted.

It is true that all the great acts of liberation of the modern age, all important changes in society in the direction of greater justice – the liberation of slaves in the eighteenth century, the abolition of serfdom in the nineteenth century, the partial solution of social problems and the partial emancipation of women in the twentieth century – took place with the active participation and even sometimes under the leadership of individual Christians. But to be honest we have to admit that they were carried out without the active participation of the churches, and often even against their express wish, although all these cases were clearly matters of putting the gospel into execution.

It is this situation which gives rise to the strange dialectic which is characteristic of the present-day relationship between the church and society. Society at the present day confronts the church in an almost hostile way with consequences and demands which can ultimately be derived from the Christian gospel, but which the church itself has omitted to derive from it. And this confrontation between the church and society is largely conducted by Christians.

At the Church Assembly in 1969 in Stuttgart a group of young people walked round the Neckar Stadium during the final assembly with a placard which read: 'The dispute about Jesus is a dispute about nothing'. Many Christians were disturbed and disgusted by this; they regarded it as an anti-christian demonstration. But in fact the young people with their placard were not demonstrating against Jesus, but only against a dispute about Jesus which was concerned with matters which they could no longer see had any relevance for us at the present day. They felt that mankind was in a situation in which such questions as the virgin birth or the divine sonship of Jesus, and perhaps even the whole of traditional christology, no longer had any meaning. What they found missing in this kind of christology was a *Sitz im Leben*, a context in present-day life. And what they demanded of christology was that it should be realized in an up to date and concrete way, and moreover not so much in the sphere of private existential life as in the field of society and politics.

They were protesting at one and the same time against the traditional division between the kingdom of God and the kingdom of the world, and therefore between 'inward' and 'outward', between eternal salvation and earthly well-being, between divine and human justice, between the private morality of the Christian and official civil morality. Instead of widening the duality evident here into a hopeless abyss by continuing to divide reality, in a non-Christian way, into two separate spheres, they were striving for an integration of the two by anticipating the future in the form of more or less real Utopias.

This historical aim puts the place and task of the church in a new light. The church no longer possesses an independent status, but is in the midst of society, as a part of it, drawn into its conflicts and to a great extent determined by its social structure. Its principal task is to be the driving force in the development of the world, for which so many long and struggle, towards a *single* humanity. For the church this is a challenge to make a serious attempt at last to apply the commandments and promises of the bible not merely to the private life of individuals, but also to the public life of society.

This new definition of the church's place in society requires that it should be present, but not represented. The church which acts through official church representatives is concerned with its identity. It therefore seeks to distinguish itself from the world around it by outward signs, but by these very signs it accommodates itself to the world around it. But the church which is present is not interested in its identity. It fits 'selflessly' into the world, and by this very solidarity hints that it has a different and a new message to bring. In short, the church acting through its representatives bears the cross on its breast, where it can be seen; but the church which is present bears the cross on its back, where it is invisible. The age of the church with its representative figures and offices is coming to an end at the present day, with the age of figureheads, parades and uniformed chauffeurs.

What the young people at the Stuttgart Church Assembly were expressing in an emotional rather than a rational way is in close accord with the new theological thinking which has been taking place at least since the second world war, and not only in Germany or within Protestantism, but within Christianity everywhere. One might describe it as a thinking through of the gospel in two directions: outwards into the world and on into the future. In both cases this has meant a rediscovery of the *social and political dimension* of Christian faith, and this has led to the rise of the *political theology*, which causes so much excitement among Christians and non-Christians.

In conscious opposition to the 'existential theology' which has been for so long dominant, the new political theology is concerned to take Christian thought and action out of the sphere of the purely private life of the individual. Behind it lies the realization that we are never concerned merely with the private life of the individual. The individual's private life, because it is located and rooted in the world, is already a 'political theme' in itself.

The life of the individual is always powerfully influenced and determined by a whole network of conditions, circumstances, demands and situations, and again by institutions, authorities, groups, associations and forces, which regulate, guide, change or preserve these conditions, circumstances, demands and situations. In short, the individual always lives in a particular political and social structure. This has always been so – the mediaeval *ordo* was a political and social structure. But today these structures have gained in power and influence; their network has a finer mesh and the relationship of men to them has also changed.

Science and technology have increased to an almost unlimited extent the purely physical power which man exercises, and have therefore given political and social structures immense possibilities of both good and evil. Just as in history the controlling of a demand on a lower level has always led at once to a new demand on a higher level, so the technological revolution, by bursting asunder the previous political, social and legal organizational forms, has thrown up a mass of new problems, especially in the field of social policy. It has created a new kind of totalitarianism, from which there no longer seems to be any way to set man free, and from which perhaps he no longer even wishes to be set free. But at the same time the growth of democracy has given us an ability to play a part in determining these structures, and a share in responsibility for them. This situation can no longer be tackled by the application of the reason to purely technical problems of means, or by mere scientific knowledge.

In association with this social and political development, and in part under pressure from it, theology has achieved a new and more profound insight into the *relation of Christian faith to the world*. The rediscovery of the Old Testament and of primitive Christian eschatology have played a major part in this. Not until our own time has theology begun to draw consequences in terms of political theology from Jesus's proclamation of the kingdom of God, or from his resurrection. At the same time the Old Testament has taken on an importance in the church and in theology which is perhaps greater than ever before in its history. Sometimes one almost has the impression that the Old Testament is no longer interpreted by the New Testament at the present day, but that instead the New Testament is interpreted by means of the Old. But together primitive Christian eschatology and the Old Testament have given Christian faith a powerful thrust in the direction of history, and therefore in the direction of this world and of the future.

The goal of divine action is the *world*, not the individual, far less the church. Characteristically, the last book of the bible, the Revelation of John, shows the fulfilment of all history not in the image of a temple – it states explicitly of the temple that it will no longer exist – but in the form of a *polis*, a political community. This image is intended to show that the aim of the redemption which God has brought about in Jesus Christ is not merely the redemption of the individual, but the salvation of the whole world. And therefore the church has failed to convey the whole message of the gospel as long as it only proclaims the personal salvation of the individual, and gives him private and individual help. The proclamation of the gospel must also be extended to political and social structures. The church has its part to play in seeing that these structures are as just as possible, and that they are maintained if they are of use, healed when they are ailing, and changed when they are unjust.

This is the reason why at the present day so many Christians in all churches and denominations are no longer concerned with the 'salvation of the soul', but principally with the 'well-being of the world', and why they therefore constantly 'interfere in politics'. For them Christian faith has something to do with every kind of conflict in the world: with the confrontation between East and West, with the economic gradient between northern and southern Europe, with the hostility between races and nations, with the contrast between industrialized and developing countries, with the mistrust between Germany and Poland, with the gap between science and morality, with Biafra, Greece, Vietnam and South America. For them faith, hope and love always include social commitment and political action.

Hand in hand with the working out of the gospel in the world goes the transformation of the consciousness of Christianity in the direction of the future; this is only the other side of the same coin. In theological studies, and particularly in ecumenical documents, one constantly comes across the same words and concepts: movement, change, development, renewal, transformation, dynamic, radical change, exodus, revolution. All these concepts are similar in their nature and associations. They all refer to a movement, and this movement is forward, in the direction of the future. In this way the vocabulary which theologians prefer betrays the position of the new political theology, or, more properly, not its position but the direction in which it is moving, its impetus.

Accordingly, the Christian virtues today are: protest, scepticism, criticism, imagination, responsibility, objective knowledge, bold assertiveness of civil rights, disobedience, mobility. Taken together, they supply the characteristics of an 'ethic of transformation', instead of the 'ethic of order' which has prevailed hitherto. This new ethic is the expression of a Christianity which no longer wishes, like the churches in the past, to belong to the 'pillars of society', the 'retaining forces' in the world, but which wishes to play its part in overcoming the political and social *status quo*, and which therefore no longer adopts a largely contemplative attitude, but exercises itself in action.

If we look for the aim underlying this new twofold working out of the gospel, in the direction of the world and in the direction of the future, we can find it in the concept of *justice*. Justice comes before mercy, declared the World Council of Churches at Uppsala (1968) and the Church Assembly in Stuttgart accepted this watchword. Through its relationship to justice, Christian love is spurred on to social criticism. It is no longer merely a 'quickening force' which assures Christians that they have fulfilled the commandment of God even in worldly ordinances, and can therefore have a good conscience. It now becomes a 'critical force', which impels Christians to recognize, in the light of the coming kingdom of God, that existing ordinances and circumstances are open to question, and urges them even now to change the present situation.

The quickening power of love means that it obliges the executioner to cut off his neighbour's head well and accurately, and to have a good conscience about it; the critical power of love means that it questions capital punishment altogether. The quickening power of love means that it encourages soldiers to fight bravely and valiantly in war; the critical power of love means that it does away with war altogether as a political instrument. The quickening power of love means that it exhorts businessmen to be honest; the critical power of love means that under certain circumstances it helps to change the whole of an unjust economic system. The quickening power of love means that it makes people conscious that they belong to their own nation; the critical power of love means that in our fast changing society it looks for forms of political organization different from those of the past age of nationalism. In short, the quickening power of love is largely concerned with the person, spurring him on to his task and giving him a clear conscience; the critical power of love is principally aimed at structures, brings them into question and demands that they be changed and healed.

The power of Christian faith for social criticism brought into play by the connection between justice and love reaches its highest point in the idea of *revolution*. And Protestant theology today, by contrast with the tradition, particularly the Lutheran tradition, which has hitherto been dominant in it, regards even revolution as a possible conception in social ethics.

Looking at the matter as a whole, one might say that the concept of revolution as it is used in theology at present is extraordinarily vague and diffuse. Under the influence of the flexible use of the word in English, 'revolution' is used to refer to every change in the *status quo* and every renewal of what already exists, from the reform of worship and the search for a new style of Christian life, through protests against racial discrimination and social injustice to the most violent political and social upheavals.

The hard core of this new revolutionary thought is the admission that, if necessary, unjust social and political situations should be altered by the use of force. There are different views, however, about which means are permitted to Christians and which are not. They range from the use of a kind of force which is still almost non-violence, through the suggestion of putting pressure on the principal organs of authority, to a willingness to take up a machine gun, plant bombs and exercise terror by torture.

All this is backed by the name of Jesus of Nazareth. But the name of Jesus can only give the impulse and the motivation to revolutionary action. The content and the aim of the revolution are derived from elsewhere, and the source once again can range from Ernst Bloch, through Herbert Marcuse and Fidel Castro to Mao Tse-tung. The radical representatives of a 'theology of revolution', however, are clearly looking for an alliance between Christianity and Marxism. For them revolution is not one problem which must be evaluated theologically amongst others, but is the principle and content of their whole theology.

But the final outcome of this development is the same as in the hall of the old grammar school; Christianity is once again used only as a source of 'inward' power, in order to help to bring about the political aims and purposes which one derives from 'outside'. Whereas in the past they were largely conservative aims and purposes, at the present day they are mainly forces working for social progress or revolution. But the danger is of transforming political theology into a theology which is nothing but politics.

2. *Theology which is Nothing but Politics*

At the present moment 'political theology' is being reduced to a 'theology which is nothing but politics', in which the newly discovered social and political dimension of the gospel becomes its sole and entire content. At the present moment the Christian element is tending to be swallowed up by its incorporation into political thought and action. And this makes society the factor which determines everything, so that society itself becomes God – following the 'death of God'.

I shall always remember the first preparatory session for the Stuttgart Church Assembly. A number of experts had been invited to help us to take a close look at current problems and to take the first steps in planning a possible general theme for the Assembly. We had spent a whole morning – on the basis of the Sermon on the Mount, of course – going over and over the subjects of common humanity, aid to developing countries, democracy, the educational crisis and the emergency law. At the end, an atheist who had been invited as it were to provide a feedback, suddenly asked: 'What is your specifically Christian contribution? If I were to come to a Church Assembly, what I would be really interested in finding out was what Christians actually believe.' The abandonment of a specifically Christian contribution is largely complete when, for example, Gert Otto bluntly describes the content of Christianity as the 'improvement' and 'humanizing of the world'.[2]

The outdated traditional proofs of God seem at the present day to have been replaced by a kind of 'sociological proof of God'. This attempts to demonstrate the truth of the Christian religion by showing that it is of use to society. The first Christians prayed for the emperor, but they refused to sacrifice on his altar. At the present day many Christians, particularly theologians, may no longer be ready to pray for the emperor, but sacrifice on his altar – except that it is no longer the altar of the emperor, but the forum of society.

This has led to a close alliance between theology and sociology. For theology at the present day, sociology plays a similar role to that formerly exercised by philosophy. And just as the categories of philosophy sometimes enmeshed and overwhelmed the Christian gospel, so in part sociology does the same today. This has given rise to the type of 'socio-theologian' for whom theology is no more than a reinforcement for sociology, who would allow the church to be swallowed up entirely by society, and who accuses those who still believe in God of 'retaining the vestiges of theism'.

The bible is considered only from the point of view of what it has to contribute to the carrying out of current social and political tasks. A typical example of this is the fate of biblical

studies at the Church Assemblies. As long as there have been
Church Assemblies in Germany, there has been a movement to
integrate biblical studies with the practical themes of the associated working parties, and quite rightly so. But this aim has
never been achieved, and there have been continual complaints
about this situation. But at the Stuttgart Assembly the integration which had been called for so long in vain was finally
to be achieved, and it was decided that in two working groups
at least, in the 'Tribunal for the Investigation of Happiness' and
the working group on 'Democracy', biblical scholars were in
each case placed on the platform with other specialists to wait
their turn to speak. What was the result? In an evaluation by
the governing body of the Church Assembly we read:

> Even where biblical study was partly or wholly integrated into the
> platform contributions, the integration intended was not carried out
> to the full. Sometimes the specialist theologians were simply not asked
> about the Sermon on the Mount, and sometimes their contribution was
> more on the fringes of the practical discussion than at its heart.

That in spite of the new procedure there was a failure to
integrate biblical study at the Stuttgart Church Assembly was
not necessarily the fault of biblical scholars. The reason may be
in the bible itself, in the fact that it contains a message which
is not written by and to our contemporaries. Perhaps its themes
cannot simply be listed under the practical problems which
concern us at the moment, but may raise questions and problems which overshadow, correct, make more profound and
enrich those we pose ourselves. The bible cannot be used like
a petrol pump to deliver usable fuel whenever certain key words
like 'development aid', 'democracy', 'participation', and 'capital
formation' are uttered. It could be that the bible has something
quite different to say to us, but that this is something of the
utmost value for our endeavours concerning development aid,
democracy, participation and capital formation. It might even
be that the bible does not merely speak to us indirectly on these
subjects, but has nothing to say to us on them at all, yet nevertheless remains for us a book which it is 'useful and good to
read'.

If the bible is only judged by what it has to offer to the politics
of present-day society, the church comes under the same judg-

ment. This can lead to such false judgments of the church as the following:

> The services it renders in this respect are either individual in their nature (birth, marriage, loneliness, sickness, funerals), or, on the other hand, albeit in a severely limited way, of a very general kind (assistance to certain groups in distress, hunger in India and Biafra, the aged, over-burdened and isolated mothers, leisure activities, marriage guidance). Taken as a whole these are matters of welfare work in the non-economic sphere of society, in the sphere of side issues and irrelevancies.[3]

What expectations, what claims! If the church today really did the things that are insolently dismissed here as belonging to the sphere of side issues and irrelevancies, it would be one of the most important and most respected institutions in our society. At any rate such a church would be doing more for the way men live together than the socio-theologians who do no more than cast the net of their abstract theories over the world and then, when they draw in the net, are surprised to find it empty. At this point, therefore, we must direct a few interjections at present-day political theology, in order to keep it from being perverted into a theology which is nothing but politics.

First interjection: A warning against slogans and abstractions.

The motto and guiding principle for political theology is the well-known saying of Karl Marx: 'All the philosophers did was to interpret the world in various ways; but what matters is to change it.' There is scarcely an essay or an article in which this saying is not quoted – but what one then reads is the very opposite: pure 'academic eschatology', theory without practice. This saying of Marx is only quoted, but never practised. Nothing is concrete, everything remains abstract, and is therefore opinion-ated, even arrogant, and basically never expected to be tried out in practice.

If one applies Max Weber's well-known distinction between 'the ethics of conviction' and 'the ethics of responsibility' to present-day political theologians, one must say that most of them put forward a pure ethics of conviction – although they urge so strongly the exercise of practical responsibility. They simply do not consider or measure the consequences of what they say; they do not ask how it fits into the existing political situation, whether it would work in the way they suppose and state, or whether its effect might not be quite different, and possibly harmful. And indeed they do not need to consider the consequences, because they will not have to suffer them, not even by losing their seat in Parliament or their job as editors. Most revolutionary theologians have a salary with pension rights; they sit safe at home and blow the trumpet to take the field for battle.

Here are three examples of the abstraction of 'political theology' of which we are complaining.

The American theologian Carl Braaten writes in an article on the 'Theology of Revolution':

> Thomas Müntzer appealed to his followers 'to stiffen their necks', in order to build a new church and a new society. Müntzer stiffened his neck and was beheaded in 1525, when the power of the princes brought his revolution to an end. This provokes the question, which also applies to our own times, whether in a particular situation we should work for a gradual change in existing institutions – regardless of how old or rotten they may be – or whether we should sweep them away by revolutionary acts, even if we are risking our necks. A religion which is based on the crucifixion should not be too quick to give the easier answer ... Judgment and chaos are becoming the eye of the needle through which we have to pass, before renewal and social progress are possible.[4]

Is the author really aware of the consequences of what he has written? How readily he calls us to revolution, and conjures up visions of beheading, judgment and chaos! One can only excuse such language with the consoling thought that they do not know what they are saying, because they never expect to have to do anything about it.

Another example. In answer to the question, what the particular tasks of Christians would be in the course of a revolution, Jürgen Moltmann replied:

> I would expect Christians who believe in the presence of God in the midst of the revolution, to laugh, sing and dance, as the first to be set free in the creation ... Christians will be oddities even in the revolution. Perhaps they will be something like the fools of the revolution. They love it, but they also laugh at it, and this will make them seem odd.[5]

Moltmann goes on to ask: 'Is this foolish?' All we can say to this is: Yes, it is foolish! A serious revolutionary would take energetic steps to stop Christians if they started singing to him when he was making his plans or danced about on the bar-

ricades. It is a consoling thought, however, that according to
Moltmann there still seems to be *one* continuity between conservative and revolutionary Christians; when the flames leap up,
they both start singing.

Finally, a third example. Johann Baptist Metz writes concerning 'The Participation of Christians in Political Work for
Peace':

> Christians must take a creative and critical part in social and political
> work for peace. For the peace of *Christ*, which is an eschatological pro-
> mise, is not the private peace of the individual, it is not a partial peace,
> a peace of isolation, but is a peace for *all*, a peace available to everyone,
> the poorest and meanest and remotest above all. It is not offered to every-
> one, no one can claim it for himself ... Nor is this peace the private
> property of the church. The church exists for this peace, not the other
> way round. It exists to infect everyone with the hope of this peace, and
> to struggle passionately against every form of contempt. And therefore
> the church itself must take part creatively in social and political work
> for peace....

He goes on and on like this.[6] The whole article contains not a
single concrete idea, not a single practical suggestion about
what a Christian can do for peace in the world in his own
situation.

But it is these concrete proposals and verifications which are
necessary. We press our questions firmly against conservative
theologians: What does it mean to be God's son? What does it
mean to say that Jesus died for us? What does it mean to say
that Jesus makes us clean from all sin? What does it mean to
pray; Come, Lord Jesus, dwell with us? We want to hear from
them exactly what they mean, and what happens in concrete
terms when what they assert takes place. We must press
some firm questions on the political theologians, in order to
force them to express and verify their statements in concrete
terms. What does it mean to say that Christians must take part
in a creative and critical fashion in social and political work for
peace? What actually takes place when the church 'infects' all
men with its hope for peace? What can bishops, ministers and
lay people do about this? What has a Christian Member of
Parliament to do at the next election?

The political theologians of the present day are all simply
playing at politics, without responsibility and with the delight
in it of naïve children. Sebastian Haffner's remark about the

publishers Lord Beaverbrook and Axel Springer applies to them too:

> The notable thing about Beaverbrook and Springer was or is, that both believed or believe that because of their press influence and by means of their press influence they could play at politics, without going to the trouble of real political thinking. But politics deals with hard realities, and anyone who ignores these realities will break his neck before he notices. But Springer, like Beaverbrook before him, takes a certain pride in a sublime ignorance of existing realities and the necessities that result from them; he believes in the power of magic formulae, and believes that he possesses miraculous trumpets before which the walls of Jericho will fall.[7]

However, there are today numerous Christians, both theologians and non-theologians, who concern themselves not with the future of the whole world, and talk about nothing else, but who, without having much to say, do in their own situation what is socially and politically necessary and possible. They do not sow the seed of righteousness over the field of the whole world, so that the wind blows it away, but are content to cultivate their own acres thoroughly. The fields they are cultivating can actually be given geographical names: Oberhausen, Mainz-Kastel, Wolfsburg, Lyons, Bumbuli/Soni, Cuernavaca, and still, as formerly, Bethel, Kaiserwerth, Neuendettelsau, Stein and Spandau.[8]

Second interjection: An exhortation to modesty.
The church today is like a station at which every train used to stop. Since then, however, there have been many changes in the timetable, and now almost all the trains pass straight through, apart from a few local and suburban trains. But every time a train passes through the station, the stationmaster still jumps out on to the platform with his flag and signals the passing train to continue.

The point of this comparison is that the church today has very little to say about public life, and that consequently it should drop all grandiloquent political gestures. The political 'watchdog role' of the church, so much spoken of after the war, has become intolerable to the generation that grew up after the church struggle was over; it displays a lack of solidarity and implies an unacceptable claim to a right to impose moral laws on others. Besides this, it is no longer backed by any reality. The days in which Christians could stand on the city walls and suppose that they could save the world by single-handed Christian effort are past. A Christian monopoly no longer exists in this respect, and all that is left is co-operation: Christians together with non-Christians, the 'children of light' hand in hand with the 'children of darkness'.

When questions of society and politics are at issue, the most the church can do is take on a *shared* responsibility. Here the church is only one voice amongst others; apart from the church there are others who have long heard and responded to the question of their 'neighbour'. Consequently, when the church speaks it should not only think *what* it has to say, but also *how* it says it *when* it says it. What it says must be as relevant to the issue as possible; how it says it, must be as modestly as possible; when it speaks, must be as rarely as possible.

We doubt very much whether the world would really be altered if for a change Christians occupied positions of power. Christians ought to exercise their political responsibility principally in the places which others prefer to avoid: where there is an attempt to change and limit the use of power and violence, where bridges have to be built between opposite views and agreements reached, where the conditions of peace in the world are being studied and even, as far as possible, brought about. If Christians went into these situations and kept their eyes open there, they would find to their surprise that they were no longer on the platform signalling the trains in and out, but were sitting in the train themselves.

Third interjection: A call to stick to the facts.

Although Christians ought ultimately to draw the social and political consequences of their belief in the gospel, they should neither try to derive recipes from it nor use it to prove the existence of God. Indeed they should not even try to give a theological justification for the content of their social and political action from the gospel. The decisive theological principle which must be recognized here is that no specific theological basis for this content exists. When the attempt is made to provide it, the inevitable result is that both Christian faith and political action are turned into an ideology. At one time the working out of this ideology could be described as the 'theology of ordinances', while today it would be known as the 'theology of revolution'. In both cases Christianity only provides the religious trimmings, while the content is derived from elsewhere.

Christians, too, have to work out with the aid of their *reason* what has to be done in politics and society. But reason has a history on which Christian belief has also had a powerful influence. And thus there is today a whole field of moral, social and political values, standards, judgments and experiences, which at one and the same time are both Christian and rational. Of course this field changes and develops continuously; and in it there are constant conflicts, disputes and disagreements. But the only place in which Christians can move is within this field, unless they are to cease being participants and become spectators.

But what is the place of Christian love in this 'field theory'? Christian love itself does not exist as a freely suspended force, as a thing in itself, but always exists only in relation to the things that actually exist in the world, and therefore in strict relation to the 'facts'. Of course reason requires love to set it in motion and to give it a goal. On the other hand, love also needs reason, if it is not to be irrelevant, dilettante and full of wild enthusiasm. Love gives reason the impulse, but reason gives love its application to a particular matter and to the historical process. And therefore the interplay of love and reason brings about 'progress' in the course of history.

But as Christian love exists only in alliance with reason and in relation to the things that actually exist in the world, this requires the church to take action which is rational and based on facts. Its knowledge of the world must therefore be better than before. And where is the church to get this better knowledge of the world if not from secular specialists? This automatically leads to a *new hierarchy between theologians and laymen*. It is not theologians but laymen who are the specialists in the church, when questions arise about society, economics, politics, culture, science and law. Each in his own situation has to say how Christianity is to be realized in a world which has become worldly. As people who can not only bring the necessary specialist knowledge to their subjects, but above all possess the essential power to do something about it, they have to recognize and carry out what is required, with mature responsibility, in the concrete situation provided by their calling.

The temptation continually exists at the present day, the Christian macrocosm having collapsed in the Middle Ages, to turn the church as it were into a Christian microcosm, into a kind of shadow cabinet of the great cabinet that runs the world, in which all spheres of life in the world, each entrusted to the governing body of a Protestant church or the head of a Catholic institute, are brought up again for discussion; a firm and devout fortress from which every now and then commando troops make sorties into foreign territory. But the 'mature world' which we hear so much about today needs not merely an occasional encounter with 'church representatives', but the constant presence of independent Christians in its midst. In the long term the measure of the church's effect in the world will be that of the number of people it has who possess the necessary practical knowledge and power to use it. It will depend on whether in parliaments and political parties, in trade unions and associations, in public authorities and private firms, universities and institutes, in broadcasting and the press, there are Christians who are ready to make use of their Christian faith. But the purpose must be not to bring back under clerical tutelage, by indirect methods, or even only to 'Christianize' various spheres of life, but for Christians to share in the responsibility for them and to help to bring to realization the forces and possibilities for good in them. Where the church lacks such people, all its efforts to share in social and political responsibility in the world, all its 'reports', and all its activity in public life will remain in the long run unconvincing and without effect, and all that will happen is that the church will fall under suspicion once again of trying to press a claim for clerical control.

Fourth interjection: A reminder of the priority of the gospel over the law.

Once again we must draw attention to the priority of the gospel over the law, and to the precedence of receiving over acting. The Christians and theologians who are nowadays so seriously rethinking the social and political consequences of the gospel, so that the gospel exists not merely for the redemption of the individual but for the renewal of the whole of society, are running the risk of turning the gospel into a law. They are quite right to ask what sort of society it is which exerts such pressure on people as happens with the striving for achievement in our own modern society. Accordingly, they draw up plans and Utopias for a new order of society in the future, in which man can finally become human and the earth can finally become his 'home'. But by concerning themselves so much with the future of man, they run the risk of making man the means and material of their plans and Utopias. The consequence is that man is once again measured by what he achieves for society, not in this case for present-day society, but for the society of the future, so that he remains as before 'under the law'.

But what happens to those who have nothing to contribute to the new order of society for which they are striving so earnestly – either because they are too weak and powerless and are unable to contribute, or because they are interested in something else and do not want to? What happens to the 'little men' who take no pleasure in Utopias, but are satisfied with their own private idylls? There must be a 'reservation' to take account of what men are like – otherwise the prophecy of Heinrich Heine will be fulfilled once again in this century:

The future has an odour as of Russian leather, blood, blasphemy and much beating with the knout. I advise our descendants to come into the world with thick skins.⁹

When I hear many Christian Utopians talking about the future, I am always reminded of this saying of Heine.

It seems to me that to maintain a 'reservation' to take account of the humanity of men is one of the most important social and political tasks of theology and the church at the present day. But the church and theology can only fulfil this task by seeing that the gospel remains the gospel and is not allowed to revert to being the law. But this can only happen where the gospel is not identified with a programme for the improvement of the world, of which there are already many, some possibly better, but where it remains a distinct and unique message which cannot be heard anywhere else, and which has something to say to men – even apart from every attempt to improve the world. What matters is this 'purposelessness' of the Christian gospel.

Only where this is achieved does the church still have a right to exist and man a chance to remain human.

3. *The Purposelessness of Christian Truth*

I remember a television discussion with Eugen Kogon in the chair, which was concerned with the question of the future of religion. Those who took part were an aggressive atheist, a weary agnostic and three concerned Christians, one of each sort: a Protestant church leader, a Catholic theologian and an ecumenical layman. The three Christians tried to demonstrate and save the future of religion against the emotional attacks of the atheist and the detached interjections of the agnostic by describing in eloquent terms how the church had improved itself, how it by no means based its claims solely on the belief in God, but was also busily engaged in exercising a concern for our fellow men, in a plea for justice, in changing society and in improving the world. Eventually the chairman of the discussion found himself obliged to step down from his impartial position and put in a personal good word for God.

Everything that the three Christians said was right; their only mistake was to argue almost exclusively on the level of aims and methods, and not on that of the truth. I wondered afterwards why in the whole discussion not one of the Christians taking part described his belief in God simply as a reality, as the natural element in which he lived, without testing it for 'effectiveness'. In this way, one would describe one's love for another person as something which, while it gives one's own life a meaning, contains its meaning in itself and cannot be subjected to a constant investigation of its use and purpose.

We have no right to try to demonstrate the truth of Christianity by pointing to the Christian origin of the standards of freedom, justice, common humanity and so forth which are held at the present day. Nor can we show that the gospel is indispensable by demonstrating that it is of use to society, through the contribution of Christianity to the scientific, technical and social achievements of the modern age. The Christian faith gave all these things to the world – and made no provision about buying them back when they were needed again.

It is perfectly proper to point to these derivations and origins from the historical and sociological point of view, but history and sociology cannot demonstrate the truth of the Christian faith in the long term. What would happen if one day Christian faith turned out to be not so useful as we try to show nowadays, and if in a few years' time it was demonstrated that freedom, righteousness, common humanity or anything else that Christianity has introduced into the world can continue to exist even though it has broken away from its origin in Christian faith – just as the human being goes on existing even after he has been weaned? Will it then be time to bid farewell to Christianity? I am sceptical about the assertion frequently made by theologians nowadays that without Christian faith the enlightenment would be unreasonable. All we have experienced so far is that the enlightenment can be unreasonable both with Christian faith as well as without it. What would happen in the long term no one can say. The game is not yet over!

The New Testament contains an illuminating test of what really matters in Christian faith, of what is its ultimate concern. This is the passage in Luke about Mary and Martha, which has always been very difficult to understand, but since the 'death of God' and the resultant 'sociological proof of God', is even less obvious than before.

Jesus went into Martha's house, where her sister Mary also lived. Mary, we are told, sat at Jesus's feet and listened to his teaching. Meanwhile, Martha had 'much serving' to do in the house, to provide for her guest. Eventually it became too much for her, and she asked Jesus why he left her to serve alone and did not ask her sister to help her. But Jesus replied: 'Martha, Martha, you are anxious and troubled about many things; but few things are needful, or only one. Mary has chosen the good portion which shall not be taken away from her' (Luke 10.38ff.; RSV margin).

Our opinion of the two sisters would be quite the reverse. We would spontaneously take the part of the active Martha and would be ready to heap on the passive Mary all the charges that are made these days against 'theistic' Christianity: quietism, pietism, a purely inward religion, individualism, preoccupation with the next world, sentimentality. Yet this is the touch-stone! It is this which shows whether for us the meaning of Christian truth depends upon its effective value, or whether the meaning of Christian faith, in the first instance at least, is contained in itself 'regardless of its purpose' – whatever consequences and effects may later result from it. Of course one must remember that Jesus of Nazareth is the central figure in this scene. For evangelist Luke he represents the presence of God, while for us, he still represents at the very least the question of God. This does not mean that Christian action, nor the responsibility of Christians for politics and society, should be regarded as of less value: nor does it demonstrate that contemplation should be regarded as having precedence in time or quality over action. More is at issue. The story is a reminder of the basic structural law of all human life, which is taken for granted when building a house, but which we so easily forget when it is a question of building our lives: that the foundation is more important than the whole building.

But the foundation of life, the basis on which everyone exists, is, whether he knows it or not, the love of God. 'Existence owed to another' – this is the truth of Christianity, which, however offensive the idea may be to many present-day Christians con-tains its own value in itself, regardless of the purpose to which it is put. This is the 'one thing that is needful', even if it cannot be shown to be so necessary for coping with our life and for running the world. When faith no longer shares the experience of the psalmist: 'Who have I in Heaven but thee? And there is nothing upon earth that I desire besides thee' (Ps. 73.25), it is running the risk of being degraded into a satisfaction for the religious needs of the individual or as a social lubricant for society. And if faith loses its purposelessness, its value for society soon disappears as well – which does not mean that one should maintain the purposelessness of faith for the sake of preserving its social usefulness. This would only lead once again to Chris-tian faith being put to use and used up.

'Politicizing' theologians should take warning from the fact that people who are not theologians and not Christians, or at least are not representatives of professional Christianity, are actually giving the church and theology urgent warnings against a one-sided and direct concentration on the political and social usefulness of Christian truth, and the consequent adaptation of Christianity to the tendencies of society and the world as it exists. They are making it clear that it is when this happens that they lose interest in the Christian message.

We quote three examples of this view, from writers whose intellectual origin is very different, but who all agree in their opinion on this point, and to whose views, in consequence, all the more attention should be paid.

The critical sociologist and philosopher Theodor W. Adorno gives the warning:

> If religion is accepted for any other reason than for the distinctive truth it contains, it undermines itself. That at the present day the positive religions are so ready to take this course, and as far as possible to compete with other public institutions, simply bears witness to the despair inherent in their own positive nature ... In my view ... what the world needs most urgently today is in fact a corrective and not the affirmative of itself which everywhere we turn flourishes much more than we like to see.[10]

The existentialist philosopher Karl Jaspers warns:

> Every chance of the churches lies in the Bible – provided they can again, in awareness of the turning point, make its original voice ring again today.... But this will only happen when the procedures of two thousand years, the prudent accommodations, the wisdom based on knowledge of human nature, the worldly 'politics', no longer take the lead.... If the churches dared thus to put themselves into jeopardy, the Word would be credible everywhere, every day, on the lips of priests and theologians... In a new earnestness, they would repeat the eternal challenge to man: to be changed in his foundations – and in conjunction with his everyday life, with all that men do or think ... They would no longer engage directly in politics but would effectively arouse the seriousness that could then motivate and support the seriousness of politics. All this would not happen on account of politics nor on account of the bomb ... but without any purpose, for the sake of God and man.[11]

Finally, the atheist existentialist Albert Camus wrote in a letter:

> I must hasten to tell you that the world needs a real dialogue, that lies and silence are the reverse of this, and that therefore there can be true dialogue only between men who remain what they are, and unconcernedly tell us the truth. This means that the present world expects of Christians that they will remain Christians in the future.

All these statements point in the same direction: they warn and indeed ask Christians to remain Christians – without any purpose, for the sake of the truth that they believe, because only then do they remain of interest to the world and play some part in it. It is almost like an echo and answer to this request and warning on the part of non-Christians or non-theologians, when the theologian Karl Barth writes:

> Can we possibly explain our existence as ministers upon any other ground than that of the existence of a basic need in other men? The people do not need us to help them with the appurtenances of their daily life. They look after those things without advice from us and with more wisdom than we usually credit them with. But they are aware that their daily life and all the questions which are factors in it are affected by a great What? Why? Where? Whether? which stands like a minus sign before the whole parenthesis and changes to a new question all the questions inside – even those which may already have been answered. They have no answer for this question of questions, but are naïve enough to assume that others may have. So they thrust us into our anomalous profession and put us into their pulpits and professional chairs, that we may tell them about God and give them the answer to their ultimate questions ... The theological problem comes into being at the *boundary* of mortality ... We cut a ridiculous figure as village sages – or city sages. As such we are socially superfluous.[12]

Karl Barth wrote these words half a century ago. They are still true – unless theologians have decided to stop being theologians any more.

To say that the Christian truth is 'purposeless' does not mean talking about God without having any regard to man; it means to talk about *God's* purpose for *men*. This dialectic warns us against using false alternatives.

4. *Heavenly Balm or Social Lubricant?*

Contemporary theologians who are responsible, that is, who say what is relevant to their situation, must when they speak of God be always as it were facing both ways.

Some of the people to whom they have to speak are frightened by the loud and emphatic proclamation of our common humanity, of social justice, political responsibility and even revolution in theology, are afraid for their identity as Christians, and ask in troubled voices what the distinctive nature of Christian faith is, and how it differs from 'mere humanism'. Theologians have to warn these people against a religion which amounts simply to contemplating their own navels, and remind them of the *good Samaritan*. He did not ask what his own distinctive part was, or what was the distinctive characteristic of being a Samaritan. Instead, he simply went and did what was necessary. But in Jesus's own words, by this very commitment he inherited 'eternal life', and this means of course that he found his ultimate identity.

But there are others who are interested only in changing society. A responsible theologian must warn them against measuring Christian faith only by its social purpose and political usefulness, and misusing it as the fuel for human society. They must be reminded of the parable of the *prodigal son*, which makes it clear that Christian faith is in fact concerned with the right relationship of man to God. All the new consideration taking place today in theology and the church of the political and social action of Christians in the world, their commitment to peace, their struggle for a better social order, their co-operation in aid to developing countries, their shared responsibility for the future, can only be an answer, a consequence and effect of the message of Jesus concerning God's purpose for men – as when a stone becomes warm by itself when it lies in the sun. But the stone of course has to lie in the sun first, before it can get warm!

On the other hand, the question must immediately be asked, whether in the absence of an answer, of such consequences and effects, Jesus's message of God's purpose for men has been rightly heard at all, and whether the relationship of man to God is really in order, because faith has remained without fruit, a theory without practice.

The close link between the two sides, between man's relationship to God and man's relationship to his fellow men, can clearly be seen in two verses from these two parables. In the parable of the Prodigal Son: 'But while he was yet at a distance, his father saw him and had compassion, and ran and embraced him and kissed him' (Luke 15.20). In the parable of the Good Samaritan we read: 'But a Samaritan, as he journeyed, came to where he was; and when he saw him, he had compassion, and went to him' (Luke 10.33). Both parables speak of a journey and a movement which is set in motion by love: the movement which the father makes towards the son is reflected and continued in the movement of the good Samaritan to the man who was lying by the road.

The necessity of always speaking in two different directions, of facing both ways, will help theology to overcome the 'uncompromising alternatives' which are posed at the present day in society and the church. We shall discuss five of them.

1. The Present or the Future?

There is no question that there is a greater affinity in the bible to the dynamic process of change than to the static principle of order, and Christianity too, at least by its origin, is more on the side of change than of preservation. The reason for the affinity of Christianity for change and transformation lies in biblical eschatology. Although the eschatological statements of the bible are very varied and even contradictory in their details, they all agree in the hope that God is guiding the course of world history and guiding it to a particular goal. It is God's will to regain his rights over his creation and thereby set man free from his self-alienation and bring him back to his own true self. This aim laid down by God gives the whole of history an orientation towards the future. This brings in to it a movement, a dynamic and an impulse, a permanent unrest, which is an impetus to change. We have only to recall once again the importance of the word 'new' in the bible. The God of the bible has on this account quite rightly been called a 'revolutionary' God. The *Magnificat* says of him: 'He has put down the mighty from their thrones, and exalted those of low degree; he has filled the hungry with good things, and the rich he has sent empty away' (Luke 1.52 f.). The exchange of power described here was later turned into something that took place in man's heart, and was spiritualized; but in the first instance it was real political and social changes which were meant.

The central figure in this history of revolution and destruction leading to renewal is the 'Messiah'. He is the agent of the divine redemption of the world. Through the coming of the Messiah in Jesus of Nazareth, a tension was introduced into history which needs to be resolved: The Messiah is at work 'even now', but he has 'not yet' completed his work. The tension between this 'even now' and 'not yet' from henceforth determines all experience of history. On the one hand, the future already exists in the present, while on the other hand the future is yet to come. Here historical existence consists of constantly going beyond the present into the future. This has created a new concept of transcendence. The Greek ontological and metaphysical concept was replaced by the historical and dynamic concept of the bible. The world beyond is not above us, but before us. But the way to this world beyond is not determined, but is laid down in co-operation between God and man. God elevates man to 'co-operate' with him in obtaining the goal of history, and where men place themselves at his disposal, history moves more rapidly towards its goal. Thus the eschatological character of Christian faith contains powerful urges and impulses in the direction of the future, tending towards a revolutionary consciousness. And it is this which in fact should determine the political and social action of Christians.

But in the history of thought, when something that has been long forgotten is rediscovered, an exaggerated significance is often given at first to the new discovery. The same has happened in present-day theology. Far too much weight is laid on the rediscovery of the future orientation of the gospel, and therefore of the character of Christian faith as hope. One can say of some theologians that they are 'future crazy'. What else can one say of a statement such as this by Harvey Cox: 'The only future that theology has, one might say, is to become the theology of the future'?[13]

Against this one-sided future orientation of theology we must point out that the future must always be firmly rooted in the *present*. The present always provides the background from which the future draws its material. And therefore Jürgen Moltmann is wrong to describe the 'new thing' of which the bible speaks in connection with eschatology as a *novum ex nihilo*, a new thing from nothing. The 'new creation' is not a 'creation from nothing', but something which is done to the world which has been created from nothing, and therefore already exists. Moltmann and those who think like him interrupt the continuity of history almost to the point of destroying its identity. The resurrection of Jesus is not something as new as Moltmann claims it to be. Hans-Dieter Bastian, who is concerned with religious education, quite rightly attacks such a 'theology of hope':

What can a theory of theological education make of an eschatology which, in pentecostal fashion, ignores empirical structures – such as inherited links, social and cultural traditions and so forth? ... The total newness of the new would be inhuman ... No exodus is permissible which shakes the past from its feet like burdensome dust ... Christian hope is related not only to the future of God, but also to the flesh of the old Adam.[14]

When man asks about the past or the future, he does so from the point of view of his position in the present. If he abandons this point of view, his questions become a flight, either upstream into the past or downstream into the future. One leads to anti-quarianism, and the other to futurism. Of course it is also possible to bury oneself in the present, but this is the danger which seems to threaten theology least of all at the present day.

Consequently, by contrast to Harvey Cox, we can only hope that the 'Hebrew-Hellenistic synthesis', and the link between the future and the present, will not be dissolved in our own time. Anyone who does not maintain the link between the future and the present is losing his grip on the finite nature of time and being carried away by his enthusiasm into infinity. But infinity is forbidden ground to man; he loses himself in it. Reaching out towards the infinite and the absolute leads to a false Utopianism which only paints pretty pictures of the future and is nowhere anchored to reality.

The necessary link between the future and the present means that *compromise* is the necessary form, under the conditions of space and time, of all political and social action. Compromise adapts itself to the situation. It does not say: 'All or nothing', but 'Here and now', and tries to strike a balance between the abstract demands of Utopia and the concrete possibilities contained in the existing situation. That is why all that is ever possible in political and social action is half measures. The only possible success is a partial realization of social justice and the establishment of a provisional peace, in a determined struggle which proceeds step by step from one provisional state of affairs to another.

But even if we succeed in this, it is necessary for our compromises to be adapted to the time factor in yet another way. They must no longer be, as hitherto, at the service of the present, and seek simply to maintain the *status quo*. They must be directed towards the future and help to overcome the *status*

quo. Everything that Christians do in the world must be judged
by the eschatological comparative of the Sermon on the Mount,
by whether they help man to *greater* righteousness.

Anyone who allows his political and social action to be
guided by this eschatological comparative is no longer forced
to proceed strictly in accordance with one of the two wings of
politics, right wing or left wing, but is free to act sometimes with
the right and sometimes with the left, and to choose his arguments and means in accordance with the demand of the
historical moment at any time – as love commands and reason
understands. This will enable him to exercise *practical criticism
of ideologies,* and to do so in every direction, and not always
against the same old enemy, be it Communist or bourgeois. In
this way he steps easily into the dialectic process of history and
goes forward with it.

Even the most perfect form of peace in the world will never
be the kingdom of God. Even if the world was full of Christians,
we would never succeed in this! For this reason we long for the
eternal peace of which the angels sang at Christmas to the
shepherds in the fields at Bethlehem. But the hope of eternal
peace does not make us disloyal to the earth and to the present,
but commits us firmly to them.

The right relationship between the present and the future is
shown by the following anecdote which Helmut Gollwitzer once
told in an interview. During a sitting of a state legislature somewhere in the Middle West in the last century, there was an
eclipse of the sun, and it seemed as though panic was going to
break out. The representative who was speaking made the
following suggestion: 'Fellow representatives! We are faced
with two questions, both of which have the same answer. Either
the Lord is coming, in which case he ought to find us at work,
or he is not coming, in which case there is no reason to interrupt
our work.'

2. *Change or Redemption?*

Any revolution, however justified, is equivocal in nature. It
contains a passion for justice and the will to liberate the
oppressed, which strives for a better and more human order of
society; but at the same time forces of violence, destruction and

oppression are at work in it, and they bring about new human suffering and new social injustices in the world. Every revolution runs the risk of simply exchanging one evil for another, in the dreary words of the old student song: 'The world goes turning round and round; and what goes up must come back down.'

But this equivocal character of every revolution only points to a characteristic of all human history. In the history of mankind there can be found guilt, suffering, meaninglessness, ruin and death, which no human power – no political democracy, however sound, and no social revolution, however complete, can remove; there is a cross that can only be borne, and can be overcome at best only by bearing it. This is not merely the 'earthly remnant' which Goethe says is hard to bear; it is the woof woven into the texture of the universe which Christian theology from early times has described by the symbol of the 'fallen creation'. This brings us back again to the problem of theodicy, and here there is also a place for Luther's doctrine of the 'two kingdoms'.

The doctrine of the two kingdoms is concerned not merely with the special problem of Christian ethics, but with the basic problem of all human existence. The doctrine of the two kingdoms reflects a basic experience of mankind: the fact that there is a chasm running through everything that exists, which cannot be closed. Men try either to bridge this chasm through cultic purification or to leap over it by means of an idealistic belief in absolute progress; or else they respect it, and thereby come to realize the relativity of all being and action, which has been given intellectual expression in the doctrine of the two kingdoms.

At the present day the criticism of Luther's doctrine of the two kingdoms is as it were the forecourt through which everyone has to pass before he reaches the palace of the new political theology. The main objection to Luther and his successors is that he neglected to draw from Jesus's preaching of the coming of the kingdom of God the appropriate consequences for the social and political ordering of the world. Instead of urging the middle classes to change the ordinances of this world, even now, in the direction of a redeemed order, they simply enabled them to do their duty within the ordinances of this world with a good conscience, and therefore to obey the 'retaining forces' instead of resisting them.

There is no doubt that this criticism has some justification. But it immediately provokes a contrary criticism if, in its turn, it emphasizes only the positive side of Christian eschatology, the changing of the world in the direction of its renewal, and thereby forgets its negative side, the constant experience of the 'end of the world', the tendency of all things to decline and decay.

The consequence is that we find in many modern theologians a blithe belief in progress and a naïve optimism about the future which is without parallel. One can certainly no longer accuse these theologians of making the world 'a vale of tears' in order to have a reason for its redemption. On the contrary, they prophesy a paradise on earth for us – if only we wanted it! Thus, for example, Harvey Cox writes about men's work: 'We could transform it from a drudgery into a delight. Yet we still cling to pious attitudes about work.' Cox expects the transformation of work from a drudgery into a delight as a result of cybernetics and automation. Of course this will make work easier, but equally certainly it will not turn it into a delight. Cox even goes so far as to prophesy:

> In all of these instances, rather than fighting and opposing secularization, we would do better to discern in it the attitude of the same One who called an earlier people out of endless toil, in a land where the task-masters were cruel, and into a land flowing with milk and honey.[15]

As though the Israelites did not have to endure any toil or any burdens in the Promised Land!

How infinitely more profound are the thoughts of the Jew and atheist Ernst Bloch, in contrast to his Christian disciples, when he piles up a series of questions about the suffering and the misery in the world:

> Where does the kingdom of necessity come from, which has oppressed men for so long? Why does the kingdom of freedom not come at once? Why must it be worked for in so bloody a fashion through necessity? What is the justification for its delay? These are matters which have still to be dealt with even in atheism, unless it is to become an unhistorical and unreal, and indeed, mindless optimism.[16]

Here Bloch is closer to Luther than he supposes and than he

would like to think. For what he looks at so helplessly is basically the same lack of consequence in the world, the same delay in the progress of its redemption, with which the doctrine of the two kingdoms is concerned. This doctrine reminds us that even the best political action can bring no perfect solutions, but only relative improvements, and that in the course of history the last word often falls to failure, powerlessness and disappointment, and that even after a particular goal has been reached there is a kind of 'melancholy of fulfilment', a feeling that the dream was really finer than the reality.

This is the point at which the difference between *change* and *redemption* becomes clear. Christians always look only for temporary changes, but never for a final fulfilment within history. But they believe that all the wretchedness of history, which we can neither understand nor ignore, is even now taken 'away' with God, and in both senses of the word. They have been taken 'away' in the sense in which we say of something that it has been safely 'put away' with someone else, perhaps a friend; but it is 'taken away' also in the sense that one fine day it will no longer exist. It is this taking away that Christian faith calls 'redemption' and to which it looks as the final goal of all history. But they do not wait for this to come about as a development which is a natural necessity, but are actively committed in a shared responsibility for bringing it about in history. And therefore the Christian, because he is aware of God's purpose for the world, goes straight to work not to redeem the world, but to change it into a better world.

3. Divine Revealer or Social Revolutionary?

In order to give a historical and biblical basis for their theological and political views, the radical adherents of a 'theology of revolution' present Jesus of Nazareth as a social revolutionary. In so far as they are also representatives of a 'theology after the death of God' they are at the same time trying to make good the theological deficit which has arisen in their christology as a result of the 'death of God', and to make clear why they still place so much importance on this Jesus of Nazareth. To justify their thesis they appeal largely to Jesus's preaching of the kingdom of God, which they describe as a 'total revolution', and which they interpret in categories drawn from Marx and Bloch.

On principle no objection can be taken to this procedure. Every theology contains numerous philosophical elements. In the past, they were generally drawn from Plato, Aristotle, Kant, Hegel or Heidegger, while today the main sources are Marx and Bloch, and more recently Hegel again. But there is always a risk that philosophical categories and conceptions used for the purpose of interpretation can swamp the gospel and take over its content. We believe that this has happened here.

Naturally one can describe the kingdom of God which Jesus preached as a 'total revolution'. But one must be quite clear that the word 'revolution' has a different meaning here from the social and political sense which it normally carries. There is no question that Jesus had ideas and carried out actions which must have seemed revolutionary to his contemporaries. He forgave sins in the name of God, he healed the sick on the sabbath, he kept company with tax collectors, Pharisees and harlots, he presented the despised Samaritans as an example to the Jews, and in the Sermon on the Mount he radicalized the Jewish law to the point where its demands seemed superhuman. But all these revolutionary ideas, words and acts on the part of Jesus were not 'political', but 'religious' in origin. The basis of them all was his message that the distant God had come close to men and that he wished, above all, to be present to those who hitherto had seemed to be excluded from his salvation and his kingdom. It was in this that Jesus's announcement of the kingdom of God consisted.

Anyone who wants to know who Jesus of Nazareth is and how he understood his mission must look at the people he gathered round him. This reflects a kind of 'indirect christology' – on the principle: 'Tell me whose company you keep and I will tell you who you are.' Dictators like to be photographed with cheerful, happy and healthy people, with laughing children and old soldiers. They would like people to draw conclusions about themselves from the people who surround them. Let us imagine such a photograph of Jesus of Nazareth – what kind of people surround him? Only people whom every devout person who thought anything of himself would go to some trouble to avoid, figures from the edge of life, people against whom both church and society were prejudiced: the sick, who, because of their sickness, were regarded on the basis of the Jewish dogma of retribution as guilty of a serious offence; lepers and the possessed, who were excluded from the fellowship of the living; heathens, who were looked down on and despised; women and children, who counted for nothing; harlots and tax collectors, that is, the morally doubtful and politically unreliable. There is a flavour of subversion about all this. Amongst the crowds Jesus gathered about himself there were in fact murmurings of revolution. But Jesus of Nazareth was not a social revolutionary, however much people today would like to brand him as one. But has not Jesus already been branded as everything? Once he was the good shepherd who kept company with the centurion at Capernaum. Now he suddenly has to pass as a revolutionary from a proletarian background, who with an angry whip drives the traders and money-changers (for which read 'capitalists') out of the temple.

But Jesus of Nazareth was more and did more than a social revolutionary. He did not stand the world and society on its head, he stood God on his head – which of course had consequences for the world and society.

And therefore we must give a warning against all undiluted messianism, and at the same time against every one-sided political use of the figure and message of Jesus. The present-day practice of virtually equating the Old and the New Testaments makes it too easy to forget that the New Testament undertakes a clear correction of the Old Testament idea of the Messiah. Its literary tradition has retained the expression of this correction in the story of the temptation of Jesus in the wilderness. In it Jesus clearly rejects the political ideal of the Messiah and thereby sets out on the way to the cross.

There is in the history of the church a story which provides a strange contrast to that of the temptation of Jesus in the wilderness. This is the well-known vision of the Emperor Constantine before his victory over his rival Maxentius in the battle of the Milvian Bridge. In the full light of midday the Emperor, together with his whole army, saw in heaven a cross formed of light, together with the words: 'In this sign you will conquer.' In the night that followed he received from Christ himself the charge to make a copy of the cross seen in the sky, and to use it in the coming battle as a protective banner. The next day, therefore, Constantine gave the order to make a standard which took the form of the cross, and which in addition, in a golden circle, bore the monogram of Christ. The emperor was told by Christian priests that this was the sign of the victory which the Son of God once achieved over death. And Constantine went into battle, and conquered his enemy and his legions in the sign of him who himself refused to call the legions of angels to his aid, or even to let a single sword be drawn. In this moment, if not before, the 'political Christ' was born. But what a perversion! He who once gave his own life to death through love was in future to appear as one who brought other people and whole nations to death.

But is there any real difference between the Emperor Constantine and the modern theologians of revolution? We cannot perceive any. Of course the modern theologians of revolution quite rightly proclaim the 'end of the Constantinian age'. Some of them, too, are pacifists, at least as far as war is concerned, though less so when it is a matter of revolution. But they too make Jesus of Nazareth a 'political Christ'. They would like to win political victories in the sign of the cross. And like Constantine, they believe that they know the will of God, and know who is God's friend and who is his enemy.

But the death of Jesus on the cross forbids every 'theology of glory'; that is, every attempt to identify the will of God by deriving it through analogy from the events of history, and then carrying it out. Consequently, the view of modern theologians of revolution that God is revealed in the most dynamic way in revolution is just as false as the conviction of those who preached at an earlier period that the most glorious witness to God is in war. We should not imagine that we can read the will of God from the course of world history. No person can say what the will of God is at any concrete historical moment. We have to acknowledge in the cross of Christ God's universal will to love, and then exercise love ourselves by doing what is objectively right, as far as our reason is able to ascertain.

At the session of the main committees of the World Council of Churches in the summer of 1969 in Canterbury, a screen was set up in the church, and during the service pictures of human suffering were projected on it – hunger, sickness, war and catastrophies. Many Christians made it clear that they were disgusted by this. We can only regard it as a legitimate interpretation of the cross of Christ. According to the New Testament, two thieves hung one on each side of the cross of Jesus, and nowadays all those who are hungry, wounded, burned, gassed, in prison, tortured and killed in the world hang with him as well. The cross of Jesus amongst the crosses of men – if anyone sees this, love makes him 'revolutionary'. It gives to our reason that 'surplus' over reason which we call 'Utopia'. But we have to ask of what spirit the Utopia is born, and whether the prognosis is a true one. For without a reasonable prognosis any Utopia is pie in the sky.

4. Justice or Mercy?

The World Council of Churches at Uppsala announced that justice comes before mercy, and the Church Assembly in Stuttgart accepted this. In the present state of the world this is certainly right and proper. The age of paternalistic charitable programmes, of mere relief campaigns motivated by mercy and representing only samples of justice, is past. In spite of this, we are constantly faced by situations in which there is no possible answer to the demand to set up just structures, and there is no alternative but the old-fashioned remedy of Christian works of mercy. We Germans experienced such works of mercy after the second world war, in part from the victorious Western allies; such acts of mercy were probably the only possible help we could give to Biafra; this mercy remains the ultimate refuge in numerous human situations presented by our modern society, based on technical and rational achievement. The best hospitals with the most modern medical apparatus and the most perfect welfare state with the most efficient social institutions remain lifeless without the breath of compassion that fills the gaps. And there will always be moments in which 'there must be direct and immediate action to save the situation'.[17] Until justice is fulfilled we constantly need mercy as well. But when has justice ever been fulfilled in this world? Consequently, human life always remains dependent upon mercy as well. A single glance at the existence we lead confirms this.

At the same time, the question of mercy also provides a touchstone of the *motive* of our efforts to bring justice to the world. It shows whether we are only making these efforts in order to put through our own ideological conceptions of a just ordering of society or to give another demonstration of the contemporary relevance and necessity of Christian faith. When someone is only trying to push through his own conceptions of justice, 'and to hell with the consequences', then the final consequences really are hellish, and the world is destroyed by this justice. And as for all our attempts to show, by our political and social commitment to greater justice in the world, that the gospel is of use to the world, others simply laugh, and quite rightly. Joachim Kahl, in his pamphlet *Das Elend des Christentums* ('The Misery of Christianity') quite rightly comments:

> No theology, whatever modern or revolutionary airs it puts on, has anything to say to a highly developed critical and atheistic theory.[18]

This recall to mercy is not a recall to a purely inward and private religion, to pure and good intentions. Christians ought to have pure hearts, but they should be ready to get their hands dirty.

5. Persons or Structures?

Our society is increasingly troubled by the problem that men live longer than before, but that at the same time many of them have to quit the productive process before they reach the 'age limit'. Sometimes people who are only 45 or 50 are 'scrapped', because, as people say nowadays, they are no longer sufficiently 'creative' and 'dynamic' to carry out certain tasks. But this means no less than that death is making its presence felt here in a new way – no longer as the *exitus*, which appears sometime or other at the end of life, suddenly or gradually, but as the shadow of transitoriness cast back from the end of life over the years of middle age.

Is the problem here a personal or a structural one? It is both. It is a personal problem, in so far as the individual is affected in his personal existence and must ask what meaning his life will now have in the future. But it is a structural question in so far as it raises the question of how a society is structured if it imposes such pressure to achieve on its members, and how its structures must be changed if everybody's justified claim to a meaningful life can be fulfilled.

When, under the pressure of an organization and the adaptation and achievement it demands of him, a person cries out: 'I cannot bear it any longer'; his cry has at least a threefold cause and relevance. The first is physical, in so far as the person feels that his bodily powers are no longer adequate. The second is sociological, in so far as the person feels himself pressurized and oppressed into anonymity by society and its demands. The third is personal, in so far as the person asks how he can make sure of a meaningful personal life in the midst of the organization which surrounds him. All these questions have a 'religious' relevance. All three levels concern faith.

This shows how false it is to break down the connection between persons and structures, between a change in the individual and the transformation of institutions, or even to give preference to one or the other. The kingdom of God, which Jesus proclaimed was beginning, is concerned with *the whole*; it extends to the 'world' and aims at changing all the circumstances and conditions in it, that is, it includes the transformation of institutions and structures. But the basis of this change in the 'whole', including institutions and structures, is that the *individual* should change and become a 'new man'. The law of the seed corn applies to his life; it must fall to earth and die in order to bring forth fruit. What makes possible such a change of mind and renewal of the individual is the gospel, Jesus's announcement of the kingdom of God, which 'comes' and is not 'built', which one 'receives' and does not 'make'. Its consequence is the changing of the world, the changing of the circumstances that exist in it. Structures and institutions can also die and rise again, but the 'agents' in this are always men who themselves must die and rise again.

The false division made between persons and structures can be illustrated by the distinction between 'eschatology' and 'apocalyptic', and also by the contrast between Rudolf Bultmann and Ernst Bloch. In Bultmann 'eschatology' corresponds to the 'historicity' of man. It is related to the present moment and is private and individual in nature. But 'apocalyptic' is related to the future of the world and seeks a change in the total context, in the earth as man's 'home'. The right thing is for both to be connected and related. Eschatology without apocalyptic leads to spiritualization and inwardness; it makes faith unworldly. Apocalyptic without eschatology, on the other hand, changes history into a cosmic drama, in which the individual is lost. Eschatology must learn to remember that God loved the *world*; while apocalyptic must respond to the objection, 'What will it profit a man, if he gains the whole world and forfeits his life?'

New hearts will not of themselves bring about new circumstances in the world – this is the error of pietism and Moral Rearmament. But neither can there be a renewal of the circumstances in the world without a renewal of men – this is the error of the 'socio-theologians' and their immediate allies, the Neo-Marxists. In fact both dimensions of Christian faith belong together. Just as the church must work to improve structures through persons, so it must at the same time press for a change and improvement of structures, in order to help persons. Or again, whether men in the future have enough food to live on depends in part upon whether sufficient people recognize for themselves that man does not live by bread alone.

The 'new thing' which the bible promises, and which we look for so urgently at the present day for the church and society, begins with 'reformation', that is with the renewal of the individual on the basis of a new preaching of the gospel, a new and more credible way of speaking of God. But this reformation must penetrate into the heart of social circumstances and bring about a 'revolution' in them. Without revolution, reformation lacks its social application; but it is only reformation which gives existential depth to revolution. The present-day theologians of revolution do not yet take revolution seriously enough – but this is no excuse for their opponents, the 'authorities'.

Death Comes at the Last

1. The Loss of the Next World

The 'theological learning' process which is required of Christian faith at the present day is nowhere so difficult as on the question of the next world and eternal life; for the enlightenment has nowhere brought about so fundamental a change in belief in God as on this point. For this is not just a partial aspect of Christian faith, a change in a *single* doctrine, the hope of eternal life, but a total reversal of all belief in God – so total that one must ask whether it has not turned Christian belief into its opposite.

What this reversal consists of, and the effect it has had, can be seen from an impressive and well known example. A murderer of the year 1700 had been sentenced to be broken on the wheel, that is, to the most cruel form of death at that time. But the court was prepared to show mercy if he would take part in the witches' sabbath on the Brocken on Walpurgis night. The condemned man rejected this possibility of receiving pardon and chose rather to be broken on the wheel than carelessly throw away the eternal salvation of his soul. Two hundred years later the custom began of holding a masked entertainment on the Brocken on the night which was once so feared, with the women dressed as witches and the men as devils.[1]

If we look at the theological content of this change, we can see exactly what is meant by the title we have given to this section, 'the loss of the next world'. This loss of the next world has led to a change of priorities, a total reversal of the orientation of man's life. Before the enlightenment men's attention was largely directed to the world beyond, and they asked questions about their eternal salvation. The answers they received to these questions also helped them to endure their life in this world. But at the present day men's gaze is fixed almost exclusively not on eternity, but on time, and they ask how they can best live their earthly lives. At best they hope, if they hope for anything at all, that the answers they receive to these questions will help them to stand firm in the face of death.

This change in the orientation of life could not remain without serious consequences for Christian theology and devotion. The question of death and the associated hope of eternal life, and the assertion of a world beyond formerly occupied a central place in them. The ultimate aim of everything that was believed and thought lay in the consolation it offered for death by looking beyond it to eternal life in another, better world. But at the present day one must admit that to this question theology has largely to reply: 'No answer.' If one asks younger theologians in particular what place death and eternal life have in their preaching, many of them answer in embarrassment, or even after careful thought, with a shrug of their shoulders. This question, they think, has largely been disposed of as far as our contemporaries are concerned, and they show no further interest in it. Thus it is not surprising that in the index to Harvey Cox's book, *The Secular City*, the entries 'death' or 'eternal life' do not occur at all, while characteristically, in his book, *On Not Leaving It to the Snake*, the entry is only 'death of God'. Likewise, Dorothee Sölle in her book *Christ the Representative* puts forward the view that 'post-mortal existence' – a modern expression for 'eternal life' – is an outdated conception from late antiquity and the middle ages. Numerous other theologians at the present day do the same; with regard to eternal life they profess either cautious agnosticism or open contempt.

Now we agree completely with these agnostics or despisers of belief in eternal life when they attack the unrelieved concentration on the next world from the false kind of religion which allows this world to be almost completely swallowed up by the world beyond. We are also in agreement with them when they remind us that Jesus himself answered the question of eternal life with the parable of the Good Samaritan, that is, by drawing attention to our neighbour, and when they recall that, accordingly, Christians belong not on the road to Jerusalem, but on the

road to Jericho, and that they ought to be concerned not with
the eternal salvation of their souls, but to preserve and redeem
the world.

Criticism is easy, and the choice is not difficult to make when
one considers that the following hymn was once taught in school
and sung at the graveside:

> Where does the soul find its home, its rest?
> Who covers it with protecting wings
> ... Leave the earth, to find the home,
> The home of the soul, so glorious, so beautiful!

and then compares with it the concluding words of Ernst Bloch's
work *Das Prinzip Hoffnung* (The Principle of Hope):

> The root of history is man working, creating, transforming and sur-
> passing the circumstances he is faced with. If he comes to himself and
> provides a firm foundation for his existence, without alienation and
> estrangement, in real democracy, something will exist in the world which
> is seen from afar in everyone's childhood, and where no one ever was:
> home.[2]

Here it is Ernst Bloch who has more truth on his side, and
even more Christian truth. The flight of the soul heavenwards
into eternal peace is not the perspective of the bible.

When the apostle Paul longed 'to depart and be with Christ'
he had already done a great deal in the world, and even he at
once corrects his desire, when he thinks of what still remains
to be done (Phil. 1.23 ff.). And when Jesus, according to the
legendary account of the Acts of the Apostles, ascended to
heaven, he did not carry up his disciples after him towards
heaven. They heard a voice which said to them: 'Men of
Galilee, why do you stand looking into heaven? This Jesus, who
was taken up from you into heaven, will come in the same way
as you saw him go into heaven' (1.9ff.). On hearing this the
disciples turned and set off back into the world. Thus the
promise of the 'second coming of Christ' did not make them un-
faithful to the earth, but actually sent them to work there. What
took place here was a kind of appointment to this world, an
entrusting with responsibility for the destiny of the world. Thus
the breakdown of Western dualistic metaphysics, together with
the disappearance of the concept of the world beyond which
went with it, is not simply a loss for Christian faith, but also

a purification of it. The enlightenment has restored to us something original in Christianity: the relevance of revelation to this world, and the relationship of Christian faith to the world.

But even if one affirms the present world and accepts responsibility for the earth as one's 'home', one cannot simply ignore the boundary of death, which runs throughout all life. Such an indifference towards death implies a thoughtlessness about life, for it calmly excludes from consideration the most certain fact in all life, the very event which makes this present world the mortal and finite world it is.

For death is not simply a matter of our own individual dying but is a shadow of transitoriness which lies over the whole world. Consequently, any theology which, like the 'theology after the death of God' takes so seriously its concern for our fellow men and its responsibility for the world, and seeks to follow Bloch in making the earth a 'home', is bound to face the question of death. Otherwise all creative and formative activity in the world is like water that beats up against the coast and falls back again, constantly rising and falling, endlessly moving backwards and forwards. Death seems to make everything uncertain: at first it looks as though it is worth while to work and be busy – and then it turns into nothing. 'All is vanity and is striving after wind', is the conclusion of Ecclesiastes as he weighs up his observations of the world; this is wisdom in the face of death, the wisdom of death.

Thus the consideration of death forms the touchstone of all statements which we make about man's existence in the world. No theology, philosophy, religion or world view is worth anything unless it shows at least some concern for an answer to the question of death. It may not be able to provide an answer to this question, or it may face it purely with a call to an attitude of resignation or heroism before an absurd situation; but it must at least ask the question. We cannot simply ignore or pass over it.

Not to take death seriously means not to take life, the world and its mortal and finite nature seriously.

Here we must point out that both in Heidegger's existentialist philosophy, and also in his critic Ernst Bloch, the theme of death takes up significantly more room, and plays a much larger role, than in the most recent developments of modern Christian theology. These atheist philosophers, who now as in the past pose the question of death, seem to us to be thinking in a 'more contemporary' way than the a-theistic theologians whose silence about the question of death seemed to be so up to date. But if one really talks to one's contemporaries, one gets the impression that for many of them the question of death is by no means closed, but is something in which they are still interested.

We have shown above in discussing the question of the relationship between structures and persons, how death already casts its shadow from the end of life across the years of middle age. This gives a new actuality to the mediaeval chant: 'In the midst of life we are in death'; except that the powers which surround us at the present day are no longer plague, fire, water, disease and foul air, but the decline of our productive powers, neuroses, the struggle for existence, and anxiety – although the same powers of death as in the past are still active, except that some of them have new names. At the present day they are called coronary thrombosis, cancer, accidental death, and of course, as always, war. Even in Huxley's 'Brave New World', in the best of all worlds, in the most perfect order of society, and where the progress of biological research has been most successful, man still has to die, and dying is something which each individual has to do personally, regardless of whether he is seventy, a hundred or a hundred and fifty years old.

Consequently, all honest and profound consideration of life is a rendez-vous, or rather a battle with death.

2. Life in the Horizon of Death

Because death comes at the end of everything, it is the sign which precedes and governs everything. From its very beginning, life is 'capable of death'. As soon as man is born, he is old enough to die, and one can even kill an unborn child. 'Also hangmen must die' says an American proverb, thus expressing the universality and omnipotence of death.

Death is not one event in the life of a man which simply follows the other events. It is not that man does various things in the course of his life, and at the end dies as well. Rather, death forms the horizon within which all the other events of his life take place. As soon as I have attained to the certainty of death, it accompanies everything else of which I become conscious in my life. Thus there can be no conscious life which does not include the consciousness of death. *Si vis vitam, para mortem* – if you want to live, prepare for death, was the motto which guided Sigmund Freud in the second half of his life. This is the ancient Israelite wisdom which the psalmist expresses in the words: 'Teach us to number our days, that we may get a heart of wisdom' (Ps. 90.12).

Something of the dignity of man is evident in the necessity of death. Even if a computer can be made to learn or even think, there is one thing it cannot do; it cannot die. Nor are there any moral reasons against dismantling it. This distinguishes it even from animals. When a horse is unfit for service it is put out to grass or put down; but a worn out computer is stripped down and cannibalized.

But the commonest experience of all human existence, that man must die, is at the same time a total non-experience. Death is the only thing that happens in man's life which he cannot anticipate in his thoughts. Our death is something which to some extent we can imagine; and sometimes we even experience it in others. But whether we imagine our own death or share the experience with others, we cannot understand what really happens, because what happens there is the loss of being, and this is something that one can only undergo oneself. By the very fact that one has undergone it, it is no longer accessible, as one thereby ceases to be, and is therefore no longer present.

In Children's Letters to God there is the following letter from a small boy: 'Dear God, what is it like when you die? Nobody will tell me. I just want to know, I don't want to do it. Your friend Mike.'[3] That no one told the boy what happens when some one dies was not because people did not want to tell him, in order to protect him or even themselves from frightening thoughts. The real reason was that no one could. All that one can really say about God and death is that it comes. But when it comes, it is dumb and makes us dumb, and that is why we can say nothing about it.

A simple example will illustrate this experience, or non-experience. We cannot imagine our own funeral. We may perhaps succeed in doing this for a moment; we give our ideas free vein and imagine the cemetery, the church, the relations, the minister, the candles, the coffin. But then we suddenly stop, because we realize that we cannot imagine any of this at all, because we ourselves no longer exist, and are therefore no longer present.

Here what we have said about human personality becomes apparent; that for man all being is personal in nature, because being only exists for man in the form of being in relation to somebody. That is, man is the only being who can have a relationship to himself, and even when he takes on a relationship to the world, he always does so in such a way that at the same time he is taking on a relationship to himself. Whether we think of a historical event, hear an item of news, meet someone or notice a flower, we can do nothing without taking ourselves into account. And this is why man is the 'interpreting animal', who is capable of knowing everything that exists and happens in the world only in such a way that the act of knowing includes its 'significance' for him.

This makes it clear why we cannot imagine our funeral and cannot anticipate death in our thought. In death man's relationship to himself and to the world ceases; in a single process both he himself and the world cease to exist for him. Because man then no longer has any relationship either to himself or to the world, he cannot imagine his funeral, and cannot anticipate death in his thought, because when death comes he no longer exists.

That man at the same time and the same act has a relationship to the world and to himself is what distinguishes him from animals. Animals cannot have a relationship to themselves, but only to their surroundings. That is why animals only have surroundings, but man has a world. And therefore an animal's fear of death is different in kind from man's fear of death. Ernst Bloch rightly says of animals, by contrast to men:

> They are really only afraid of dying, not of death; and this is because they have no ego which has a conscious relationship to itself and can accordingly anticipate and therefore fear its own annihilation in death.[4]

The German language expresses the same distinction by using the word *verenden* of the death of animals, and the word *sterben* of the death of men. The former word, or such expressions as 'to kick the bucket', or 'snuff it', should really never be

used of men: when we do so use them, we do so only to express
the fact that here man has been most profoundly misused. And
there is a further distinction between men and animals which
we must make with regard to death. Only man can commit
suicide, not animals, because only man can have a relationship
to himself and of his own accord end his relationship to himself.

Because it is part of human nature for man to have a relationship in one and the same action to himself and to the world, and
because this ability to have a relationship to himself ends in
death, man is afraid of death. Or at least, he ought to be afraid
of death, because this is the mark of conscious life. Of course we
try again and again to hide our fear of death from ourselves,
because we lack the courage to fear death. Perhaps there is no
greater courage than the courage to be afraid of death and
consciously to accept this fear. I can have very little respect for
those who boast that they have no fear of death, but want to
die standing like a tree in a forest. I cannot avoid the suspicion
that even in life they have rarely condescended to help their
fellow men, because in reality they have been constantly pre-
occupied with themselves, and therefore unconsciously with
warding off their fear of death.

Even if we succeed in hiding from ourselves our fear of death,
it is the secret companion to everything we do. Because death is
so certain, life is so uncertain – and man tries to protect himself
against this uncertainty of life, which derives from the certainty
of death, in order to achieve permanency. And therefore he
resists the coming of death with all his might. Perhaps one could
write a whole history of the world from the point of view of
man's attempts to conquer death. There have been many
attempts of this kind. At the end they all come out to the choice
on the part of man of an absolute value in life, to which he
clings firmly. This can be almost anything: a wide-ranging
Utopia or the success of his own ambitions; an ideal which is
binding upon him or the latest medical discovery, a lofty
morality or the love of a woman, the future of his children or
a well-filled bank account, or even an illness or his own fear.
What a miserable contradiction: in order to avoid the fear of
non-being, one engages in a passionate relationship with nothing-
ness, and so is driven deeper into the fear of death.

At this point we can see why the bible makes a connection

between death and human sin. The apostle Paul describes death as 'the wages of sin'. If this expression means anything to us at all, we can no longer take it in the traditional dogmatic sense, that because God punished the father of mankind with death for his 'fall', all men since have had to die. Even before it was thought of, this idea was contradicted by the biological fact that death existed even before man came into the world, and that there is never any life without death. Yet there is a profound truth implicit in the mythological conception of death as the wages of sin. We can perceive this truth if we do not take it historically as a causal derivation of death from a fact in the past, but interpret it existentially, as a fact of our present human existence.

It is man's attitude to his destiny at death which finally decides what is the basis of his life: whether he creates it himself or whether he receives it; and from what he derives his existence: whether from what he already has, or from somewhere else. Thus when we look at the essence of the question of death, we are faced with the question of trust.

3. *The Question of Trust*

The question of trust which is posed by death is answered by Christian faith in the following way: *In the moment in which man ceases in death to be able to have a relationship to himself and to the world,* God's relationship to him continues.

There has to be some reason for this assertion of faith. Hitherto a distinctive event in the past has been regarded as the backing for it: the resurrection of Jesus Christ from the dead – just as man's condemnation to death was attributed to Adam's fall. In both cases a particular event, accepted as 'historical', came first and initiated a kind of causal nexus in history. Just as, in consequence of the sin and death of Adam, all men descended from him had to die, so now, as a result of the resurrection of Jesus Christ, all his followers attained to eternal life. The world view which this theory assumed was in both cases the spatial and temporal conception of a divine world above and beyond this world.

But the resurrection of Jesus Christ signifies something different, and something more than merely the return of a dead person from the world beyond it to life. Anyone who conceives of the resurrection of Jesus merely as the bringing back to life of a body is separating it from his message and his work and making it no more than a partial miracle. In itself, an event of this kind, even if it had taken place in such a way, means nothing – for in numerous myths people return from the dead in this way. Anyone who wants to place the right interpretation on the event which – with the aid of the metaphor taken from contemporary late Jewish apocalyptic – we call the 'resurrection from the dead', that is, anyone who wishes to interpret it in a 'Christian' sense, must look at it in the context of the whole mission of Jesus Christ. There its meaning is: 'This man Jesus of Nazareth was right, his cause continues in history and the grass no longer grows over his grave.'

In what respect was this Jesus of Nazareth right? What was the cause he stood for and which ever since has continued in history, so that one can say that no grass grows over his grave?

Here we must go back to what we said about the life and death of Jesus of Nazareth, and compare it to the death we have to undergo. In what happened to him – in his preaching and attitudes, in his life and death – Jesus of Nazareth revealed the love of God as the ultimate and unconditional power over our existence. But he did not do this superficially and in a general way, as an abstract doctrine or an eternal idea, but in the concrete assurance that God loves man and seeks fellowship with him; and this he does, again, not as an isolated act in some divine place apart, but as the revelation of the ultimate ground of all being.

If we take seriously Jesus's affirmation of the love of God and confront it with the fact of death, it follows that the relationship between God and man cannot be broken even in death. The conventional and sentimental assertion, so often made in romantic melodramas and on gravestones, that love is stronger than death, here takes on a clear and serious meaning. And thus the answer that faith gives to the question of trust posed by death is that in the very moment in which man ceases in death to have a relationship to himself and to the world, God's relationship to him continues.

We can make this eschatological fact even clearer with the aid of the concept of the 'in between' worked out by Martin Buber.

We already used this concept in interpreting the personality of God, and distinguished between the lesser 'in between' of our relationships with our fellow men and the greater 'in between' of the relationship between God and us. In death all the lesser 'in betweens', all our relationships to men and to objects in which we have passed our life, now disappear. All that remains is the great, all-embracing 'in between', God's relationship to us, which is the basis of our personal existence. And thereby love has succeeded in conquering death. Even death is taken over by the great divine 'in between' and so made a 'phenomenon of God'. Wherever it leads, God is there.

It is this which we call 'eternal life'. This means that eternal life is not simply one additional article of faith, but is something implicit in Christian faith in God, and derives from its inner logic. Anyone who takes seriously the relationship between God and man as a fellowship with men desired and revealed by God must necessarily face the question whether this fellowship of God with us is destroyed in death like all our other relationships. The answer will be that even in the certainty of his death, the believer remains certain of God. Eternal life, then, means nothing less than that the love of God remains present even in death.

The experience that belief in God is contrary to the appearance of the world, and is therefore always marked by an element of contradiction and defiance, is at its most acute when faced with death. This is the point at which all the guarantees, supports and links with which man tries to bring security into his life break down; all ground slips away from under his feet and he sinks into complete unconsciousness; no relationship exists any longer, either to himself or to the world. But at this very point faith becomes total and the final exodus out of everything visible takes place; and the 'last surrender' comes about. There our life is finally revealed for what it is, 'existence owed to another'.

In this act of trust, which takes the form of the final exodus and last surrender, man ultimately achieves the *identity* for which he has longed all his life. Augustine writes, Eckhart quotes Augustine, and Ernst Bloch once again requotes Eckhart's words:

I become aware of something which is half formed and half visible to my soul; if this could be brought to completion and permanence in me, it would surely be eternal life.[5]

There is nothing more that we can say about eternal life. We have nothing to say about the next world. We have no detailed picture to give of it, and we shall not even assert its existence. All we offer is the faith that even in death God continues to have a relationship to us. Anyone who asks for more is a religious glutton. He should ask himself whether his desire for 'eternal life' and the 'world beyond' is really aimed at God, or is it not simply a wish for continuation of his earthly existence without any sorrow, with greater material comforts, and on a higher metaphysical level. But a faith of this kind takes Christians away from the presence of Jesus to the reserve of the Creek Indians, who believe that after death we go to a place where there is an abundance of wild animals, the corn grows throughout the year, and streams full of clear water never dry up.

In the face of all atheist and Christian materialism, the only answer we can give to the question of eternal life and the next world is that of Eberhard Jüngel:

God is our beyond. In his life our life too is hidden. And this must satisfy us. Our death is nothing more interesting than this.[6]

From this point of view, the disappearance of all spacial and temporal conceptions of the next world as a result of the enlightenment is not a loss to Christian faith, but a purification of it. This is no reason to lament the loss of the next world, but good reason for a curious and expectant certainty of God. In this certainty we can set to work not to redeem the world and make it in the highest sense man's 'home', but to use our love and reason to make it a little better and to build man a slightly more habitable dwelling place in it. The final victory over the disorder of the world is God's and not ours. But we bear responsibility for the preliminary victories and defeats. We cannot see the ultimate meaning of our existence in victories and defeats on this earth, but neither can we renounce this earth.

A Concluding Remark

Instead of giving the usual summary at the end of the book, I would like to conclude simply with a special personal word to those readers who find it difficult to believe in God, and who no longer think that they can believe in God. I feel a particular close link with them, and therefore I venture to address them personally.

I assure you of my respect for your honesty. But so that you can remain honest, I allow myself to ask you something; Keep a place open for God in your lives. Do not fill it with anything else. Go on asking and looking for God. Scold God if you like, abuse and revile him as Job did – but go on waiting for him. Keep the place open for God in your lives. For whether we believe or do not believe, God cannot die. And therefore we are never done with the question of God.

Notes

INTRODUCTION

1. *The Future of Man*, Collins, London, 1964, p. 260.
2. 'The Critique of Hegel's Philosophy of Right' in *Karl Marx: Early Writings*, tr. and ed. T. B. Bottomore, Watts, London, 1963, p. 44.
3. *Die Zeit*, No. 30, 25.7.1969.
4. *The Eclipse of God*, Gollancz, London, 1953, pp. 17f. (reissued as a Torchbook, Harper and Row, New York, 1967).
5. *Stadt Lucca*, Werke V, ed. O. Walzel, Leipzig 1914, p. 59; E.T. by C. G. Leland, '*The City of Lucca*', Works III, Heinemann, 1891, p. 315.

CHAPTER ONE

1. *Zur Geschichte der Religion und Philosophie in Deutschland*, Werke VII, pp. 291f.; E. T. *From Luther to Kant*, Works, V, pp. 130ff.
2. *Existentialism and Humanism*, tr. P. Mairet, Methuen, 1948, p. 33.
3. Op. cit., p. 56.
4. Edward Schillebeeckx, *Gott – die Zukunft des Menschen*, Mainz, 1969, p. 51.
5. *Atheismus im Christentum*, Frankfurt a.M., 1968, p. 37.
6. *But that I can't believe*, Fontana, 1967, p. 44.
7. *Theologische Jugendschriften*, ed. H. Nohl, p. 225; E.T. by T. M. Knox, *Early Theological Writings*, Peter Smith, Gloucester, Mass., 1970, p. 159.
8. *Werke* VII, ed. Witkowski, p. 214.
9. 'Über Bedingungen und Möglichkeiten eines neuen Humanismus', in *Rechenschaft und Ausblick*, Munich, 1958, p. 340.
10. Ernst Bloch, *Atheismus im Christentum*, pp. 17f.
11. *Schriften zur Theologie* III, Einsiedeln, 1956, p. 461; E.T. *Theological Investigations* III, Baltimore and London, p. 390.
12. Dorothee Sölle, *Christ the Representative*, SCM Press, London, 1967, p. 140.

CHAPTER TWO

1. Monica Furlong writing in the *Guardian* (January 11th, 1963). Quoted in *The Honest to God Debate*, edited by David L. Edwards and John A. T. Robinson, SCM Press, London, 1963, pp. 246f.

2. *Christ the Representative*, p. 152.
3. *On not Leaving it to the Snake*, SCM Press, 1968, p. 13.
4. *Erlebter Kirchentag Köln 1965*, Stuttgart/Berlin, 1968, p. 94; 'Theologie nach dem Tode Gottes', in *Merkur* 18, p. 1105.
5. Weimar Edition, 18, p. 784.
6. *Gesammelte Werke XV*, p. 189; E.T., *Standard Edition of the Complete Psychological Works*, Hogarth Press, London, vol. XXII, p. 174.
7. *Also sprach Zarathustra*, Kröner, Leipzig, 1925, p. 318; E.T., *Thus Spake Zarathustra*, by T. Conman, in O. Levy, ed. *The Complete Works of F. Nietzsche*, London and Edinburgh, 1910, Vol. 4, p. 351.
8. *Lectures on the Philosophy of Religion*, tr. and ed. E. B. Speirs and J. Sanderson, London, 1895, vol. III, p. 98.
9. *Glauben und Wissen*, *Werke I*, ed. H. Glockner, p. 433.
10. Hans Küng, *Menschwerdung Gottes. Eine Einführung in Hegels theologisches Denken*, Freiburg, Bâle, Vienna, 1970, p. 215.
11. *Was kommt nach dem 'Todes Gottes'?*, Stuttgart and Berlin, 1968, p. 58.
12. Werner Jetter, *Was wird aus der Kirche?* Stuttgart and Berlin, 1968, p. 58.
13. *Des Christen Zukunft*, Munich, 1955, p. 148.
14. Jean Lacroix, *The Meaning of Modern Atheism*, M. H. Gill, Dublin, 1965, p. 63.
15. Philosophische Bibliothek 33, ed. Georg Lasson, 5th ed., Leipzig, 1949, p. 40; *Werke VIII*, ed. H. Glockner, p. 50.
16. Ed. Rudolf Otto, Göttingen, 6th ed., 1967, p. 92. E.T., 'On Religion', ed. J. Oman, Harper and Row, 1958, p. 91.

CHAPTER THREE

1. *Homiletik*, 1966, p.77.
2. Weimer Edition 56, p. 234.
3. Weimar Edition 37, p. 451ff.
4. E.g. Weimar Edition 7, p. 24; 56, p. 79; 40.I, p. 360.
5. Weimar Edition 40. I, p. 360.
6. Erich Seeberg, *Grundzüge der Theologie Luthers*, Stuttgart, 1940, p. 49.
7. *Theologie des Alten Testaments* I, Munich, 1957, pp. 36f., 141ff.; E.T. by D. M. G. Stalker, *Old Testament Theology* I, Oliver and Boyd, 1962, p. 136, 138f.
8. S. Freud, *Gesammelte Werke XIV*, p. 373; XV, p. 181: *Standard Edition*, XXI, p. 49; XXII, p. 168.
9. *Systematic Theology* I, Nisbet and Co., 1953, p. 235.
10. 'Wie kann heute glaubwürdig von Gott geredet werden?' Address to the 14th German Protestant Church Assembly, in Stuttgart, 1969, Stuttgart and Berlin, 1970, p. 147.

Notes

269

11. *Über das Wesen der Religion, Werke* VIII, Leipzig 1851, p. 257. Cf. E.T. by Ralph Madison, *Lectures on the Essence of Religion*, Harper and Row, 1967, p. 256.

CHAPTER FOUR

1. Max Horkheimer, 'Die Funktion der Theologie in der Gesellschaft', in *Die Funktion der Theologie in Kirche und Gesellschaft*, ed. P. Neuenzeit, Munich, 1969, pp. 225, 229.
2. Hans-Dieter Bastian, *Theologie der Frage*, Munich, 1969, p. 51.
3. Wolfhart Pannenberg, 'The Question of God', in *Basic Questions in Theology* Vol. 2, SCM Press, London, 1971, pp. 222f.
4. A. Camus, *The Rebel*, Penguin, Harmondsworth, 1962, p. 14.
5. *The Honest to God Debate*, edited by David L. Edwards and John A. T. Robinson, SCM Press, London, 1963, pp. 57f.
6. Op. cit., p. 96.
7. Quoted by H.-D. Bastian, op. cit., p. 280f.

CHAPTER FIVE

1. *Gesammelte Schriften* I, ed. E. Bethge, Munich 1958, p. 61.
2. *Zeitschrift für Theologie und Kirche* 65, 1968, p. 117.
3. See Peter Biehl, 'Zur Aufgabe eines verantwortlichen Redens von Gott im Religionsunterricht', in *Die Religionspädagogische Frage nach Gott*, ed. W. G. Esser, Freiburg, Bâle and Vienna, 1969, p. 150.
4. Heinrich Ott, *Wirklichkeit und Glaube* II, Göttingen and Zürich, 1969, p. 146.
5. *Die Wahrheit ist konkret*, Olten and Freiburg, 1967, p. 17.
6. In a sermon, 26.1.1969, in the Luther Church in Hamburg-Wellingsbüttel.
7. Here and on what follows see Siegfried Müller-Markus, 'Der Glaube als Voraussetzung der Wissenschaft', *Neue Züricher Zeitung*, 8.2.1970.
8. Quoted in E. Jones, *Sigmund Freud, Life and Work*, Hogarth Press, 1955, p. 465.
9. *Der Spiegel* No. 1/2, 1970.
10. Cf. G. Ebeling, 'Theologie und Wirklichkeit', in *Wort und Glaube*, Tübingen, 1960, p. 198; E.T. by J. W. Leitch, *Word and Faith*, SCM Press, 1963, pp. 196f.
11. *Aus einer philosophischen Rechenschaft, Werke* I, Munich, 1962, p. 1114.
12. Op. cit., p. 68.
13. *The Shaking of the Foundations*, SCM Press, 1949, p. 19.

CHAPTER SIX

1. *Die Lehre vom Worte Gottes; Prolegomena zur christlichen Dogmatik*, Munich, 1927, p. 215.

2. House Sermon, Whit Monday 1532, Weimar Edition 35, p. 184.
3. Hubertus Halbfas, *Fundamentalkatechetik*, Düsseldorf and Stuttgart, 1968, p. 76.
4. A. Camus, *The Fall*, Hamish Hamilton, London, 1957, pp. 85f.
5. Karl Barth – Eduard Thurneysen, *Ein Briefwechsel*, Siebenstern-Taschenbuch 71, pp. 92f.; E.T. by J. D. Smart, *Revolutionary Theology in the Making*, Epworth, 1964, p. 105.
6. Op. cit., p. 117.
7. Ingo Hermann, 'Die Theologie vor dem Anspruch der Öffentlichkeit', in *Die Funktion der Theologie in Kirche und Gesellschaft*, Munich, 1969, p. 214.
8. Norbert Greinacher, 'Theologie im Spannungsfeld von Theorie und Praxis', in *Die Funktion der Theologie in Kirche und Gesellschaft*, p. 33.
9. Paul Audet, 'Eine Theologie für eine Zeit des Neuaufbaus', in *Die Funktion der Theologie in Kirche und Gesellschaft*, p. 33.

CHAPTER SEVEN

1. Rudolf Bultmann, 'Neues Testament und Mythologie' in *Kerygma und Mythos* I, 2nd ed. Hamburg, 1951, p. 48; E.T. by R. H. Fuller, *Kerygma and Myth*, SPCK 1953, p. 44; 'Zum Problem der Entmythologisierung' in *Glauben und Verstehen* IV, Tübingen, 1965, p. 136.
2. 'Der Gottesgedanke und der moderne Mensch', in *Glauben und Verstehen* IV, Tübingen 1965, pp. 125f.
3. Ernst Bloch, *Atheismus im Christentum*, p. 318.
4. *Widerstand und Ergebung*, ed. E. Bethge, Munich, 1951, p. 259; E.T. *Letters and Papers from Prison*, p. 210.
5. 'Botschaft und Erkenntnis', in *Funktion der Theologie in Kirche und Gesellschaft*, p. 315.
6. Sigurd M. Daecke, 'Welcher Gott ist tot?', in *Ev. Kommentare*, 2, 1969, p. 192.
7. Helmut Thielicke, *Der evangelische Glaube* I, Tübingen 1968, p. 347; cf. pp. 341ff.
8. Karl Rahner, 'Meditation über das Wort "Gort"', in *Wer ist das eigentlich – Gott?* ed. H. J. Schultz, Munich 1969, p. 17ff.
9. No. 1/2, 5.1.1970.

CHAPTER EIGHT

1. P. M. van Buren, *The Secular Meaning of the Gospel*, SCM Press, 1963, p. 169.
2. Bloch, *Atheismus im Christentum*, p. 21.
3. *Die Sprache des Menschengeschlechts* I, Heidelberg, 1963, pp. 416f.
4. *Gesammelte Schriften* III, Munich, 1960, p. 174; E.T. by J. S. Bowden, *Christology*, Collins, 1966, p. 35.
5. *Theologie für die Zeit. Wider die religiöse der Wirklichkeit in der*

modernen Theologie, Stuttgart, 1969, p. 154.

6. Blaise Pascal, *Pensées* 555, Everyman edition, trans. W. F. Trotter, 1908, reprinted 1943, p. 154.

7. Quoted in Helmut Gollwitzer, *The Existence of God*, SCM Press, 1965, p. 252.

8. Camus, *The Fall*, p. 107.

9. H. Thielicke, op. cit., p. 150ff.

10. Quoted by Hans-Dieter Bastian, 'Verfremdung und Verkündigung', in *Theologische Existenz heute*, N.S. 127, Munich, 1965, p. 69.

11. Weimar Edition 47, pp. 705, 19ff.; 49, pp. 366, 1ff.

12. *Stadt Lucca, Werke* V, pp. 35f.; E.T. *Works* III, pp. 282f.

13. E. Schillebeeckx, op. cit., p. 171.

14. 'Unmittelbarkeit zu Gott', in *Die Relionspädagogische Grundfrage nach Gott*, pp. 17f.

15. Eberhard Jüngel, 'Das dunkle Wort vom "Tode Gottes"', in *Ev. Kommentare* 2, 1969, p. 106.

16. H. Thielicke, op. cit., p. 221.

17. *Glaube und Erfahrung*, Tübingen, 1965, p. 308.

CHAPTER NINE

1. 'Das Wort "Gott" in christlicher Theologie', in *Theologische Literaturzeitung* 92, 1967, col. 164.

2. *Luther, Einführung in sein Denken*, Tübingen, 1964, pp. 220ff.; E.T. by R. A. Wilson, *Luther: an Introduction to His Thought*, Collins, 1970, pp. 193ff.

3. *Wirklichkeit und Glaube* II, p. 77.

4. *Systematic Theology*, Nisbet, 1953, p. 271.

5. In an address quoted in *Die Welt*, 2.3.1969.

6. *Wirklichkeit und Glaube* II, p. 251.

7. Op. cit., pp. 161ff.

8. Gert Wendelborn, 'Die Wirklichkeit Gottes', in *Ev. Pfarrerblatt in der DDR*, 1965, pp. 319ff.

9. *Politisches Nachtgebet in Köln*, Stuttgart and Mainz, 1969, p. 24.

10. Antichrist, No. 52; E.T. *Complete Works*, 1911, p. 206.

11. *Predigten*, Reutlingen 1835, p. 31; E.T., *Selected Sermons of Schleiermacher*, Hodder and Stoughton, 1890, p. 38.

12. Op. cit., p. 127.

13. *Atheistisch an Gott glauben*, pp. 113f.

14. *Politisches Nachtgebet in Köln*, pp. 24f.

15. Op. cit., p. 23.

CHAPTER TEN

1. *Vom Geist des Ausgehenden Mittelalters*, Halle, 1929, p. 225.

2. 'Urdistanz und Beziehung', *Werke* I, p. 423.

3. A. Camus, *The Myth of Sisyphus*, Hamish Hamilton, London, 1955, p. 99.

4. *The Courage to Be*, Nisbet, 1952, p. 9.

5. Op. cit., p. 21.

6. *Widerstand und Ergebung*, p. 242f.; E.T., *Letters and Papers from Prison*, pp. 197ff.

7. E. Fuchs, op. cit., pp. 170f.

8. Walter Schmithals, 'Jesus und die Weltlichkeit des Reiches Gottes', in *Ev. Kommentare* I, 1968, pp. 570f.

CHAPTER ELEVEN

1. Quoted from H. Ott, *Wirklichkeit und Glaube* II, pp. 280f.

2. *Vernunft. Aspekte zeitgemässen Glaubens*, Stuttgart and Berlin, 1970, p. 40.

3. Edmund Weber, 'Die Forderung nach Auflösung der Kirchenorganisation', in *Menschlich sein – mit oder ohne Gott*, ed. M. Lohse, Stuttgart, 1969, pp. 114f.

4. *Lutherische Monatshefte* 7, 1968, pp. 216ff.

5. 'Gott in der Revolution' in *Ev. Kommentare* I, 1968, pp. 570f.

6. *Zur Theologie der Welt*, Mainz and Munich, 1968, p. 128.

7. *Stern*, 7/1970, p. 146.

8. Areas of particular importance in pioneering work of the church and industry; see e.g. Horst Symanowski, *The Christian Witness in an Industrial Society*, Collins, 1966.

9. *Lutetia. Werke* IX, p. 236. E.T., *Works* VIII, p. 305.

10. 'Offenbarung und autonome Vernunft'. Discussion between Theodor W. Adorno and Eugen Kogon, in *Frankfurter Hefte*, 13, 1958, pp. 400, 485.

11. *Die Atombombe und die Zukunft des Menschen*, Munich, 1958, pp. 356ff. Shortened E.T. by E. B. Ashton, *The Future of Mankind*, University of Chicago Press, 1961, pp. 258f.

12. *Das Wort Gottes und die Theologie*, Munich, 1924, pp. 158ff.; E.T by D. Horton, *The Word of God and the Word of Man*, Hodder and Stoughton, 1928, pp. 187ff.

13. *On not Leaving it to the Snake*, p. 12.

14. *Theologie der Frage*, pp. 144f.

15. *The Secular City*, SCM Press, 1965, pp. 183, 191.

16. *Atheismus im Christentum*, p. 165.

17. Walter Dirks, 'Offenbarung und autonome Vernunft', loc. cit., p. 487.

18. rororo aktuell, Hamburg, 1968, p. 15.

CHAPTER TWELVE

1. Recounted by Ernst Bloch, *Atheismus im Christentum*, pp. 338f.

2. Frankfurt am Main, 1959, p. 1628.

3. *Children's Letters to God,* edited by Eric Marshall and S. Hample, Collins, London, 1967.

4. *Atheismus im Christentum,* p. 335.

5. Ibid., p. 332.

6. Op. cit., p. 202.

Index of Biblical References

Index of Names

Thielicke, Helmut, 138, 154, 168, 270, 271
Thurneysen, Eduard, 125, 270
Tillich, Paul, 67, 113, 132, 181, 193, 204
Troeltsch, Ernst, 53

Unamuno, Miguel de, 5

Vahanian, Gabriel, 38

Weber, Edmund, 225, 272
Weber, Max, 21, 225
Weizsäcker, Carl Friedrich von, 102
Wendelborn, Gert, 185f., 271
Werner, Anton von, 214
Wiesner, Heinrich, 93, 122

Xenophanes, 61

Zundel, Rolf, 7